The Shopaholic's Top 1000 Websites

Patricia Davidson

CAPSTONE

Other Wiley Editorial Offices
John Wiley & Sons Inc., 111 River Street, Hoboken, NJ 07030, USA
Jossey-Bass, 989 Market Street, San Francisco, CA 94103-1741, USA
Wiley-VCH Verlag GmbH, Boschstr. 12, D-69469 Weinheim, Germany
John Wiley & Sons Australia Ltd, 42 McDougall Street, Milton, Queensland 4064, Australia
John Wiley & Sons (Asia) Pte Ltd, 2 Clementi Loop #02-01, Jin Xing Distripark, Singapore 129809
John Wiley & Sons Canada Ltd, 22 Worcester Road, Etobicoke, Ontario, Canada M9W 1L1

Wiley also publishes its books in a variety of electronic formats. Some content that appears in print may not be available in electronic books.

A catalogue record for this book is available from the British Library.

Library of Congress Cataloging-in-Publication Data
Davidson, Patricia.
  The shopaholic's top 1000 websites / Patricia Davidson.
     p. cm.
  Includes index.
  ISBN 978-1-906465-36-0 (pbk. : alk. paper)
  1. Teleshopping--Guidebooks. 2. Shopping--Computer network resources--Guidebooks. I. Title. II. Title: Shopaholic's top one thousand websites. III. Title: Shopaholic's top thousand websites.
  TX335.D38565 2008
  381'.142--dc22
                                                                                                      2008031721

ISBN: 978-1-90646-536-0

Typeset by Sparks, Oxford – www.sparkspublishing.com
Printed and bound in Great Britain by Bell & Bain, Glasgow

Substantial discounts on bulk quantities of Capstone Books are available to corporations, professional associations and other organizations. For details telephone John Wiley & Sons on (+44) 1243 770441, fax (+44) 1243 770571 or email corporatedevelopment@wiley.co.uk

For Sam

*'Whoever said money can't buy happiness
didn't know where to shop'*

Bo Derek

Contents

Acknowledgements

A great big thank you to Jason Dunne, Sarah Sutton, Katie Moffat, Julia Lampam, Iain Campbell, Megan Verrily, Grace O'Byrne and everyone at John Wiley for their continued belief that I will spend most of my life browsing and shopping the world online. Needless to say, your belief is totally justified. Also to Jonny Geller, Doug Keane and Alice Lutyens at Curtis Brown, and to Sara Norman and Lalla Dutt at BgB. I'm extremely fortunate, and grateful, to have such a great team behind me.

Thanks also to Lee, Simon and Chris of E2E Solutions for their great work with thesiteguide.com.

About the Author

After twelve years in international designer fashion mail-order, Patricia Davidson started www.thesiteguide.com, the online luxury fashion, beauty and lifestyle website directory described by Condé Nast's Glamour.com as 'the web's best shopping directory.'

She has written six books on online shopping. Her first, *The Shopaholic's Guide to Buying Online*, was published by Capstone in October 2006. She has also written features for magazines and newspapers and been interviewed for TV and radio. Described by Eamon Holmes as 'the fairy godmother of online shopping'. She lives in Buckinghamshire with her husband, three children and two dogs.

John Wiley/Capstone have published the following books:

The Shopaholic's Guide to Buying Online
The Shopaholic's Guide to Buying Fashion and Beauty Online
The Shopaholic's Guide to Buying for Mother and Child Online
The Shopaholic's Guide to Buying Gorgeous Gifts Online
The Shopaholic's Guide to Buying Online 2008
The Gift Book – September 2008

Introduction

L et me tell you a story. Once upon a time, not so very long ago, if you wanted to buy something you actually had to go out to do so. You had to get dressed, put on your coat and leave home for hours at a time, and sometimes longer if what you were looking for could only be found in a far-off land.

Then, yes really, trust me – you had to carry what you had bought from the store back to your car or, even worse, all the way home on the train and then transport it into your house where you might even need to rest for a time before admiring your trophy purchase/s.

Fairytale land? Maybe, but it really wasn't that long ago that you had to go out shopping for absolutely everything, from silly but essential things such as dog food and loo rolls to the far less prosaic champagne, cashmere and cosmetics.

We've now travelled at a spanking pace to the opposite end of the spectrum, where you can buy all you could possibly need or want without ever leaving home, with a vast number of stores just the touch of a button away and far too much choice of everything.

For me shopping has to be fun. It's a little bit (or a lot) of therapy ready whenever I need it and the pleasure is there when I'm out in the shops or when shopping from home. I do both, outstandingly well.

However, I do think that we've reached a stage when it's pretty well impossible to steer clearly through what has become the overabundance of shops online. Do you really want to wade through the 88 million or so search results you'll get for 'cosmetics' if you type that into a search engine, or the 150,000 that are the result of asking for 'designer handbags UK only?' Not if you have any sense.

Having already established a directory of over 2000 websites myself, just for fashion, beauty, lifestyle products and travel, I decided it was time to ruthlessly pare those down to my 1000 personal favourites. These may have become favourites because of their beautifully designed websites, the special range of products they offer, their excellent prices, their superb service (many of them personally tested by me, I promise – hope that neither my bank manager nor my husband is reading this), or because there's simply something wonderfully stylish and clever about them that makes them a pleasure to visit.

There are some great household names here that undoubtedly you will have heard of and quite possibly shopped from. There are also some online-only secrets that you won't have come across before. I hope you enjoy them all.

Patricia

About this Book

I wrote this book to make it quick and easy for you to get to the best shopping websites. When you're browsing through you can see immediately who will deliver worldwide, who offers express delivery and who will gift wrap your choice and send it out for you. I've also given special awards to my all-time favourites who I consider to be the best of the best.

I've picked online retailers who work really hard to offer you pleasurable shopping online; they all have attractive and frequently glamorously designed websites, offer a really good range of products, an excellent service and make shopping online clear and simple for you. In fact, they're all a joy to buy from.

However, the aim of this book is not just to take you straight to the ultimate online stores so you don't have to search any more but also to give you a snapshot of each retailer's website so you can decide quickly whether or not you want to pay it a visit.

For example, when you're in a flat panic because you've forgotten that important birthday, you want to know immediately that the online retailer you're intending to buy from will deliver your gift tomorrow, by guaranteed delivery, beautifully wrapped on your behalf. You want to have an idea of the price range before you start to browse, where they're based and where they deliver to.

With this book you can shop from just about anywhere in the world and take delivery anywhere in the world. The world wide web has made the globe a much, much smaller place, so for a little entertainment and a great deal of temptation just turn the page and read on.

Shopping Online for Less

You probably know already that you can save a great deal of money by buying online when you're looking for products such as computers, cameras and other electrical equipment by using a price-comparison website (I'll explain how to get the best out of them later). My advice, particularly with the amount of competition that there is between online retailers, is that you don't consider buying any kind of appliance without price comparing – you can get such excellent deals when you do.

You can also save in the sale sections of many fashion websites which are available all year round. No more delving through the rails with the rest of the crowds on the high street – just click and see immediately whether that perfect jacket is available in your size and in a couple more clicks it's yours. You may never want to pay full price again! Be aware that these virtual 'sale rails' are being added to on a weekly, if not daily basis. Pick your favourite online boutiques and then keep checking back.

Don't expect to find this season's designer fashion collections discounted until the end of the season and if you do come across somewhere that claims to be offering you the latest fashion for less, take a good hard look. If the price seems too low to be true I suggest that you don't dream of unleashing your credit card unless you are cast-iron certain that what you are being offered is authentic – it may well not be. I'm sure you'll gasp (being sarcastic, here) when you learn that there are some companies that take pictures of the real thing and then sell you something different, but I have to confess I've given up gasping and now believe just about all the horrors I've been told.

You can save lots of money online on many products, crazy amounts of money in fact, particularly if you don't mind that your new camera is last season's purple instead of this season's hot pink. So enjoy using this book, and learn the best places to shop and save, and the best products to look for discounts on.

Then you can go out (or shop online) and use all that money you've saved to purchase that Marc Jacobs handbag you've been coveting. Last seen in *Vogue* – now on your arm. Now what could be better than that?

Decision Time – The Top 1000

These are, in my opinion, the top 1000 places to shop online.
So what makes an online store great?

- They have to be extremely attractive to look at and offer a wide range of products with a good selection within each range.
- They have to be easy for you and I to navigate – in other words, we don't want to have to think too hard to find what we're looking for.
- They have to offer their service details on the home page – how long they take to deliver, where they deliver to and extra services such as express delivery and gift wrapping.
- They have to make it easy for us to contact them if we need to, and not just with an email address.
- They need to demonstrate their online security to let us know straight away that we're safe shopping there, particularly if they're not a household name.
- They need to have put a great deal of thought into persuading us to shop within the first few clicks of us arriving at their website.
- If they do all of these they'll be one of the best.

There are bound to be other, great web shopping stores out there that I haven't heard of. If you have your own favourites please email me at phd@thesiteguide.com and tell me which they are so they can be included next time.

I spend an incredible amount of time looking at site after site (as you can probably imagine). Over the years of reviewing websites I've developed my own pet hates and I never fail to be annoyed by the following:

- Sites with long flash intros – who has the time? We're there to shop so let us get on with it. We want to get to the products now!
- Online retailers who don't bother to update their sites on a realistically frequent basis – we don't want to read about Christmas in May the following year. Get off the web if you can't be bothered.
- Retailers who don't make it obvious that it's secure for us to shop with them.
- Retailers who think we should be clever enough to find our way round their confusing websites.
- Those who expect us to wait until check-out to discover that they do offer express delivery but they won't deliver to France/the US or Hong Kong. Tell us everything right at the start, please.
- Poor photography. Now that it's extremely easy to photograph everything digitally on a small set even when products are changing regularly, the pictures should be clear and all on the same background. There – I've said it. I have a real dislike of scruffy photographs and an even greater dislike of the 'some of these and some of those' variety where there are lots of different types of substandard pictures – why should we buy from them?

I'm sure there are more but I'll let you get on.

Section 1
Spoilt for Choice – the Department Stores

This is the first time I've been able to dedicate a section to department stores, which, in the UK at least, have been reticent in putting themselves properly online. John Lewis and Debenhams were the first to go for it and both now have clear and easy-to-navigate websites with a wide range of products. I have to confess that John Lewis gets my award here because they do it so very well and have a constantly increasing selection of products. I don't think they will ever be first for fashion but there are certainly items on offer that you won't find easily anywhere else so they're well worth a look. This is a wonderful place to shop for home accessories, appliances, fitness equipment, cameras and just about everything else you can think of, including flower deliveries and lovely toiletries.

Happily also (for fashionistas in particular) Harrods and Harvey Nichols also have attractive retail sites now, and again you should 'watch this space' as their collections can only grow.

Take a look below and see what's available now, then keep your eyes wide open for more. We may be behind Neiman Marcus, Saks, Bloomingdales and Nordstrom in the US, and they have a huge start on us, but we're going to be catching up fast from now on. Happy times!

www.debenhams.co.uk

The excellent range from 'Designers for Debenhams' includes designers such as Betty Jackson, Jasper Conran, Ben De Lisi, John Rocha, Julien MacDonald and more. Then you can also find lots of other, less expensive brands such as Principles and Red Herring, lingerie, menswear, childrenswear, electricals and beauty by brands like Estée Lauder, Lancôme, Benefit and Elemis.

Prices:	Very Good Value	Express Ship?	No
Delivers to:	UK	Gift Wrap?	No
Based:	UK		

www.fortnumandmason.com

At the Fortnum and Mason online store you can order their gorgeously packaged teas, coffees, chocolates, hampers and deli products such as caviar and cheese, dip into their extensive wine cellar and visit their 'At Home' department, which is packed full of lovely gift ideas and home décor items. Then pay a visit to Fashion and Beauty to find their own-brand toiletries plus other exclusive ranges.

Prices:	Luxury/Medium	Express Ship?	48 hours
Delivers to:	Most worldwide	Gift Wrap?	Automatic
Based:	UK		

www.harrods.com

Where else online can you find the clothes of Roberto Cavalli, John Galliano, Theory, Moschino, VJC Versace and more? Well, Harrods, of course. If you haven't looked at their well-designed website recently and the excellent and constantly increasing range, then you should do so now. Alongside the clothing there are the beauty ranges, men's and kidswear, toys, home accessories and lots of gift ideas.

Prices:	Luxury/Medium/Very Good Value	Express Ship?	No
Delivers to:	Most worldwide	Gift Wrap?	No
Based:	UK		

www.harveynichols.com

You've almost certainly visited this great fashion and beauty store, whether in London, Dublin, Edinburgh or elsewhere. The list of modern brands they offer is always excellent, up-to-the-minute and totally in line with each season's trends. At the stylish online store you can buy bags by Marc Jacobs, Botkier, YSL and more, belts, jewels, gloves and scarves, your next pair of Prada or Chanel shades and exclusive beauty must-haves.

Prices:	Luxury/Medium	Express Ship?	Yes
Delivers to:	UK	Gift Wrap?	No
Based:	UK		

3

www.houseoffraser.co.uk

The product range at House of Fraser's well-designed online store includes fashion by designers such as Max Mara, Joyce Ridings and Miss Sixty, accessories by Coccinelle and Adrienne Vittadini, and beauty, bath and body products by brands like Banana Republic, Nars and Urban Decay. Plus there's much more for men, kids and your home.

Prices:	Very Good Value	Express Ship?	Yes
Delivers to:	UK	Gift Wrap?	No
Based:	UK		

www.johnlewis.com

The fashion and beauty ranges at this excellent online store are growing all the time. You can browse through contemporary handbags by Francesco Biasia and DKNY, jewels by Dower & Hall and Lola Rose, a wide selection of beauty products, plus everything for your home – furniture, accessories, kitchen appliances, fitness gear, computers and hi-fi … all online from one of the best sites on the web.

Prices:	Medium/Very Good Value	Express Ship?	Yes
Delivers to:	UK	Gift Wrap?	No
Based:	UK		

www.libertyoflondon.co.uk

At present this is a small range of beautiful accessories, including handbags, travel bags, scarves and ties. I expect this to grow – it's about time this wonderful London store was properly online, as I'm sure you'll agree. Take a look at the collection now and then keep checking back to see what's been added.

Prices:	Luxury/Medium/Very Good Value	Express Ship?	No
Delivers to:	UK, EU, USA	Gift Wrap?	No
Based:	UK		

www.marksandspencer.com

Together with an outstanding lingerie collection and the special clothing ranges by Autograph, Limited Collection, Per Una and more, you can order luggage and other travel goods, beauty products and your next sofa or fridge freezer. Then there are all the home accessories such as lighting, rugs and cushions, plus flowers and gifts. So what can't you order here yet? Well, food of course. Cross your fingers that that's coming next.

Prices:	Very Good Value	Express Ship?	Yes
Delivers to:	UK	Gift Wrap?	No
Based:	UK		

www.shop.com

Shop.com is a virtual shopping mall where you can buy from lots of different stores using just one shopping cart or through being linked to one of the partner retailers. There are few brands and fewer products that you can't find here and the list is growing by the day. Browse here for everything from fashion, beauty and jewels to your next kettle.

Prices:	Medium/Very Good Value	Gift Wrap and Express Ship depends on the retailer
Delivers to:	Dependent on retailer	
Based:	UK	

Section 2
The Fashionista's Paradise

ashion retailers may have taken longer than most to get online, but now they are catching up with a vengeance. You'll find boutiques and stores such as Karen Millen, Reiss, Ghost, Hobbs and Whistles all available online, so here's an irresistible list of stylish and glamorous stores and designers just waiting for you to visit.

Not only that, but they want to preview each new season's collections for you, to break down the often confusing catwalk trends so you know if and how each will suit you, sell you the pieces that make the new looks work and then advise you on what to wear with them. Clever, eh?

All of this gives you so much more choice – you can trek to London (or your nearest city, depending on where you are, of course), go to your local shopping mall where you know exactly which stores you'll find, or shop online from famous brands, chic boutiques and the special discoveries which I've brought together for you here.

Visit your favourite fashion brands early in the season to make sure that perfect leather jacket is available in your size and order it then and there; wait and you may well find that the only size left is an 8. The best trend pieces will always sell out first and you have no guarantee that there'll be more.

The services offered by most online fashion retailers include express 1–2-day delivery and gift wrapping. The temptation begins here.

Sheer Luxe

This is the place to browse and buy from the collections of all those designers you read about each month in *Vogue*, *Glamour* and *In Style*. There are beautiful, signature pieces you'll have seen in the catwalk reports of the new season's collections, some of which (I find) are quite hard to understand and others which you just immediately think 'that's me'. Some of the websites are extremely idiosyncratic, which does not always make it easy to properly see the clothes and accessories on offer. Others just use beautiful photographs of the products to get the message across, which to my mind makes them far more irresistible.

If you're thinking of investing make sure that you check the size charts before you buy, as premium designers have a tendency to size smaller than main market brands. Many of the retailers here specify that you should return goods in their packaging and some will ask you to call or email them first to obtain a returns authorisation code. If this sounds tricky it really isn't and it's worth following their instructions.

Just a note: many of the luxe retailers here do not specifically offer express delivery as a service on their sites, although they usually deliver extremely fast. If you want something urgently give them a call and ask if you can have your order tomorrow – provided you're ordering early enough in the day you usually can. In many cases also they don't offer gift wrapping but if you've shopped at any of these stores you'll know that the packaging is always in line with the clothes – beautiful, luxurious and a joy to receive.

www.amandawakeley.com

On Amanda Wakeley's stylish, black-based website you can click through to the e-store where you can order from her luxuriously chic collection of dresses and separates, plus accessories such as shoes, belts and stoles. If your taste is for body-skimming silk jersey dresses, butter-soft leather jackets and seriously beautiful eveningwear in understated neutrals, you'll be visiting the right place.

Prices:	Luxury	Express Ship?	No
Delivers to:	Most worldwide	Gift Wrap?	No
Based:	UK		

www.brownsfashion.com

The Browns website offers a mouthwatering list of contemporary designers including Lanvin, Balenciaga, Missoni and Paul Smith, plus Dolce & Gabbana, Roberto Cavalli, Ann Demeulemeister and Issa. There are several views of each item plus lots of essential information and size charts. Look here too for your next Luella handbag fix (or Fendi or Marni) or pair of heels (Christian Louboutin or Marc Jacobs).

Prices:	Luxury/Medium	Express Ship?	Yes
Delivers to:	Most worldwide	Gift Wrap?	Yes
Based:	UK		

www.burberry.com

You can buy from Burberry online through their beautifully designed website. Browse the luxuriously photographed collections including Burberry Prorsum, Burberry London and the Icons Collection, then click through to the online store and choose from menswear, womenswear, bags and accessories. If you want to see what's coming next you can preview the new collections. Expect superb quality and gorgeous packaging.

Prices:	Luxury/Medium	Express Ship?	Yes
Delivers to:	Most Europe, US	Gift Wrap?	No
Based:	UK		

www.dvf.com

Although you can find a wonderful collection of her famous wrap dresses here, Diane von Furstenberg also has a full collection of glamorous separates which include up-to-the-minute jackets, trousers, tops and skirts. In the Vintage section you'll find her covetable vintage print silk jersey wraps and tops – I want them all, so no surprise there then.

Prices:	Medium	Express Ship?	Yes
Delivers to:	Most worldwide	Gift Wrap?	Yes
Based:	UK and US		

www.lineafashion.com

Linea started life as a boutique in London's Hampstead offering designer brands from around the world. At the online store the range is photographed so you can see each item clearly. You will find collections from international designers such as Blumarine, Celine, Etro, Gharani Strok, Juicy Couture, Missoni and Emanuel Ungaro, plus handbags and shoes by Hogan, Tods and Celine.

Prices:	Luxury/Medium	Express Ship?	Yes
Delivers to:	Most worldwide	Gift Wrap?	No
Based:	UK		

www.luisaviaroma.com

This excellent luxury Florence-based online boutique offers worldwide shipping on a wonderful range of designers including Burberry, Chloe, Balenciaga, Lanvin, Narcisco Rodruigez, Roberto Cavalli and Missoni. Prices are exactly as you would expect them to be but the range is exceptional and the pictures are clear, with several views of each item.

Prices:	Luxury/Medium	Express Ship?	Fedex Express
Delivers to:	Most worldwide	Gift Wrap?	No
Based:	Italy		

www.marni.com

At luxury brand Marni's high-tech 'virtual store' everything is clearly photographed and you can see different views of each item. Register with them so that you can create 'My Style

Notes,' where you can view all the pieces you've selected together in one place and then see if you can resist putting them all in your basket. Be warned that most items don't go beyond size 44/10.

Prices:	Luxury/Medium/Very Good Value	Express Ship?	Yes
Delivers to:	Most worldwide	Gift Wrap?	Yes
Based:	Italy		

www.matchesfashion.com

Luxury designer boutique Matches is famous for offering a unique, personal service together with a mouthwatering choice of designers such as Dolce & Gabbana, Bottega Veneta, Chloe, Christian Louboutin, Lanvin, Marc Jacobs, Missoni and Stella McCartney. You can find this excellent service and the full range of designers online and they'll be delighted to help you choose the essential pieces for each season.

Prices:	Luxury/Medium	Express Ship?	Yes
Delivers to:	Most worldwide	Gift Wrap?	Yes
Based:	UK		

www.mytheresa.com

The talent list here is exceptional, with designers such as Anna Sui, Catherine Malandrino, Christian Louboutin, Dolce & Gabanna, Temperley, McQueen and Vera Wang being just a few of the names. Prices are all in euros and are totally at the designer end of the spectrum, but the choice of clothes, bags, shoes and other accessories is wonderful. Now would my bank manager still speak to me if I bought those Dolce shoes? No, didn't think so.

Prices:	Luxury/Medium	Express Ship?	Germany only
Delivers to:	Most worldwide	Gift Wrap?	Yes
Based:	Germany		

www.netaporter.com

Here you'll find the most impressive range of designer clothes and accessories available online and a retailer that's becoming increasingly well known for its clever buying, excellent service and attractive packaging. So if you're searching for something special with a designer label, such as Marc Jacobs, Alexander McQueen, Burberry, Roland Mouret, Alberta Ferretti, Marni, Jimmy Choo or Paul Smith, you should definitely have a look here.

Prices:	Luxury/Medium/Very Good Value	Express Ship?	Yes
Delivers to:	Most worldwide	Gift Wrap?	Yes
Based:	UK		

www.paulsmith.co.uk

One of the most successful and internationally well-known British designers, with several collections including Paul Smith Black, Jeans and fragrance, his website is, as you would expect, different and idiosyncratic. Here you'll find a selection of his jeans, shoes, knitwear, t-shirts and accessories, plus a small amount of tailoring, and there are several clear views of each item.

Prices:	Luxury/Medium/Very Good Value	Express Ship?	Yes
Delivers to:	Most worldwide	Gift Wrap?	Yes
Based:	UK		

www.pollyanna.com

Here's one of the longest-established fashion retailers in the UK, with a premium list of designers for men and women including Comme des Garcons, Issey Miyake, Junya Watanabe and Yohji Yamamoto, plus Jil Sander and Lanvin. Shop on this modern, clean website and choose where to go by designer, garment type or season.

Prices:	Luxury/Medium/Very Good Value	Express Ship?	No
Delivers to:	Most worldwide	Gift Wrap?	No
Based:	UK		

www.smythson.com

For over a century Smythson has been famous as the Bond Street purveyor of top-quality personalised stationery and accessories, including diaries, leather journals, albums, frames and gold-edged place cards. They also have a luxurious small collection of handbags, briefcases, wallets and small leather goods at totally frightening prices.

Prices:	Luxury	Express Ship?	No
Delivers to:	Worldwide	Gift Wrap?	No
Based:	UK		

www.viviennewestwoodonline.co.uk

You may not be able to order her iconic clothing here. However, on Vivienne Westwood's simply designed website you will find her handbags, jewels, shades, belts, fragrance and ties. To view the main collections take a look at www.viviennewestwood.co.uk. Delivery is to the UK, EU and US.

Prices:	Luxury/Medium	Express Ship?	No
Delivers to:	UK, EU and US	Gift Wrap?	No
Based:	UK		

Boutique Bliss

This is quite a mix of online retailers, from clever stores you'll almost certainly have heard of to upscale brands such as Coast and Reiss and great little boutiques offering you a bit of everything – that Farhi jacket, Chloe bag, Cavalli belt and Strutt Couture shoes, all tied together with small but fascinating collections of jewels which, when you take the whole look into account, clearly define each season.

Some of these sites give you the lowdown on the latest trends and how to wear them, others assume you've already got the idea. With everything from modern classics to next season's must-have, you need to allow quite a time for a good browse when you reach this section. Make that cup of tea or pour yourself that glass of wine and boot up your PC now for a really good time.

www.agnesb.com

This site is a must for Agnes B fans as you can order most of the collection online and find the ranges for women, men, children and accessories. Order beautifully cut, fitted white shirts, superbly designed t-shirts and chic trousers, which are staples of this collection, plus each season's new fashion pieces.

Prices:	Medium/Very Good Value	Express Ship?	Yes
Delivers to:	Most EU, China, USA and Japan	Gift Wrap?	No
Based:	France		

www.apc.fr

Browse through the looks here, click on one you like and then order from the component parts at this chic young French store. You can find some unique pieces such as baby llama wool stoles, bamboo and cotton-mix knits and contemporary outerwear. The collection is for men, women and children and it's a very specific style.

Prices:	Medium/Very Good Value	Express Ship?	Yes
Delivers to:	Worldwide	Gift Wrap?	No
Based:	France		

www.asos.com

ASOS has exploded over the past few years from its As Seen On Screen early days to one of the largest fashion sites on the web. Just click to the brand list to find All Saints, French Connection, Just Cavalli and Rock and Republic, alongside bags by Balenciaga, watches by Michael Kors and footwear by Kurt Geiger, Strutt Couture and UGG. You could spend hours browsing here, so make sure you have plenty of time when you start.

Prices:	Luxury/Medium/Very Good Value	Express Ship?	Yes
Delivers to:	Worldwide	Gift Wrap?	No
Based:	UK		

www.brittique.com

This is a beautifully designed online boutique featuring designers such as Amanda Wakeley, Maria Grachvogel and Louise Amstrup, and the list is growing all the time. You'll also find accessories and jewellery by Vinnie Day, Lucy J, Deal and Wire and more, some of which would make perfect gifts, particularly with the speedy delivery and high-quality packaging.

Prices:	Luxury/Medium/Very Good Value	Express Ship?	Yes
Delivers to:	Worldwide	Gift Wrap?	Yes
Based:	UK		

www.coast-stores.com

You may well have heard of Coast, retailer of gorgeous and accessibly priced occasion and eveningwear. Now you can browse and buy from the collection online, with everything from your next Little Black Dress to full-length evening gowns. Take a look here in advance of the next party season as the best dresses will disappear fast.

Prices:	Medium/Very Good Value	Express Ship?	Yes
Delivers to:	UK and Ireland	Gift Wrap?	No
Based:	UK		

www.coggles.com

There's a really good range of modern brands here at this online boutique based out of York, but the list is far too long to give you them all. As an idea you'll find Joseph, Seven for all Mankind, Nicole Farhi, Paul Smith and Ralph Lauren. Not only that but you can immediately see whether your size is available. Look out for some excellent discounts in the end-of-season sales.

Prices:	Luxury/Medium	Express Ship?	Yes
Delivers to:	Worldwide	Gift Wrap?	No
Based:	UK		

www.crocandco.co.uk

Here's a multi-brand designer boutique offering collections by Issa, Hudson, Vivienne Westwood, Paul Smith, Valentino, Nicole Farhi and more, with the range changing regularly. Unlike some online boutiques they're not trying to overwhelm you with products and on one page you can select by designer, by men, women or children's clothes and by type of garment.

Prices:	Luxury/Medium	Express Ship?	Yes
Delivers to:	Worldwide	Gift Wrap?	No
Based:	UK		

www.cruiseclothing.co.uk

Cruise offers an excellent range of contemporary fashion for men and women, specialising in casualwear, trainers, bags and shoes. With brands such as Gina, Chloe, Marc Jacobs, Dior and DKNY there's plenty to choose from and you can expect more great brands to be added in soon. The shoes and handbags are definitely the strongest offers here. Call for express delivery, standard UK delivery is free.

Prices:	Luxury/Medium/Very Good Value	Express Ship?	Yes
Delivers to:	UK	Gift Wrap?	No
Based:	UK		

www.fredafashion.com

Freda is a beautifully finished and wearable selection of each season's essentials from Matches of London, including chic coats, jackets, skirts, trousers, tops and knitwear, all totally in line with fashion's latest trends and all of which you'll probably want to buy immediately. Sizes are 8–14.

Prices:	Luxury/Medium	Express Ship?	Yes
Delivers to:	Worldwide	Gift Wrap?	Yes
Based:	UK		

www.ghost.co.uk

Ghost has a stylish, easy-to-navigate website full of flattering, wearable temptations. You can shop from the basic crepe range for your holiday trousers, skirts and tops and then pay a visit to the dress section to find your next little cocktail number. Ghost is not inexpensive, but with a range designed to suit all shapes and sizes that not only travels beautifully but will always make you feel your best, it's well worth it.

Prices:	Luxury/Medium	Express Ship?	No
Delivers to:	Worldwide	Gift Wrap?	No
Based:	UK		

www.hobbs.co.uk

You may well have shopped at Hobbs for beautifully cut tailoring, chic eveningwear or casual separates (not to mention excellent accessories). On their attractive website you can order everything online. Shop by item or visit specific areas such as partywear, gifts and jewellery. The choice is yours.

Prices:	Medium	Express Ship?	No
Delivers to:	UK	Gift Wrap?	No
Based:	UK		

www.jaeger.co.uk

The Jaeger website is far more modern than the stores, so you get a completely different feel to the clothes on offer. They are very wearable and there's a range of styles for just about everyone. Take a look at Jaeger London for their view on the key looks of the season or the excellent basics in the Jaeger Collection.

Prices:	Medium	Express Ship?	Yes
Delivers to:	UK	Gift Wrap?	Yes
Based:	UK		

www.jigsaw-online.com

Jigsaw always has one of the very best collections each season of contemporary mix-and-match dressing, with unique toning colours and layering essentials that you won't be able to live without. Buy just one piece here or your complete new wardrobe and add to it as the season and the new ranges arrive.

Prices:	Medium/Very Good Value	Express Ship?	Call them
Delivers to:	UK plus US site	Gift Wrap?	No
Based:	UK		

www.josephm.com

Here's a women's and children's designer boutique based in Darlington and offering ranges from See by Chloe, Issa, Alexander McQueen, Matthew Williamson and James Lakeland, to name but a few. Children's collections are by Burberry, Chloe, DKNY and D & G Junior. Cleverly you can see the site in French, German, Italian, Spanish, Korean, Japanese and Chinese.

Prices:	Very Good Value	Express Ship?	No
Delivers to:	UK	Gift Wrap?	No
Based:	UK		

www.julesb.co.uk

Brands here include Armani Jeans, Nicole Farhi, Diane von Furstenberg, Mulberry and Oska alongside Crea Concept and Hoss Intropia. The site is easy to navigate, with several views and a zoom-in facility on all products. The next time you find that one of the better-known stores has sold out of your favourite DVF dress or Mulberry handbag, take a look here, you just never know. There's an excellent menswear collection here as well.

Prices:	Luxury/Medium	Express Ship?	Yes
Delivers to:	Worldwide	Gift Wrap?	No
Based:	UK		

www.karenmillen.co.uk

At Karen Millen you can buy your stretch-satin, one-shoulder evening dress, sequinned cocktail frock and leopard-print coat well in time for the party season. I'm sure you don't need me to tell you that you can find great occasionwear, smart everyday tailoring, relaxed but contemporary weekend separates and wonderful accessories, but I thought I'd remind you anyway.

Prices:	Medium	Express Ship?	Yes
Delivers to:	UK	Gift Wrap?	No
Based:	UK		

www.misamu.com

Citizens of Humanity, Gold Hawk, Ella Moss, Pyrus, Rebecca Taylor and Velvet are just some of the modern brands stocked by this Ireland-based online boutique willing to ship to you anywhere in the world. Prices are, as you'd expect, at the designer level, but the clothes are well photographed on actual models rather than just as stills. Delivery is free if you spend over £100.

Prices:	Medium	Express Ship?	No
Delivers to:	Worldwide	Gift Wrap?	No
Based:	UK		

www.my-wardrobe.com

This is a well laid-out designer clothing and accessories website offering FrostFrench, Cacharel, Ann Louise Roswald, Sara Berman, Tocca and See by Chloe. For each item you can see several different views, plus a close-up of details such as embroidery and prints. There is also excellent description and commentary under 'My-Advice.'

Prices:	Luxury/Medium	Express Ship?	Yes
Delivers to:	Worldwide	Gift Wrap?	No
Based:	UK		

www.reiss.co.uk

Buy this fast-expanding, reasonably priced and fashion-forward brand online on their excellent website. Choose from outerwear, dresses, tailoring and casual separates, plus excellent chic accessories. This is a great place for stylish workwear and after-dark dresses, plus grown-up weekend dressing.

Prices:	Medium	Express Ship?	No
Delivers to:	UK	Gift Wrap?	No
Based:	UK		

www.shopatanna.co.uk

With stores based in London, Norfolk and Suffolk, Anna is an innovative boutique offering clothes and accessories by Betty Jackson, Seven, Issa London, Orla Kiely, Gharani Strock and lesser-known designers such as Day and Noa Noa. This is an eclectic and modern collection combining elegance and quirkiness and designers are being added all the time, so keep checking back.

Prices:	Luxury/Medium	Express Ship?	Yes
Delivers to:	Worldwide	Gift Wrap?	Yes
Based:	UK		

www.shoptommy.co.uk

There's an excellent selection of modern daywear and accessories available from the Tommy Hilfiger website, from cashmere/cotton cable knitwear, jeans and winter jackets and coats to bags and wallets, snow boots and shoes and chic skiwear. There's also a gift section and the option of gift boxing for all items.

Prices:	Medium	Express Ship?	No
Delivers to:	Worldwide	Gift Wrap?	Yes
Based:	UK		

www.start-london.com

'Where Fashion meets Rock'nRoll' is the mission statement here and you'll see why immediately when you visit the site, where Marc Jacobs and Mulberry mix happily with Josh Goot and Pink Soda. You'll find an eclectic selection of clothes and accessories for both men and women, totally different from what's available elsewhere, so it's well worth a look.

Prices:	Luxury/Medium/Very Good Value	Express Ship?	Yes
Delivers to:	Worldwide	Gift Wrap?	No
Based:	UK		

www.stylebop.com

German-based Stylebop offers speedy worldwide delivery and a mix of clothing and accessory designers who go under the headings of Great Luxury (Celine, Burberry, Calvin Klein, Valentino), Contemporary (Isabella Fiore, Kenneth Jay Lane, Kors, Juicy Couture, Day Birger et Mikkelsen) and Young and Trendy (C & C California, La ROK, Ella Moss and Coast).

Prices:	Luxury/Medium/Very Good Value	Express Ship?	Within Germany Only
Delivers to:	Worldwide	Gift Wrap?	No
Based:	Germany		

www.whistles.co.uk

Whistles' online store is a well-designed, clever and fun place to shop where you can clearly see the full collection, check out what's new and choose what to buy to go with each item. There are separates, day and evening dresses, outerwear and accessories, all in their own idiosyncratic contemporary style. Take a look now – you're bound to want to shop here.

Prices:	Medium	Express Ship?	Yes
Delivers to:	Worldwide	Gift Wrap?	No
Based:	UK		

www.zenggi.com

Keep your credit cards firmly locked away when you start to look at this Netherlands-based website as the temptation levels are extremely high. Zenggi is a new online luxury clothing and accessories store offering a chic, high-quality, covetable range. When you click on an item you can see a stylish model pic plus your chosen piece and how to accessorise it. Gift packaging is standard.

Prices:	Luxury/Medium	Express Ship?	No
Delivers to:	EU	Gift Wrap?	Yes
Based:	Netherlands		

Style Secrets

If you're the kind of gal who likes to find a little bit of everything together in one place then this is the section for you. Whether you want hard-to-find designer pieces, pretty lingerie, unusual pamper pressies (and treats for yourself) or clever accessories all brought together in a totally different way from the mainstream boutiques, just sit down here and have a look through.

These 'gems' are often wonderful for gifts as not only have the ranges been brought together by a group of single-minded, luxury-loving buyers, but their attention to detail is also very special. You can expect your order to arrive gorgeously wrapped, boxed or bagged in a way that states that not only is there something special inside but that you, the giver, must have great taste to have discovered such an unusual place to buy from.

You'll notice that there are some overseas-based online shops included here and of course if you choose to buy from them you'll have to wait that little bit longer for your order to arrive. But often there are reasonably priced ideas you simply won't find elsewhere, so if you want to appear really, really clever …

www.allegrahicks.com

Allegra Hicks offers beautiful and contemporary designs, with a fashion collection aimed at the woman who travels a lot and needs stylish clothes that work in many climates and travel and pack easily. There are lovely home accessories and gifts here as well. Delivery is free if you buy more than three products, but it's extremely expensive otherwise.

Prices:	Medium	Express Ship?	No
Delivers to:	Worldwide	Gift Wrap?	No
Based:	UK		

www.anthropologie.com

US brand Anthropologie has over 100 stores throughout the US and now delivers to most countries in the world. Shop their attractive online store for special and different clothes and accessories such as rose trimmed cardis, peasant blouses, appliquéd skirts, stamped leather bags and more. With Anthoropogie you see everything in your currency plus duty and shipping charges. Prices are not cheap once you've added everything in but there are some very special pieces.

Prices:	Medium	Express Ship?	No
Delivers to:	Worldwide	Gift Wrap?	No
Based:	US		

www.anusha.co.uk

Here's a boudoir-style online boutique where you can buy pretty and indulgent designer pieces, from clothes, luxurious loungewear, vintage-inspired jewellery and unique accessories to pampering gifts. When your order arrives it'll be beautifully wrapped in layers of fuchsia tissue paper and finished off with a feather butterfly and chocolate-brown Anusha label. So come here for a treat for yourself or for perfect presents.

Prices:	Medium	Express Ship?	No
Delivers to:	Worldwide	Gift Wrap?	Yes
Based:	UK		

www.cocoribbon.com

Calling itself London's lifestyle boutique, Coco Ribbon offers a selection of contemporary clothing by designers such as Collette Dinnigan, Rebecca Taylor and Cynthia Vincent. There is pretty, modern lingerie and swimwear, a small but beautiful range of handbags and jewellery, plus unusual girly gifts and candles.

Prices:	Medium	Express Ship?	Yes
Delivers to:	Worldwide	Gift Wrap?	Yes
Based:	UK		

www.ladress.com

This is a novel idea from a Netherlands-based retailer offering you beautifully styled simple dresses in a variety of lengths and fabrics, from polka-dot satin silk to lace, crepe jersey and fine wool. So if you've been searching for that perfect dress for a while you may find it here. There's a choice of a chic wrap style or flattering button front and they're designed to be an easy fit. Your dress will arrive beautifully packaged and ribbon tied and you can order slips and sashes here as well.

Prices:	Medium	Express Ship?	Yes
Delivers to:	EU	Gift Wrap?	No
Based:	Netherlands		

www.plumo.co.uk

At Plumo you'll always find something different and interesting, from crystal flower tealights to a beaded clutch. They also offer homewares, clothes and accessories including shoes and jewellery. It's not a huge collection but beautifully edited to be feminine and chic at the same time. There are some lovely gift ideas here as well and express delivery and gift wrapping are just two of the services offered.

Prices:	Medium/Very Good Value	Express Ship?	Yes
Delivers to:	Worldwide	Gift Wrap?	Yes
Based:	UK		

www.reddirect.co.uk

What started as a small offshoot of *Red* magazine has now become a treasure trove of cleverly chosen jewellery, watches, handbags, shoes, belts and pretty leather accessories by designers such as CC Skye, Rebecca Lau, Belen Echandia, Osprey and Ollie and Nic, with interior ideas by Jan Constantine, Orla Kiely and Missoni. There are also cute, well-priced kids' toys and gifts.

Prices:	Very Good Value	Express Ship?	Yes
Delivers to:	Worldwide	Gift Wrap?	No
Based:	UK		

www.shopbop.com

Shopbop is a clever, modern online boutique offering a wide lists of brands, including Ella Moss, Beatrix Ong, Juicy Couture, Diane von Furstenberg, Chip and Pepper, Marc by Marc Jacobs, Hudson, Kooba and Seven For All Mankind to name just a few, and offering to ship them just about anywhere in the world by express delivery.

Prices:	Luxury/Medium	Express Ship? (UK)	Yes
Delivers to:	Worldwide	Gift Wrap?	Yes
Based:	USA		

www.sundancecatalog.com

Inspired (and initiated) by Robert Redford, Sundance is a truly American catalogue which has now become a worldwide online store. You'll discover wonderful jewellery by American craftsmen, a wide range of high-quality classic American clothing including shirts, tops, ts, skirts and trousers, ranch-style boots, home accessories (gorgeous quilts and throws) and lots of ideas for gifts.

Prices:	Luxury/Medium	Express Ship? (UK)	No
Delivers to:	Worldwide	Gift Wrap?	Yes
Based:	USA		

Take a Walk on the High Street

I'm sure you'll have heard of all of these and passed them frequently on your strolls down the high street. Now's your chance to buy from them online and avoid that Saturday morning/late night shopping crush. You won't necessarily be the first to find out what's in the stores, nor will all the range be available here, but when you take into consideration the amount of choice, the excellent trend advice and the ease with which you can shop, you may well find these stores irresistible for a weekly non-bank-breaking fashion fix.

www.allsaintsshop.co.uk

All Saints offers up-to-the-minute styling totally in line with each season's different looks on their funky urban-appeal website. There are lots of well-photographed views of every item, including both model shots and basic product close-ups. Sizing goes from 6 to 14 in most items (although expect general sizing to be on the small size). You can shop by collection or by item and see straight away what's available in your size.

Prices:	Medium/Very Good Value	Express Ship?	No
Delivers to:	Worldwide	Gift Wrap?	No
Based:	UK		

www.dorothyperkins.co.uk

Dorothy Perkins' clothes and accessories are modern and amazingly well priced. They use some natural and some man-made fabrics and sizing goes from 8–22 for most items. You'll find wearable new looks each season plus some colourful knits, tops and accessories. Take a good look at the start of the season if you're likely to want something here as once a product has sold out they probably won't replace it.

Prices:	Very Good Value	Express Ship?	Yes
Delivers to:	UK	Gift Wrap?	No
Based:	UK		

www.esprit.co.uk

Susie and Doug Tompkins started selling Esprit clothes out of the back of their station waggon in San Francisco. You can now find the brand all over the world, with its young, fun, well priced and wearable ranges of t-shirts, jeans, basics, separates and accessories

Prices:	Medium	Express Ship?	No
Delivers to:	UK, some EU and US	Gift Wrap?	No
Based:	UK		

www.frenchconnection.com

This is a company where the words 'young' and 'contemporary' come straight to mind. They always have one of the best selections of new wardrobe must-haves alongside their very good basics such as knitwear and t-shirts, which are well priced, good quality and available in a range of colours. French Connection is definitely not cheap, but they deliver up-to-the-minute styling for men and women and the site is well worth a look.

Prices:	Medium	Express Ship?	Yes
Delivers to:	Worldwide	Gift Wrap?	No
Based:	UK		

www.joebrowns.com

This is a really fun website, where you'll find well-priced contemporary sportswear for men and women. Think vintage-style tops, ruffled shirts, sporty gilets and colourful polos and you'll get my drift. The pictures are extremely clear and there's plenty of description and information about each item. Alongside the clothing there are lots of accessories including sunglasses, jewellery, bags and purses and belts.

Prices:	Medium/Very Good Value	Express Ship?	No
Delivers to:	UK	Gift Wrap?	No
Based:	UK		

www.mango.com

Spanish label Mango offers inexpensive, up-to-the-minute clothes and accessories which they'll ship to you just about anywhere in the world. Their clever, modern website shows you everything at a glance. With jackets at around €60 and t-shirts from around €13 you can find plenty here to help you get the latest look without breaking the bank. Delivery is from Spain but is usually extremely quick.

Prices:	Very Good Value	Express Ship?	No
Delivers to:	Worldwide	Gift Wrap?	No
Based:	Spain		

www.missselfridge.co.uk

An integral part of the high street since the 60s, Miss Selfridge has always been a mainstay for young, modern style. There's nothing quiet about the clothes on offer but plenty of information and guidance on how to put together the latest looks and the background to the trends. They do go up to a size 16 but most of the clothes are designed for smaller sizes.

Prices:	Very Good Value	Express Ship?	Yes
Delivers to:	UK	Gift Wrap?	No
Based:	UK		

www.monsoon.co.uk

With its well-known presence on the high street almost everyone has heard of Monsoon, offering attractive, not inexpensive but still good-value clothing including some extremely wearable and different occasionwear. Sizing in a lot of cases goes up to a 20. The childrenswear selection is smaller but has the same look, including candy-coloured skirts and tops, sugar-striped swimwear and the prettiest partywear.

Prices:	Very Good Value	Express Ship?	No
Delivers to:	UK	Gift Wrap?	No
Based:	UK		

www.oasis-stores.com

The Oasis website allows you to shop simply and easily by garment, where you can zoom right in to see every detail and find all the information on sizing and fabric you could need. Alternatively you can shop by trend, where all the relevant pieces are brought together for you, or visit the glamorous Vintage collection.

Prices:	Very Good Value	Express Ship?	No
Delivers to:	UK	Gift Wrap?	No
Based:	UK		

www.principles.co.uk

With an easier-to-wear selection than some of the high street retailers Principles offers a stylish, well-priced collection of separates, dresses and coats on this attractively designed website. You'll find dresses, skirts, tops, jeans, knitwear, some attractive tailoring and occasionwear and a petite collection which goes from size 6–16.

Prices:	Very Good Value	Express Ship?	Yes
Delivers to:	UK	Gift Wrap?	No
Based:	UK		

www.riverisland.com

This young, stylish everyday, workwear and evening range is one of the best around. The site is great to look at and easy to use, and with a constantly updated range you can come back often and always find something new. Allow extra time for their standard delivery at busy times. One of the best things about shopping here is that you don't have to go through the trial of finding something you love and then discovering that your size isn't there.

Prices:	Medium/Very Good Value	Express Ship?	Yes
Delivers to:	UK	Gift Wrap?	No
Based:	UK		

www.store.americanapparel.co.uk

All the t-shirts and related products at hugely successful US based American Apparel have been photographed very simply and you can find just about every shape, neckline and sleeve and an amazing selection of colours. There are also daytime separates, sleepwear, swimwear, an organic range and options for men, kids and babies.

Prices:	Medium	Express Ship?	No
Delivers to:	Most Worldwide	Gift Wrap?	No
Based:	UK this site		

www.topshop.co.uk

This is the place to go if you want the latest fashions at the best prices and can't stand the scrum of the shops. Can't afford Marc Jacobs or Miu Miu? Go straight to Top Shop, and if you can't bear the heaving crowds in the store, desperately seeking the last pair of the latest and absolutely must-have heels in your size, you can order them online and have them sent to you by express delivery. www.topman.co.uk is the men's online store.

Prices:	Medium/Very Good Value	Express Ship?	Yes
Delivers to:	UK, USA, Australia and ROI	Gift Wrap?	Yes
Based:	UK		

www.urbanitystore.com

This is a hip website offering urban sportwear for girls and boys. Brands include Pop Clothing, Ichi, Boxfresh, Power Puff Girls and loads more offering jeans, dresses, skirts, tops and jackets, plus bags, belts and jewellery. They regularly have new stock so it's worthwhile checking back if this is the kind of fashion for you.

Prices:	Medium/Very Good Value	Express Ship?	No
Delivers to:	Worldwide	Gift Wrap?	No
Based:	UK		

www.urbanoutfitters.co.uk

Fast-growing US-based brand Urban Outfitters' young website is clearly targeted directly at their 18–30-year-old audience with a wide range of chic 'urban-styled' clothes and accessories for girls and boys. There's designer wear from Alice McCall and See by Chloe, an eclectic, well-priced range of separates, hosiery, scarves and gloves, right through to shoes, jewellery and underwear. Get the look now.

Prices:	Medium/Very Good Value	Express Ship?	Yes
Delivers to:	UK	Gift Wrap?	Yes
Based:	UK		

www.wallis-fashion.com

Wallis offers a small selection from its stores on the website and just about everything goes up to a size 20, so styles on the whole are easier to wear for most people. They give clear information right from the start about each and every product, right down to washing information, fabric content and sizing, as well as telling you about each season's looks and how to put them together.

Prices:	Very Good Value	Express Ship?	Yes
Delivers to:	UK	Gift Wrap?	No
Based:	UK		

www.warehouse.co.uk

Shop online at Warehouse for the latest trends and stylish must-haves. You'll find excellent seasonal collections as well as Warehouse Maternity, Denim and the Spotlight collection – a glam range of pieces for special occasions. The website is very user friendly and they deliver to all UK and ROI addresses.

Prices:	Very Good Value	Express Ship?	Yes
Delivers to:	UK and ROI	Gift Wrap?	No
Based:	UK		

Easy on the Eye

I had a real problem coming up with a name for this section. To me the word 'classic' is a total put-off (and in many cases these stores aren't classic so I'd be misleading you), so I thought that Easy on the Eye would probably confuse you enough to make you read these few words. Here goes.

This is a quirky group of online stores to bring together, where you can find easy-to-wear separates for everyone plus very good accessories. They're for those who love clothes but don't necessarily want to sport the very latest shape/colour/style and also want beautiful additions to their wardrobe without spending huge amounts. Buy your complete wardrobe here? Well, you certainly could, but you can also order perfectly cut trousers, non bank-breaking cashmere, your next shearling jacket and that Little Black Dress to take you from day through to night, plus loads more.

www.artigiano.co.uk

At Artigiano the emphasis is on modern/classic clothes and accessories with easy rather than very fitted shapes and reasonably generous sizing. You'll find lovely, fine and chunky knitwear, excellent t-shirts and tops, trousers in a selection of styles and fabrics, and unique jackets, outerwear and occasionwear you can't buy anywhere else.

Prices:	Medium/Very Good Value	Express Ship?	Yes
Delivers to:	Worldwide	Gift Wrap?	Most Items
Based:	UK		

www.boden.co.uk

It would be surprising if you hadn't already seen the Boden catalogue and you may well already have shopped from them online. Provided you like the colourful relaxed style you'll probably be extremely tempted. If you're into minimalist chic black, don't go there. There's Mini Boden and menswear as well. The site is always full of fun ideas and makes you feel good just having a browse.

Prices:	Medium/Very Good Value	Express Ship?	Yes
Delivers to:	Worldwide	Gift Wrap?	No
Based:	UK		

www.celtic-sheepskin.co.uk

There are some excellent clothes and accessories here, particularly for the winter months, including chic Toscana shearling jackets and coats, gloves, scarves and sheepskin lined boots and slippers, waistcoats and gilets and cute shearling duffles and boots for children. Prices are reasonable and everything's really clearly photographed.

Prices:	Luxury/Medium	Express Ship? (UK)	No
Delivers to:	UK	Gift Wrap?	No
Based:	UK		

www.ewenique.co.uk

This is a very attractive and comprehensive range of leather, suede and shearling coats and jackets for men and women plus flying jackets and accessories such as scarves and stoles, hats, hide bags, gloves and snuggly slippers. Everything is beautifully photographed with close-ups of the sheepskins so that you can see exactly what you're buying.

Prices:	Medium	Express Ship? (UK)	No
Delivers to:	Worldwide	Gift Wrap?	No
Based:	UK		

www.kew-online.com

Kew offers modern, versatile, well-priced separates in a wide choice of colours and styles. There's a very good selection on this website and there are some great tops and fine knitwear plus easy jackets and skirts with most items being available in a selection of colours, which they show you very clearly.

Prices:	Very Good Value	Express Ship?	Yes
Delivers to:	Worldwide	Gift Wrap?	Most Items
Based:	UK		

www.landsend.co.uk

This leading catalogue company originates in the US and offers a wide range of high-quality, well-priced clothing for men and women. Signature collections include stylish co-ordinates, casualwear, linen wear, swimwear, outerwear, cashmere and footwear with lots of essentials for your new season's wardrobe.

Prices:	Medium/Very Good Value	Express Ship?	Yes
Delivers to:	Worldwide	Gift Wrap?	Yes
Based:	UK		

www.lauraashley.com

If you haven't visited Laura Ashley's attractive website recently then now would be a good time; there's an excellent range of pretty and wearable clothing in contemporary prints and colours and often some very good special offers. You can see straight away what the latest arrivals are and if you like something be aware that they can sell out fast. The home furnishings range is excellent too.

Prices:	Very Good Value	Express Ship?	Yes
Delivers to:	Worldwide	Gift Wrap?	Yes
Based:	UK		

www.peruvianconnection.co.uk

Each season Peruvian Connection offers a richly photographed collection of separates using Peruvian alpaca and jewel coloured pima cotton. The look is very elegant with a choice of fine tops and knits to wear with gorgeously patterned skirts, art knit jackets and sweaters, beaded jewellery, scarves and bags. You'll find excellent quality and in some cases quite steep prices.

Prices:	Medium/Very Good Value	Express Ship?	Yes
Delivers to:	Worldwide	Gift Wrap?	Yes
Based:	UK		

www.phase-eight.co.uk

For reasonably priced and beautifully thought-out occasion dressing Phase Eight has always been one of the best, with a particularly good selection of dresses that fit and flatter to perfection. Browse the range and don't miss the printed wrap and tapework dresses, bead- and sequin-trimmed camisoles and shrugs in a lovely choice of colours and fine gauge knits.

Prices:	Medium/Very Good Value	Express Ship?	Yes
Delivers to:	Worldwide	Gift Wrap?	Yes
Based:	UK		

www.planet.co.uk

I'm sure you've heard of this brand but if it's not one you normally shop from offline you should stop now and take a quick look round. They've made it very easy to see everything on offer and they tell you straight away all the sizes that are available. Styles tend to be classic and there are quite a lot of (high-quality) man-made fabrics, but it's a very good range, particularly for the jackets and outerwear.

Prices:	Medium/Very Good Value	Express Ship?	Yes
Delivers to:	UK	Gift Wrap?	No
Based:	UK		

www.toastbypost.co.uk

Toast has long been well known for simple, beautifully made clothes in natural colours and natural fabrics. The range of separates includes skirts, tops, knitwear and trousers, plus nightwear and gowns, beachwear and a small collection of bed linen. Don't expect lots of bright colours here – this designer is about quiet, easy style.

Prices:	Medium/Very Good Value	Express Ship?	Yes
Delivers to:	Worldwide	Gift Wrap?	Yes
Based:	UK		

www.wallcatalogue.com

If you like high-quality, easy-to-wear clothing in unusual fabrics then you should take a good look at this well-photographed website. It's a very different and attractive range of modern, flattering separates in muted colours such as barley, oyster, pale grey and, of course, black for winter. The clothes aren't inexpensive but you're buying into real quality and the service is excellent.

Prices:	Medium/Very Good Value	Express Ship?	Yes
Delivers to:	UK	Gift Wrap?	No
Based:	UK		

www.wraponline.co.uk

There's always a very good selection of tops, knitwear, trousers and skirts here using mainly natural yarns such as cotton, silk and cashmere, you can see how they all work together and also tell at a glance whether what you want to order is in stock or not. Check out the new accessory range of casual bags and belts. There are separate websites for the UK, USA and Germany.

Prices:	Medium/Very Good Value	Express Ship?	Yes
Delivers to:	UK	Gift Wrap?	No
Based:	UK		

Jean Machine

If you're not a dedicated jeans wearer then I recommend you just turn the page and move on to the next section. This is the first time that jeans have had their own special section and for anyone who treasures their jeans as friends beyond just about any other article of clothing, this is yet another perfect place to shop. This is provided you either know which make, style and size is right for you or you don't mind shelling out for several different pairs to start with so that you can try them all on at home and swiftly despatch back the ones that don't fit.

If you know and love a specific designer brand you probably will be able to find it online at one of the stores below, plus some easier fit and quite hard to find imports such as Not Your Daughter's Jeans – the non skinny-fit jeans person's answer to designer jeans.

www.acnejeans.com

Swedish-based Acne Jeans have created a versatile wardrobe for men and women which includes basic cotton t-shirts, jackets, knitwear accessories and footwear. In the jeans collection there's a wide range of styles and you can see everything from front and back. Prices are at the high end but the styling is different and innovative, so if you're in the market for a new casual wardrobe you should take a look.

Prices:	Luxury/Medium/Very Good Value	Express Ship?	No
Delivers to:	Most worldwide	Gift Wrap?	No
Based:	Sweden		

www.diesel.com

There's so much going on at Diesel's stylish website that it's hard to get away without buying something, particularly if you're a Diesel fan. Visit the unusual flash-driven 'Style Lounge' to take a peek at the new season's collections or just buy from the clearly photographed ranges of jeans, tops, t-s, accessories and more for men and women. There's footwear and luggage as well on this seriously good casualwear website.

Prices:	Medium/Very Good Value	Express Ship?	Yes
Delivers to:	UK, Europe and US	Gift Wrap?	No
Based:	UK		

www.ilovejeans.co.uk

Those of you who aren't a perfect size 8, 10, or in fact a perfect size anything should rush to this online store, one of the few places on the web where you can find the current fashion favourites, otherwise known as Tummy Tuck Jeans (or Not Your Daughter's Jeans). They also offer Made in Heaven, Ruby, !IT and Hudson Jeans and there's a good range of styles and washes and lots of information on fit.

Prices:	Medium	Express Ship?	Yes
Delivers to:	Worldwide	Gift Wrap?	No
Based:	UK		

www.jeans-direct.com

If you're a jeans addict you should take a look at this website, where there's a selection by Levi, Ben Sherman, Wrangler and Diesel, although by far the greatest choice is by Levi. Personally I think you really have to know your size in each brand to be sure you won't have to send them back, but obviously you can try lots of different styles at home which is a great benefit if you, like me, would rather try your jeans on in private than in a public changing room.

Prices:	Medium	Express Ship?	No
Delivers to:	EU	Gift Wrap?	No
Based:	UK		

www.eu.levi.com

For Levi fanatics this is the place for you to buy your next pair of jeans. It's a young, busy and friendly website offering every style and introducing the new ones as they come into the collections. So if you're into skinny/straight/bootcut/low-rise/high-waist or whatever, you'll find them all here. As well as the jeans there's a great selection of denim jackets, sweaters and tops plus bags and belts.

Prices:	Medium	Express Ship?	No
Delivers to:	Most worldwide	Gift Wrap?	No
Based:	UK		

www.trilogystores.co.uk

Trilogy is devoted to helping you find the perfect pair of jeans. If you can't get there, take a look at their excellent website where you can find (and find out about) brands such as Seven for All Mankind, Citizens of Humanity, Joe, Rich and Skinny, and Vince. If that all sounds a bit confusing you can just click through to their Denim for You section to find your favourite style, rinse and type of leg and to discover what's new now.

Prices:	Medium	Express Ship?	Yes
Delivers to:	Worldwide	Gift Wrap?	No
Based:	UK		

www.usc.co.uk

USC is one of the UK's leading retailers of 'youth culture' branded clothing, footwear and accessories, offering brands such as Diesel, G-Star, Replay, Henri Lloyd, Lacoste, Miss Sixty, Firetrap and Vila. With a list like this you'll no doubt be able to guess that jeans are not all you'll find here – you'll find your up-to-the-minute separates and accessories here as well.

Prices:	Medium	Express Ship?	No
Delivers to:	UK	Gift Wrap?	No
Based:	UK		

Knitwear Queen

Most of the online fashion stores offer knitwear as part of their collection, but for the really good cashmere ranges you should take a look here where you'll find a wide choice of prices and styles. With cashmere, inevitably, you get what you pay for, so when you're gasping for joy at that amazing hot pink v-neck cashmere top at what seems to be a ridiculously low price, do not expect it to wash as well or last for the same length of time as something that's going to set you back around four times the price. It'll be fun to wear but may well not last you more than one season.

My advice is for new season's colours and 'interesting styles' go cheap and cheerful but for classics spend as much as you can afford. That black slim-fit roll-neck sweater will be with you for ever but you'll probably tire of hot pink as soon as they tell us that purple's going to be the new black this year.

www.belindarobertson.com

Award-winning Belinda Dickson goes by the affectionate title of 'Queen of Cashmere'. On her website you'll find her two different labels – the White Label collection, offering affordable but beautifully designed cashmere, and her signature 'Cashmere Couture' range of the finest cashmere, made exclusively in Scotland and sparkling with Swarovski crystals and satin trims. All available in up to 120 colours.

Prices:	Luxury/Medium	Express Ship? (UK)	Yes
Delivers to:	Worldwide	Gift Wrap?	Yes
Based:	UK		

www.berkcashmere.co.uk

David Berk opened his shop at 46, Burlington Arcade, off London's Piccadilly, more than 50 years ago and though initially the shop stocked Shetland knits and tartan kilts, scarves and rugs, the focus has gradually shifted to cashmere. Brands on offer include their own wide range of styles and colours, Balantyne cashmere and John Smedley plus cashmere and silk and camelhair.

Prices:	Luxury/Medium	Express Ship? (UK)	Yes
Delivers to:	Worldwide	Gift Wrap?	No
Based:	UK		

www.brora.co.uk

Brora offers classic fine-quality Scottish cashmere with a contemporary twist, with prices that offer real value for money. Although they are not the cheapest, they offer some of the best quality available and in designs and a selection of colours that you won't find anywhere else. The pictures are beautifully clear and you'll find them hard to resist. The collection extends to men, children and babies.

Prices:	Luxury/Medium	Express Ship? (UK)	Yes
Delivers to:	Worldwide	Gift Wrap?	Yes
Based:	UK		

www.cashmere.co.uk

Purely Cashmere is one of Scotland's longest-standing online cashmere retailers. They offer high-quality single-, two- and three-ply knits for men and women in a good range of colours and there's a combination of classic designs and modern styles plus some luxurious throws for the home. They also have cashmere care products such as Cashmere Wash and clear zipped bags for storing and travelling.

Prices:	Luxury/Medium	Express Ship? (UK)	Yes
Delivers to:	Worldwide	Gift Wrap?	No
Based:	UK		

www.crumpetengland.com

This is a small range of beautiful and modern cashmere, ranging from fine, almost lingerie-inspired pieces to chunky knits. Most pieces are available in a range of new season's colours and all are beautifully photographed. There are plenty of places to find your everyday cashmere classics. Here you'll find something special and different, so take a look.

Prices:	Luxury/Medium	Express Ship? (UK)	No
Delivers to:	Worldwide	Gift Wrap?	No
Based:	UK		

www.ejk.biz

Emma Jane Knight's collection is uniquely detailed, high quality (and high-end priced) with cashmere sweaters, wraps and jackets in a good range of colours. You need to download and fill in their order form or call them to order. The styling is unusual and the quality quite exceptional.

Prices:	Luxury	Express Ship? (UK)	No
Delivers to:	Worldwide	Gift Wrap?	No
Based:	UK		

www.figcashmere.com

Here you can find reasonably priced cashmere in both classic and modern designs, many of which you won't find anywhere else and sometimes with assymetric hems, fluted cuffs and semi-precious stone trims. Most items are available in a range of seasonal colours. There are cute baby cashmere tops here as well and they offer a gift-box service.

Prices:	Medium	Express Ship? (UK)	No
Delivers to:	Worldwide	Gift Wrap?	Yes
Based:	UK		

www.johnsmedley.com

John Smedley is a family-owned business established in 1784 and specialises in the highest-quality fine-gauge knitwear. It's expensive but unbeatable for quality and fit. Whether you want a simple shell to wear underneath a jacket or a modern-cut fine merino cableknit top with the perfect neckline and three-quarter sleeves, it's better to buy just one piece from here than several cheaper versions.

Prices:	Luxury/Medium	Express Ship? (UK)	No
Delivers to:	Worldwide	Gift Wrap?	No
Based:	UK		

www.johnstonscashmere.com

No trip to the north of Scotland is complete without visiting Johnston's Woollen Mill in Elgin, where you can buy gorgeous, high-quality cashmere in modern and traditional styles and a very good of colours. On their easy-to-navigate website you can choose from cashmere for men, women, kids and babies, plus seriously beautiful blankets and throws, and other home textiles.

Prices:	Luxury/Medium	Express Ship? (UK)	Call
Delivers to:	EU	Gift Wrap?	No
Based:	UK		

www.purecollection.com

This is chic, high-quality cashmere in a wide range of styles with the emphasis on modern shapes and new season's colours. Alongside their less expensive range they offer 'Superfine' cashmere at a higher price, which is perfect for layering or wearing on its own. The delivery and service are excellent and the prices are good too.

Prices:	Luxury/Medium	Express Ship? (UK)	Yes
Delivers to:	Worldwide	Gift Wrap?	Yes
Based:	UK		

www.uniqlo.co.uk

Here's an excellent, extremely well-priced online store, where you can find cashmere knits in a marvellous range of colours. There are also fun t's and tops, jeans in lots of different styles and some excellent accessory gift ideas such as scarves, Argyll-patterned hats and gloves and a wonderful selection of belts including metallic leathers.

Prices:	Very Good Value	Express Ship? (UK)	No
Delivers to:	UK (this website)	Gift Wrap?	No
Based:	UK		

Big is Beautiful

There are quite a number of places to find larger sizes in this book as well as here, particularly from the US/UK-based online stores such as Orvis, Lands End and Peruvian Connection where they really understand about sizing up.

Then there are the stores listed below that have specialised in a wide range of sizes. Some, such as Spirito, part of Artigiano, offer their own brand, while others such as Gray and Osbourn have the clothes of designers such as Gina Bacconi, Basler and Gardeur.

www.annascholz.com

For those looking for fashion in sizes up to a UK 28 life has just got a whole lot easier. Anna Scholz is a German-born designer who studied at the Central St Martins College of Art and Design and who has created a collection of glamorous clothes in sizes 12–28 incorporating silk, velvet and cashmere, animal prints and feathers. If you're looking for something really special this is an excellent place to browse.

Prices:	Luxury/Medium	Express Ship? (UK)	No
Delivers to:	EU	Gift Wrap?	No
Based:	UK		

www.grayandosbourn.co.uk

Here you'll find labels such as Basler and Gerry Weber plus their own well-priced Gray and Osbourn range. Most items are available in sizes 12–22 and some go up to 26. The range is essentially classic but in tune with each season and you can dress here from holiday/cruise, country weekends, smart tailoring, tops and accessories to really chic eveningwear.

Prices:	Luxury/Medium	Express Ship? (UK)	No
Delivers to:	UK	Gift Wrap?	No
Based:	UK		

www.longtallsally.co.uk

As someone who's always been quite a bit shorter than they'd really like to be, when I click onto this modern, stylish website I always wish that they offered clothes I could wear as well (foolish, I know, but there it is). Here you'll find a range of clothes for women over 5ft 7in from casual to smart and everything in between, also swimwear, maternity wear, shoes and accessories

Prices:	Medium	Express Ship? (UK)	Yes
Delivers to:	Worldwide	Gift Wrap?	No
Based:	UK		

www.pennyplain.co.uk

Penny Plain (who you've probably already heard of) have a clear website where you can order their clothes from size 10 to size 26. The collection of separates, dresses and eveningwear is essentially classic and combines pretty fabrics with reasonable (although not cheap) prices. There's a small range of attractive shoes as well.

Prices:	Medium	Express Ship? (UK)	Yes but expensive
Delivers to:	Worldwide	Gift Wrap?	No
Based:	UK		

www.rowlandsclothing.co.uk

The first Rowlands shop opened in Bath in 1983 with the aim of providing a range of high-quality, reasonably priced, smart-casual classic country clothing. From their successful mail-order catalogue they've now put their collection online with a simple, easy-to-use website offering smart coats and jackets, dresses and a selection of separates from day to evening.

Prices:	Medium	Express Ship? (UK)	No
Delivers to:	UK	Gift Wrap?	No
Based:	UK		

www.spirito.co.uk

This is the top end of the online plus-size clothing ranges offering a high-quality selection in sizes 10–20, including smart daywear, knitwear, casualwear and eveningwear. Everything is beautifully made in Italy and smartly photographed to make you really want to buy, as you would expect from Artigiano's sister company. Shoes, accessories and jewellery are from the main Artigiano ranges and footwear goes up to a size 9.

Prices:	Medium	Express Ship? (UK)	Yes
Delivers to:	Worldwide	Gift Wrap?	Yes on some items
Based:	UK		

Lingerie and Swim

This is one of my all-time favourite areas for buying online (alongside handbags and shoes, jewels, cashmere, gorgeous pampering … OK, so I won't go and and bore you with the rest of the list).

You may think that buying swimwear and lingerie online could be tricky but I can assure you that it's not. There simply isn't any store offline where you could find the choice that's available here, whether you want designer or less expensive brands. The other really good thing about buying these products online, apart from the obvious – that you can try them on at home when you choose to – is that you'll always find a much wider range of sizes online. Forget finding that perfect little bordeaux lace number, falling in love with it, and then searching in vain through the rail to find your size – that simply doesn't happen online. You can see in an instant if it's available or not, how long you'll have to wait for it if it isn't yet in stock and whether you should move on and find something else.

Lingerie

www.agentprovocateur.com

Joseph Corre and Serena Rees opened the first Agent Provocateur shop in London, UK in December 1994 and have never looked back. The look is overt and sexy and at their online store you'll find their gorgeous lingerie displayed with attitude on the most perfect bodies. Don't come here if you're looking for something in a size larger than a 36E. Do come here if you love their products and don't want to have to go out to find them.

Prices:	Luxury/Medium	Express Ship? (UK)	Yes
Delivers to:	Worldwide	Gift Wrap?	No but packaging is very
Based:	UK		attractive

www.belladinotte.com

Bella di Notte has a pretty website offering one of the best collections of classic, lace-trimmed thermal, silk and cotton camisoles, vests and tops online in a range of colours such as ruby red and chocolate that you're unlikely to find elsewhere. You can buy Italian wool and silk tops, loungewear and nightwear here too plus hosiery and shapewear. Lingerie is by Triumph, Chantelle, Lejaby and more.

Prices:	Medium	Express Ship? (UK)	Yes
Delivers to:	Worldwide	Gift Wrap?	Yes
Based:	UK		

www.bravissimo.com

Bravissimo offers a wide selection of lingerie in D–JJ cup plus bra-sized swimwear in D–J cup making it the essential site for the fuller figure. You'll find strappy tops and sports bras and fitting advice as well. Their service is excellent and if you have any queries you can email them and they'll come back to you immediately.

Prices:	Medium	Express Ship? (UK)	Yes but you need to call them
Delivers to:	Worldwide	Gift Wrap?	No
Based:	UK		

www.coconuttrading.com

There's a great deal of beautiful beachwear here, from swimwear, sarongs, sundresses and kaftans by Melissa Odabash and Cia Maritima, exclusive sandals by Jack Rogers of the US and covetable bags by Serpui Marie. This is not a collection that you'll find together anywhere else and so definitely worth a look round before your next trip.

Prices:	Luxury/Medium	Express Ship? (UK)	No
Delivers to:	UK	Gift Wrap?	No
Based:	UK		

www.figleaves.com

If you can't find it here, you may well not be able to find it anywhere else as this is one of, if not the, best collection of lingerie, swimwear and sportswear available online. Almost every lingerie brand name is offered, from DKNY, Dolce & Gabbana and Janet Reger to Sloggi, Gossard and Wonderbra, and delivery is free throughout the world.

Prices:	Luxury/Medium/Very Good Value	Express Ship? (UK)	Yes
Delivers to:	Worldwide	Gift Wrap?	Yes
Based:	UK		

www.glamonweb.co.uk

Here you'll find the lingerie, hosiery, nightwear and the clothing ranges by La Perla and its associated brands, so if you're a La Perla devotee you'll definitely have come to the right place. All the items here are beautiful and luxurious, mostly with prices to match, and the sizing on the whole is on the small side.

Prices:	Luxury/Medium	Express Ship? (UK)	Yes
Delivers to:	Europe	Gift Wrap?	No
Based:	UK		

www.glamorousamorous.com

Glamorous Amorous specialises in lingerie you won't easily find anywhere else – think animal print and scarlet trim from Fifi Chachnil, sequin and silk camisoles from Guia La Bruna and a lace bustier and thong from Bacirubati and you'll get the kind of idea – extremely glam in other words. Everything arrives in a silk organza bag, wrapped in tissue paper scented with Provencal lavender.

Prices:	Luxury/Medium	Express Ship? (UK)	Yes
Delivers to:	Worldwide	Gift Wrap?	Yes
Based:	UK		

www.janetreger-online.com

On Janet Reger's beautiful website there's the most gorgeous selection of lingerie, where the prices are not for the faint hearted. Once you've picked the style you like you can immediately see all the other items in the range plus colourways and size options. This brand is totally about luxe and glamour so be prepared to spend a small fortune on wonderful quality and style.

Prices:	Luxury	Express Ship? (UK)	Yes
Delivers to:	Worldwide	Gift Wrap?	Yes
Based:	UK		

www.lasenza.co.uk

At La Senza you'll find a large choice of lingerie and nightwear ranging from beautiful basics to seriously sexy styles as well as bra accessories. It's great to know that retailers are actually catering for those who want something larger than a C cup as sizes also go from 30A to 38F. Yes you can buy colours, plunge bras and diamante-trimmed bras even if you're a DD or above and you'll also find cleavage enhancers, extra bra straps and strap extenders.

Prices:	Very Good Value	Express Ship? (UK)	Yes
Delivers to:	Worldwide	Gift Wrap?	Yes
Based:	UK		

www.myla.com

If pearl nipple tassels are just what you're looking for then you've probably come to the right place. Alternatively you can steer clear of the toys and accessories here and just browse the seriously beautiful and feminine lingerie within which the bras go up no further than a D cup. You'll find robes, camisoles, suspenders and baby dolls plus accessories such as feather boas and silk mules. Oh yes, and there's chocolate body paint here as well.

Prices:	Luxury/Medium	Express Ship? (UK)	Yes
Delivers to:	Worldwide	Gift Wrap?	No but packaging is lovely
Based:	UK		

www.mytights.co.uk

My Tights offer the hosiery brands of Aristoc, Charnos, Elbeo, Gerbe, La Perla, Levante and Pretty Polly, to name but a few, plus maternity tights by Spanx and Trasparenze. So whether you want footless or fishnet tights and stockings, support tights, shapewear, knee highs or suspenders you'll find it all here, and provided you order before 3pm you'll probably get it the next day.

Prices:	Luxury/Medium	Express Ship? (UK)	Yes
Delivers to:	Worldwide	Gift Wrap?	No
Based:	UK		

www.rigbyandpeller.com

You may know their shop just round the side of Harrods where you can be properly fitted for your next bra and choose from a chic selection of lingerie. You can also see the range on their website where they offer a wide range of brands such as Aubade, Lejaby, La Perla plus their own, and a superb service.

Prices:	Luxury/Medium	Express Ship? (UK)	Yes
Delivers to:	Worldwide	Gift Wrap?	Yes
Based:	UK		

www.tightsplease.co.uk

Whether you want fishnets and crochet tights, bright colours, knee highs, stay-ups, stockings or footsies you'll find them all here plus leg warmers, socks and flight socks, maternity and bridal hosiery. This website really caters for all your hosiery needs and with names such as Aristoc, Pretty Polly and Charnos offered you should never run out again.

Prices:	Luxury/Medium	Express Ship? (UK)	Automatic
Delivers to:	Worldwide	Gift Wrap?	No
Based:	UK		

www.wolfordboutiquelondon.com

Wolford are world famous for their top-quality hosiery, bodies, tops and lingerie and you can now purchase their collection online, through their London South Molton Street shop. The range includes sexy and beautifully photographed seasonally inspired pieces and is being updated all the time.

Prices:	Luxury	Express Ship? (UK)	Yes
Delivers to:	Worldwide	Gift Wrap?	No
Based:	UK		

Swimwear

www.cocobay.co.uk

If you'd rather not be bedazzled by the huge amount of choice you can find on some swim and resortwear websites then take a look here at Coco Bay, where you can browse through the well-priced range by Seafolly, Moontide and Sunseeker which includes bikinis, one-piece swimsuits and Coco Bay's own range of kaftans, beach dresses and sun hats.

Prices:	Medium	Express Ship? (UK)	Yes
Delivers to:	EU	Gift Wrap?	No
Based:	UK		

www.elizabethhurley.com

You may well have read in the press about Elizabeth Hurley's resortwear range and here it is online. There's wonderful, sexy, stylish swimwear, chic kaftans, dresses and tops and a choice of knitwear and t-shirts. Then there are the totes, sarongs and towels to help complete the collection. It's an expensive range but you'll almost certainly want something. There's adorable swimwear for kids as well.

Prices:	Medium	Express Ship? (UK)	No
Delivers to:	Worldwide	Gift Wrap?	No
Based:	UK		

www.espadrillesetc.com

Whether or not you're an espadrilles fan, if you're going on holiday you really should take a look at this summer shoe website, where there's every colour, fabric and style you can think of, including soft-coloured suede and brightly coloured fabric espadrilles, plus some very pretty sandals, brightly coloured beach bags and totes and children's espadrilles.

Prices:	Medium/Very Good Value	Express Ship? (UK)	No
Delivers to:	Worldwide	Gift Wrap?	No
Based:	Spain		

www.heidiklein.com

Heidi Klein offers beautiful holidaywear all the year round. The range includes chic bikinis and one-piece swimsuits, pretty and flattering kaftans, dresses and sarongs plus all the accessories you could need for your next trip away to the sun (flip-flops, hats, bags and more). They offer a same-day delivery service in London and express delivery throughout the UK.

Prices:	Luxury/Medium	Express Ship? (UK)	Yes
Delivers to:	Worldwide	Gift Wrap?	Yes
Based:	UK		

www.kikoy.com

For holidays and trips abroad you'll want to know about this colourful website, offering fine cotton and muslin shorts, kaftans, cover-ups, trousers, hats and bags plus beach towels. There are some excellent summer/holiday gift ideas here but if you see something you want in a hurry give them a call to make sure that they have it in stock. If they do, they'll ship it to you for next-day delivery.

Prices:	Medium/Very Good Value	Express Ship? (UK)	Yes, call them
Delivers to:	Worldwide	Gift Wrap?	No
Based:	UK		

www.louisesandberg.com

Whether they're in fashion or not, kaftans are an essential part of your holiday packing and they're great for wearing over a swimsuit when you want something to give more cover than a sarong. Here's an excellent collection – long, short, colourful or neutral and beautifully embroidered.

Prices:	Medium	Express Ship? (UK)	Yes
Delivers to:	Worldwide	Gift Wrap?	No
Based:	UK		

www.odabash.com

Melissa Odabash offers beautifully chic one-piece swimsuits and bikinis in her online store, together with cover-ups and kaftans, beach bags, t-shirts in a great choice of colourways, plus swimwear for children. You won't find the full range here but a well-edited selection. I would expect that the sizing for this designer range will be on the small side so if in doubt order a size up.

Prices:	Luxury	Express Ship? (UK)	Yes, call them
Delivers to:	Worldwide	Gift Wrap?	No
Based:	UK		

www.sandinmytoes.com

Sand in My Toes offer carefully edited selections by Seafolly, Melissa Odabash, Jets, Papillon Bleu and Princess Tam Tam, among others. You can shop by brand, shape (yours), style or colour and although there are far more bikinis here than one-pieces, there are enough seriously gorgeous cover-ups and kaftans to make it worth your while having a look before your next trip to the beach.

Prices:	Luxury/Medium	Express Ship? (UK)	Yes, call them
Delivers to:	Worldwide	Gift Wrap?	No
Based:	UK		

www.simplybeach.com

Simply Beach is devoted just to swimwear and includes designer brands Banana Moon, Salinas, Verde Veronica and Lisa Ho, with swimsuits and bikinis in all shapes and sizes. There's a wide range of accessories as well including cover-ups, towels, beach bags and inflatables and direct links through to their other website where you'll find everything for scuba diving and snorkelling.

Prices:	Medium	Express Ship? (UK)	Yes
Delivers to:	Worldwide	Gift Wrap?	No
Based:	UK		

Also visit www.figleaves.com for one of the best collections of swimwear.

Sensational Sportswear

Here are all the clothes you love to wear to live in, lounge in and take you to the lido and back – the casual polos, stylish trackies, branded hoodies and, most important of all, those Nike, Adidas or Puma casual (or serious) trainers it's easy to wear far too much of the time.

Here you'll find young brands such as Abercrombie, White Stuff, Jack Wills and Joules alongside Sweaty Betty and Casall. The only problem with wearing these clothes is they're so comfortable you can forget how to do that fashionista 'of the moment' look – so keep reading those glossy mags even if you're totally dressed down to do so.

Lounge and Play Here

www.uk.abercrombie.com

The style here at this US-based brand is very 'casual luxury'. Take a look around if you can tear yourself away from the outstanding photographs of the most beautiful models (mostly men). Sizing is small, particularly for fitted items, so if in any doubt go up a size. Of course, you can now shop in their Savile Row, London store, but if you can't get there – and for all those of you who are complaining about the prices – at least you don't have to pay the air fare (or duty) to buy here now.

Prices:	Medium	Express Ship?	Yes
Delivers to:	Worldwide	Gift Wrap?	No
Based:	UK		

www.crewclothing.co.uk

Crew have a really attractive and modern online store with a constantly expanding range offering all the Crew gear, from the full collection of sailing-inspired and casual clothing to lots of other choices including flip-flops, deck shoes, cowboy boots, belts and socks and well-priced luggage. The Limited Edition collection for women is also well worth a look.

Prices:	Medium	Express Ship? (UK)	Yes
Delivers to:	Worldwide	Gift Wrap?	No
Based:	UK		

www.jackwills.co.uk

Take a look at this website, offering 'cool' and idiosyncratic sportwear including jeans, hoodies, fun, printed t-shirts, polo shirts and accessories for girls and guys. The website is beautifully designed and great fun to browse and if you have a teenage daughter, as I do, you'll probably have seen a great deal of this clothing brand about.

Prices:	Medium	Express Ship? (UK)	Yes
Delivers to:	Worldwide	Gift Wrap?	No
Based:	UK		

www.joulesclothing.com

Joules is a clothing website with a difference: beautifully photographed and well laid out and there are some excellent fun sporty separates for just about everyone provided you like stripes and colours (although lots of items are available in black/jet as well). It's mainly aimed at the riding fraternity, although many of the clothes, particularly the jackets and fleeces, have a much wider appeal.

Prices:	Medium	Express Ship? (UK)	Yes – call them
Delivers to:	Worldwide	Gift Wrap?	No
Based:	UK		

www.ruehl.com

I will freely admit that this is a very dark site, but for an Abercrombie vibe from a new brand that most likely no one you know will be aware of this is a great place. Ruehl is based in the US, is part of the Abercrombie and Fitch group and having chanced on one of the stores a short while back is, I can tell you, a hard place to resist. The range is for both girls and guys. They'll ship to most worldwide destinations and shipping is not extortionate.

Prices:	Medium	Express Ship? (UK)	No
Delivers to:	Worldwide	Gift Wrap?	No
Based:	US		

www.whitestuff.com

This young, urban clothing company sells casual sporty lightweight gear in the summer months for guys and girls, plus trendy skiwear in the winter (hence the name). There are colour options for just about all the clothes, from the Flawless T to the Java Jive pant and you can see straight away what's available in stock or what you'll have to wait for. This isn't a huge collection but it's fun and well priced and definitely worth having a look at.

Prices:	Medium	Express Ship? (UK)	Yes
Delivers to:	Worldwide	Gift Wrap?	No
Based:	UK		

The Real Thing – Sports Fanatics Only

www.adidas-shop.co.uk

At Adidas's contemporarily designed online store you can find all their footwear and clothing together in one place and much better than that, you can also read up on all the latest sports innovations from this famous brand. There's sports clothing and footwear for men, women and kids plus the Adidas by Stella McCartney line. Go there and be prepared to start training – soon.

Prices:	Medium	Express Ship? (UK)	Yes
Delivers to:	UK	Gift Wrap?	No
Based:	UK		

www.elliegray.com

This is an excellent sportwear destination whether you're looking for exercise clothes for the gym or just for relaxing in. Offering brands USA Pro, Pure Lime, Deha and their own, you'll find a selection of hoodies and jackets, sweatshirts, pants, outerwear, sports bras and accessories in a good range of colours and styles. Everything is easy to see and described in details and even better, you can immediately see what's in stock.

Prices:	Medium	Express Ship? (UK)	Yes
Delivers to:	Worldwide	Gift Wrap?	No
Based:	UK		

www.jdsports.co.uk

There's sports footwear and clothing here for men, women and kids, with brands including Adidas, Animal, Asics and Converse, Lacoste, Nike and Lee Crow. You can expect to find a very good selection whichever area you're looking in and with such a lot of products to go through make sure you have time to spare before you start.

Prices:	Medium	Express Ship? (UK)	No
Delivers to:	UK	Gift Wrap?	No
Based:	UK		

www.nike.co.uk

I love Nike but hate long flash intros so be warned, you'll have to wait a bit to get to the products themselves. Go and make a cuppa or something while it's loading. This is probably one of the most beautiful and cleverly designs sports stores of all but boy, do I hate having to wait. All the clothing and footwear is here for everyone and you can customise your shoes as well.

Prices:	Medium	Express Ship? (UK)	No
Delivers to:	UK, EU and USA	Gift Wrap?	No
Based:	UK		

www.puma.com

You'll find pretty well the full range at the Puma online store, and once you've hung about for a while for the flash intro to pass (grrr) you can order their unbelievably comfortable casual trainers (of which I am a huge fan), serious sports shoes and casual and sporting gear for both men and women. There are also sports bags, shades, belts and watches for real Puma addicts.

Prices:	Medium	Express Ship? (UK)	No
Delivers to:	EU	Gift Wrap?	No
Based:	Switzerland		

www.sportswoman.co.uk

Don't visit this website unless you're feeling energetic (although if you're not it'll definitely push you in the right direction). Here you can see, beautifully photographed, the Casall range of sportwear, which includes basic activewear, tennis, running, yoga and Pilates and golf clothing plus underwear and accessories such as socks, waterbottles and kit bags. In the accessories section there are gym balls, ab rollers, gloves and more.

Prices:	Medium	Express Ship? (UK)	Yes
Delivers to:	Worldwide	Gift Wrap?	No
Based:	UK		

www.sweatybetty.com

Here's another website to get you going, where you'll find an excellent and stylish range of clothes for the gym and for yoga, available in basic colours such as black, grey and pink. They also offer sleek (and minimal) beachwear, chic and well-priced skiwear plus accessories such as leg and arm warmers and books on yoga. Postage is free on orders over £50 (UK) and they'll deliver worldwide.

Prices:	Medium	Express Ship? (UK)	No
Delivers to:	Worldwide	Gift Wrap?	No
Based:	UK		

Green is the new Black ...

... or so we're told, and whether you want to go along with it or not there's no doubt that the green, organic and eco-friendly tide is definitely flowing our way. You may or may not be ready to buy clothes and accessories made out of bamboo or hemp but you can have no objection to fairly traded and organically farmed cotton, or tencel, which is made of wood pulp but drapes beautifully. Whatever you decide the choice is yours but choice is now the buzzword here as for the first time there's a great deal of it, much of what's on offer is beautiful and wearable and well worth taking a serious look at.

Here are my favourites among the environmentally friendly online retailers. Some have larger collections than others but throughout all of them you're conscious of their determination to help you help them to protect the planet and the people who trade there.

www.adili.com

Adili offer a superb range of clothing for everyone from well-priced separates to designer dresses. They give you the provenance of every product they sell and although you may not be interested in finding out where that pretty top came from (you just want to click and buy), if you have the time it's worth a read.

Prices:	Medium	Express Ship? (UK)	Yes
Delivers to:	Worldwide	Gift Wrap?	No
Based:	UK		

www.amana-collection.com

The aim at Amana is to combine beautiful design with ethical production practices and all their garments are made by women artisans in a village perched high in the Middle Atlas Mountains in Morocco. The collection includes printed tops, dresses and tailoring in clever blends of silk, cotton, hemp and tencel.

Prices:	Medium	Express Ship? (UK)	Yes
Delivers to:	Worldwide	Gift Wrap?	No
Based:	UK		

www.ciel.co.uk

There's a small but beautiful range of clothes, lingerie and spa products here that is seriously worth a browse. Ciel carefully selects environmentally and ethically produced fabrics and production throughout the design and making process to produce a range that is tempting to say the least, and they include the smallest details such as garment labels and hang tags within their policies. Take a look for yourself.

Prices:	Medium	Express Ship? (UK)	Yes
Delivers to:	Worldwide	Gift Wrap?	No
Based:	UK		

www.howies.co.uk

Here you'll find contemporary casualwear made from organic cotton, bamboo and merino wool, sometimes with a bit of essential Lycra and spandex thrown in (well you want them to stay up, don't you?). This is very much a young collection for the environmentally thoughtful and there's a great selection of t-shirts and jeans for kids as well.

Prices:	Medium	Express Ship? (UK)	Yes
Delivers to:	Worldwide	Gift Wrap?	No
Based:	UK		

www.karencole.co.uk

Karen Cole is a New Zealand designer specialising in using mainly natural fibres and ethically sourced fine New Zealand merino wool. She offers an extremely pretty and wearable collection of dresses and separates in contemporary colours and prints which is much more fashion forward than many of the 'natural' collections.

Prices:	Medium	Express Ship? (UK)	No
Delivers to:	Worldwide	Gift Wrap?	No
Based:	UK		

www.katherinehamnett.com

British designer Katherine Hamnett is well known the world over not just for her clothing but also for her insistence on ethical manufacture and peace-themed t-shirts with slogans such as 'Peace and Liberty' and 'Stop the War'. On her modern website you can order from a selection of her designs including the organic cottan slogan ts for both men and women which are available in a range of colours.

Prices:	Medium	Express Ship? (UK)	No
Delivers to:	Worldwide	Gift Wrap?	No
Based:	UK		

www.peopletree.co.uk

People Tree work closely with fair trade organisations throughout the world and aim to pioneer ecologically sound methods of production. Not only is most of their cotton certified organic and Fairtrade, all their clothes are dyed using safe and natural dyes. Their designers in the UK and Japan help them to produce clothes that are both beautiful and caring, incorporating handwoven fabrics with screen printing and embroidery.

Prices:	Medium	Express Ship? (UK)	Yes
Delivers to:	Worldwide	Gift Wrap?	No
Based:	UK		

www.seasaltcornwall.co.uk

Although not everything here is organically produced, Seasalt was the first fashion company to have garments certified to Soil Association standards. The collection is extensive, attractive and extremely reasonably priced and they immediately tell you what everything is made from. There's a range of t-shirts, tops and outerwear for men and kids here as well.

Prices:	Medium/Very Good Value	Express Ship? (UK)	No
Delivers to:	Worldwide	Gift Wrap?	No
Based:	UK		

www.untouchedworld.co.uk

New Zealand fashion brand Untouched World has a passion for ethical design which flows through every element of their collections, from their textiles and buttons to how and where each item is produced. The collection offers contemporary casual dressing for men and women with fashion forward but wearable styles in each new season's palette of colours.

Prices:	Medium	Express Ship? (UK)	No
Delivers to:	Worldwide	Gift Wrap?	No
Based:	UK		

Section 3
The Accessory Place

Arm Candy

Carry These without
Breaking the Bank

Bag a Bargain

Kick Your Heels

Shade Shop

All That Glitters

Designer Jewels

Gorgeous and Accessible

Fashion Rocks

Tic Toc

Wraps and More

Gloved and Waisted

Small Accessory Store

It's much easier to buy most accessories online than it is clothes, and so much easier to flash your plastic and order that Chloe Paddington bag, knowing exactly what's going to arrive, than your next Little Black Dress. All of which, of course, makes this area of online shopping not just more accessible but totally tempting too.

There are huge numbers of accessory stores appearing all the time and while some are extremely clever, others seem still to have a lot to learn. Take a look at Gucci.com, Forzieri.com or any of the other well-established online retailers and take in how much information you're offered on anything you look at – how close up you can get to the fabric, the different shots of each item, how you can see inside (handbags) and every which way (shoes) – and don't spend a lot at anywhere that doesn't offer you those facilities. Why should you? I'm still amazed there are places trying to sell you hugely expensive items with just one picture – we've already moved a long way on from there.

You'll find three price ranges for bags, shoes and jewels: sheer luxury (warn your bank manager first unless he's your best friend), still gorgeous but more accessibly priced where you can regularly treat yourselves and others on your gift list, and non-investment, contemporary ranges which fit in with the trends and are great for a quick, guilt-free fashion fix.

Arm Candy

Is it a frightening thought that a designer handbag will now set you back the best part of £1,000 or quite possibly more? I think it is. The trouble is that there are so many people buying them at this level as the ultimate feel-good buy that no self-respecting designer is going to charge much less. So if, like me, you have a hankering for the 'real deal' you better start saving now.

My advice here is that unless spending £800+ on a 'superbrand' handbag is a breeze, make sure that when you do make that investment you buy something that's not 'of the moment' – purple patent, animal print or neon bright – but something you'll be happy to carry for years, which probably means it'll have to be black, chocolate or beige. Buy your wonderfully expensive contemporary classics first and then, if you've anything left, go for broke on something outrageous.

To have one of these gorgeous designer handbags in your wardrobe can give that lovely warm feeling just knowing you own it, and when your other half says 'new bag dear?' you can simply say, 'what, this old thing? Of course not, I've had it for years.' Unless he's a real follower of fashion he won't be able to tell, I promise.

www.anyahindmarch.com

Anya Hindmarch's collection of beautiful, unique and sometimes quirky handbags have long been glossy magazine fashion editor's favourites and on her website you'll find everything from summer straw totes to contemporary day bags and glossy evening purses. There's also a covetable shoe collection to take you from day to night, all with her signature quilted lining.

Prices:	Luxury	Express Ship? (UK)	No
Delivers to:	Worldwide	Gift Wrap?	No
Based:	UK		

www.dior.com

At luxury brand Christian Dior's online boutique you can purchase from their range of beautiful, covetable handbags, shoes and boots, small leather accessories, scarves, watches and fine jewellery. Prices are steep as you would expect but if you want to be carrying the latest version of their instantly recognisable handbags on your arm this season you'll no doubt be prepared.

Prices:	Medium	Express Ship? (UK)	Yes
Delivers to:	UK but US and other sites available	Gift Wrap?	No but beautiful packaging is standard
Based:	UK		

www.gucci.com

As one of the ultimate 'superbrands' available online you visit this website at your peril. As you would expect the site is very modern and beautiful (and heartstoppingly expensive) and the products irresistible. You can look through the range and then when you find what you're looking for get right close up and place your order. Shop here for handbags, luggage, jewellery, men and women's shoes and gifts such as key rings and lighters.

Prices:	Luxury	Express Ship? (UK)	Yes
Delivers to:	Worldwide most places	Gift Wrap?	Automatic
Based:	UK		

www.launer.com

Launer handbags and small leather goods are handmade by skilled craftspeople in the softest calf, exotic lizard, ostrich and alligator skin. Every attention is paid to detail, and the gold plated fittings all feature the signature Launer rope emblem. Launer's trademark is understated, elegant and classic. This is not the place for the up-to-the-minute look but for really beautifully made investment pieces that will last for years.

Prices:	Luxury	Express Ship? (UK)	No
Delivers to:	Worldwide	Gift Wrap?	No
Based:	UK		

www.louisvuitton.com

Louis Vuitton's unmistakable, covetable (and luxuriously expensive) handbags, small leather goods, sunglasses, watches, scarves and belts are now available online directly through their quick and clear website. So you don't have to go into one of their stores any more and ask for help and information, you'll find everything you could possibly need to know here.

Prices:	Luxury	Express Ship? (UK)	Yes
Delivers to:	Worldwide	Gift Wrap?	Automatic
Based:	UK		

www.luella.com

Any member of the handbag cognoscenti will tell you that Luella's handbags are all gorgeous and covetable. Take a look at her website and you can view the collection with all the colourways, from the well-known Stevie and Gisele bags to the studded Joni and whatever's new this season. The clothing collection is now online as well.

Prices:	Luxury	Express Ship? (UK)	Yes
Delivers to:	Worldwide	Gift Wrap?	Automatic
Based:	UK		

www.luluguinness.com

'Be a glamour girl, put on your lipstick' is the phrase welcoming you to this elegant website, from which exquisite handbags and accessories from famous British designer Lulu Guinness can be shipped to you anywhere. With unique styling, sometimes very quirky, sometimes just plain gorgeous, and a selection of cosmetic bags in stylish prints, this is a website you should take a look at if you're in the mood for a treat or special gift.

Prices:	Luxury/Medium	Express Ship? (UK)	No
Delivers to:	Worldwide	Gift Wrap?	No but everything is beautifully packaged
Based:	UK		

www.mulberry.com

Mulberry is a truly British luxury brand with an extensive line of highly crafted bags which combine stylish, standout design with the finest leathers and highly wrought detailing. Stuart Vevers, Design Director, has used Mulberry's 1970s' bohemian roots as a reference point in many of his designs and styles like the Bayswater, Emmy and Brooke have become covetable fashion classics for consumers and celebrities alike. Buy one if you can.

Prices:	Luxury	Express Ship? (UK)	No
Delivers to:	Worldwide	Gift Wrap?	No
Based:	UK		

www.temperleylondon.com

There's no doubt that within a very short space of time Alice Temperley has become well known throughout the fashion world for her totally desirable dresses and separates, including her fabulous collection of evening dresses. Although you can only view her clothing online you can buy her accessories, including handbags, gloves, belts and scarves.

Prices:	Luxury	Express Ship? (UK)	Yes
Delivers to:	Worldwide	Gift Wrap?	No
Based:	UK		

Carry These without Breaking the Bank

www.angeljackson.co.uk

You'll find an irresistible collection of extremely well-priced and well-made handbags here in an excellent range of colours plus weekenders, purses and day to evening clutches. You can see all the items in a lot of detail with close-up and different view pictures. This is a great place to shop if you want to carry something totally different to everyone else.

Prices:	Medium	Express Ship? (UK)	No
Delivers to:	Worldwide	Gift Wrap?	No
Based:	UK		

www.belenechandia.com

Here are soft leather handbags in a choice of colours with names such as Rock Me, Hold Me and Take Me Away by accessory label Belen Echandia. Choose your style of handbag, check out the measurements and detailing and then use their semi-bespoke service to select your particular choice of leather, from croc finish to metallics and brights to neutrals. Nothing here is inexpensive, but unique and different – an investment that'll last you for years.

Prices:	Luxury	Express Ship? (UK)	Yes
Delivers to:	Worldwide	Gift Wrap?	Yes
Based:	UK		

www.forzieri.com

If you haven't yet taken a look at this Florence-based fashion retailer you should visit there now, but be warned: it's hard to escape without buying. They have a marvellous range of mainly Italian designer handbags and shoes plus jewellery, watches, leather coats and jackets and other accessories for both men and women. They also offer next-day delivery to most countries.

Prices:	Medium	Express Ship? (UK)	Yes
Delivers to:	Worldwide	Gift Wrap?	Yes
Based:	Italy		

www.ignesbags.com

The next time you're looking for a new handbag, take a look here, where you can find unique designs in unusual South American leathers. This is a small, high-quality collection priced mostly at between £150 and £200 and ranging from large day bags to small, idiosyncratic evening bags with chain handles.

Prices:	Medium	Express Ship? (UK)	No
Delivers to:	Worldwide	Gift Wrap?	No
Based:	UK		

www.lizcox.com

Liz Cox offers a collection of unique bags and luggage hand-made in her own workshops in the UK using exclusive fabrics, bridle and saddle leathers and incorporating exotic patterns and innovative designs. Click on the design you like and you'll be able to see all the colours and fabrics that it's available in. Call for express delivery and gift wrapping.

Prices:	Medium	Express Ship? (UK)	Yes
Delivers to:	Worldwide	Gift Wrap?	Yes
Based:	UK		

www.ollieandnic.com

Ollie & Nic offer a stylish and chic range of accessories at excellent prices including pretty bags for day, evening and holiday, plus umbrellas, sunglasses, scarves, brooches and other accessories. The collection is very seasonal, with new products being introduced all the time, and each season will have a specific theme so you can visit this website regularly and you'll never be bored.

Prices:	Medium	Express Ship? (UK)	No
Delivers to:	Worldwide	Gift Wrap?	No
Based:	UK		

www.orlakiely.com

Orla Kiely designs unique, instantly recognisable clothes and accessories, using bold and colourful patterns that are always fresh and appealing. On her website there is a small selection from her ready-to-wear clothing range, but a much wider choice of her unusual, attractive and highly functional accessories including handbags, purses and luggage.

Prices:	Medium	Express Ship? (UK)	No
Delivers to:	Worldwide	Gift Wrap?	No
Based:	UK		

www.osprey-london.co.uk

For many years Osprey have created beautifully crafted handbags and small leather accessories in high-quality leathers, all designed by Graeme Ellisdon in Florence. The range includes classic and business handbags – but think modern business, so although they'll take all the papers you need to carry, they look like great bags as well.

Prices:	Luxury/Medium	Express Ship? (UK)	Yes
Delivers to:	Worldwide	Gift Wrap?	No
Based:	UK		

www.radley.co.uk

'Truly Radley Deeply' is the statement here from the company with the Scotty dog logo and a wonderful, cleverly designed website with a wide range of classic to modern, reasonably priced arm candy. There's a great deal of choice here, from the whimsical Cupcakes bag to the woven leather Corsica and the seriously beautiful Soho. Radley offer luggage, purses and wallets, brollies, scarves and shades as well.

Prices:	Medium	Express Ship? (UK)	No
Delivers to:	UK	Gift Wrap?	No
Based:	UK		

www.tabitha.uk.com

At Tabitha you can see some covetable, not overpriced but very unusual bags and accessories in a choice of coloured leathers and metallics. Whatever the season's trends are you'll find them here with handbags and weekenders in a wide range of sizes plus some very good gift ideas such as wallets and washbags in unusual finishes.

Prices:	Medium	Express Ship? (UK)	No
Delivers to:	Worldwide	Gift Wrap?	No
Based:	UK		

Bag a Bargain

www.branded.net

Handbags, wallets and purses by Gucci, Christian Dior, Chloe, Fendi, Dolce & Gabanna and Prada are on offer here, all at discounted prices and from recent seasons' collections. You always have to be careful when buying discounted designer labels in case they're not the real thing. However, there are a number of re-sellers who are able to sell on ends of lines and overstocks of real designer products and these are what you'll find here.

Prices:	Luxury/Medium	Express Ship? (UK)	Yes
Delivers to:	Worldwide	Gift Wrap?	Yes
Based:	UK		

www.handbagcrush.co.uk

This company buys from designer resellers to enable you to buy authentic handbags and accessories from designers such as Gucci, Prada, Fendi and Versace. They clearly state the RRP (which I always suggest you should double check if you can) plus the discount on offer and there are good, detailed pictures and lots of information. Worth having a look round.

Prices:	Luxury/Medium	Express Ship? (UK)	Yes
Delivers to:	Worldwide	Gift Wrap?	No
Based:	UK		

www.koodos.com

Web retailer Koodos offers you the opportunity of buying clothes, shoes and accessories by designers such as Gucci, Prada, Fendi, Feraud, Amanda Wakeley, Beatrix Ong and Nicole Farhi at amazing discounts. You need to check back often to see what's there and if there's something you like, snap it up straight away or you'll get back to it with the frustrating 'just sold out' notice clearly visible.

Prices:	Luxury/Medium	Express Ship? (UK)	Yes
Delivers to:	UK	Gift Wrap?	No
Based:	UK		

www.yoox.com

At Yoox you'll find end-of-season designer pieces at very good discounts – usually 50% off the designer's original price. It's a huge site and there are lots of designer clothes and accessories to choose from so it's best to have some sort of idea of what you're looking for before you start. Click on your favourite designer, search for a specific type of item and you're away.

Prices:	Luxury/Medium	Based:	USA but use UK website
Delivers to:	Worldwide but click on the country for delivery to see that range	Express Ship? (UK)	Yes
		Gift Wrap?	Yes

Kick Your Heels

A lot of people think that buying shoes online is difficult because of the sizing. This is a total misconception. If you're a size 38 you'll almost certainly be that size in anyone's shoes unless they're known for being exceptionally wide or narrow.

It's for this reason that nearly all the major shoe brands are now online and, OK, you're not going to be able to see exactly what they'll look like on your feet but you almost certainly have a good idea of what you like to wear, what shape toe, what heel height and which colours, which makes buying here a breeze.

If you land on a site that doesn't give you the heel height, or what the sole is made of, don't buy. This is also probably not the place to try out a 10cm heel if you're used to 5, nor the latest huge platform or daft heel shape (and I really do think some of them are daft, as are some of the prices).

With Kurt Geiger, Carvela, Nine West, Jimmy Choo, Gina et al all available online you're really spoilt for choice. You can also find some chic and stylish shoes at Artigiano, Boden, net-a-porter, Browns Fashion and many of the designer boutiques above, so have a browse there as well.

Just in case you're in doubt here are the size conversions for UK, European and US women's shoes.

Women's shoe size conversions									
US	5.5	6	6.5	7	7.5	8	8.5	9	9.5
UK	3	3.5	4	4.5	5	5.5	6	6.5	7
European	36	36.5	37	37.5	38	38.5	39	39.5	40

Luxury Heels

www.emmahope.com

On her pretty website you can now see the full range of Emma Hope's beautiful designer shoes at real designer prices, so if you're in the mood to invest for your feet this is very much a place to explore. You'll find ballet flats, evening heels and modern platforms in a choice of colours, plus bags and accessories and an elegant wedding collection.

Prices:	Luxury	Express Ship? (UK)	Yes
Delivers to:	Worldwide	Gift Wrap?	No
Based:	UK		

www.envycouture.com

Shoe designer Annabel Leung has created the ultimate shoe lovers' fantasy, a place where you can either buy from her hand-made (and not unreasonably priced) collection of glamorous heels or select one of her basic designs and then make it totally yours by choosing your heel height and then from her wide range of fabrics and colours. Sizes go from 33 to 43 and heel heights from 1.5" to 4". There are beautiful bridal shoes here as well.

Prices:	Luxury/Medium	Express Ship? (UK)	No
Delivers to:	Worldwide	Gift Wrap?	No
Based:	UK		

www.exclusivefootwear.com

Gina, Moschino, Beatrix Ong, Pedro Garcia and Patrick Cox head up the list of designer-label footwear you'll find here, alongside Stuart Weitzman and lots of other stylish brands plus a good selection of casual footwear, boots and bridal shoes. The website is extremely quick to browse round with temptation everywhere. Men's ranges include Oliver Sweeney, Jeffery West and Patrick Cox.

Prices:	Luxury/Medium	Express Ship? (UK)	Yes
Delivers to:	Worldwide most countries	Gift Wrap?	Yes
Based:	UK		

www.gina.com

Gina was established in 1954 and named after Gina Lollobrigida. If you want the couture look and a seriously special pair then click no further. Here you'll find a truly wonderful collection of sexy shoes in the softest leather and with out-to-lunch and dinner heels. There's a price to match as you would expect, but the shoes are worth it and they'll last a long time. There's also a small selection of handbags.

Prices:	Luxury	Express Ship? (UK)	No but 2 days is standard
Delivers to:	Worldwide	Gift Wrap?	No
Based:	UK		

www.jimmychoo.com

Needless to say the Jimmy Choo website is beautifully and provocatively designed and makes you want to browse right through even though the prices are quite frightening in most cases, to say the least. This is always a covetable collection, including diamante-encrusted sandals, killer-heel peep-toe slides, gorgeous boots and wonderful, right-on-trend handbags.

Prices:	Luxury	Express Ship? (UK)	Yes
Delivers to:	Worldwide	Gift Wrap?	Automatic
Based:	UK		

www.struttcouture.co.uk

For those of you who like high, glam, killer heels this is probably the place for you, where chic and very sophisticated sum up the style. There's nothing for the faint hearted here but if you like to make an impression you should definitely take a look round. The shoes are extremely chic and there are some wonderful boots here you won't find anywhere else.

Prices:	Luxury	Express Ship? (UK)	Yes
Delivers to:	EU	Gift Wrap?	No
Based:	UK		

Affordable Heels

www.dune.co.uk

Here you can buy from a range of trendy, affordable and stylish shoes and accessories including glitzy sandals, dressy pumps and flats, modern casual shoes and ballerinas and excellent boots. As well as all of this there are handbags, belts and sunglasses. The website is well photographed and easy to use, and provided you place your order before 10am you'll receive it the next day.

Prices:	Medium/Very Good Value	Express Ship? (UK)	Yes
Delivers to:	UK	Gift Wrap?	No
Based:	UK		

www.duoboots.com

If you've ever (like me) gone into a shoe shop, discovered the perfect pair of boots and found that the zip won't do up to the top, you'll welcome this website. Duo Boots offer 21 calf sizes, from 30cm to 50cm. You just select your style and colour from their wide range, check out the pictures which are excellent, then input your normal shoe size and calf measurement.

Prices:	Medium	Express Ship? (UK)	Yes
Delivers to:	Worldwide	Gift Wrap?	No
Based:	UK		

www.faith.co.uk

This contemporary shoe brand that you've almost certainly heard of offers a wide range of styles for every occasion at extremely good prices. They also stock designers Olivia Morris, Gil Carvalho and their own Faith Solo so if you want something a little more different you should take a look at them as well. Check out the small but extremely pretty bridal range as well, which has matching bags.

Prices:	Very Good Value	Express Ship? (UK)	No
Delivers to:	UK	Gift Wrap?	No
Based:	UK		

www.footlux.com

Footlux offers you an eclectic range of footwear and accessories by designers such as Michael Kors, Pedro Garcia, Barbara Bui and Chie Mihara. Don't worry if you don't know some of them, there's excellent information here and best of all when you browse the collections you'll discover modern designs, always at the forefront of fashion. Clothing and accessories are offered here as well.

Prices:	Luxury/Medium	Express Ship? (UK)	Yes
Delivers to:	Most worldwide countries	Gift Wrap?	No
Based:	Spain		

www.frenchsole.com

If you've been looking for the perfect ballet flat to update your spring/summer or autumn/winter wardrobe you need search no more. French Sole are well known for offering a wide range of styles, from the classic two-tone pump to animal print and metallic versions, and each season they bring out new styles and colours that are totally on trend. They also offer driving shoes and loafers.

Prices:	Medium	Express Ship? (UK)	No
Delivers to:	Worldwide	Gift Wrap?	No
Based:	UK		

www.helenbateman.com

This Edinburgh-based shoe designer offers a pretty and unusual selection of shoes for all occasions. There's a great deal of choice from beaded Shantung silk evening shoes and stylish sandals to funky espadrilles in a range of colours. One of the great advantages of ordering shoes here is the amount of information on each style, from fit to fabric and heel height plus different views.

Prices:	Medium	Express Ship? (UK)	Yes
Delivers to:	Worldwide	Gift Wrap?	No
Based:	UK		

www.kurtgeiger.com

Browse the Kurt Geiger online store for shoes and accessories from many of your favourite designers, including Kurt Geiger, Marc Jacobs, Stuart Weitzman KG, Gina and Carvela. With new arrivals daily, you can find styles ranging from young contemporary to modern classic, with the site also featuring a sale area. They currently deliver to the British Isles and Eire, and offer a next-day service.

Prices:	Luxury/Medium/Very Good Value	Express Ship? (UK)	Yes
Delivers to:	UK	Gift Wrap?	No
Based:	UK		

www.lkbennett.com

LK Bennett's covetable collection of shoes, accessories and clothing is available to buy online from their beautifully designed, clear and easy-to-navigate website. Here you'll find all the new season's trends converted into wearable styles which you can see in each colour choice and check immediately if your size is available. Then you can buy the bag too and have your order shipped to you wherever you are in the world.

Prices:	Medium	Express Ship? (UK)	No
Delivers to:	Worldwide	Gift Wrap?	No
Based:	UK		

www.modainpelle.com

Moda in Pelle offers an excellent range of fashionable and well-priced shoes, boots and bags including trendy daytime bags and shoes and a very good evening selection. They aim themselves at a young, high street audience (think River Island, Jane Norman and Morgan) but with their up-to-the-minute styling have a much wider appeal.

Prices:	Very Good Value	Express Ship? (UK)	No
Delivers to:	Worldwide	Gift Wrap?	No
Based:	UK		

www.prettyballerinas.com

Established in 1918 to make ballet shoes, Pretty Ballerinas offer a wide selection of colours and prints including animal prints (zebra, leopard, or tiger) metallics, sequins, prints such as purple butterflies and fuchsia, green or blue satin. When you look at the site you need to be aware that all the prices are in euros so you'll need to do the conversion to pounds, dollars or whatever currency you want to buy in.

Prices:	Medium	Express Ship? (UK)	No
Delivers to:	Worldwide	Gift Wrap?	No
Based:	UK		

www.rubbersole.co.uk

On this excellent casual shoe website you can order your Havainas flip-flops, stylish Cubanas (flip-flops with heels), Pare Gabia espadrilles, Crocs and Birkenstock shoes plus Vans and Converse trainers and Hunter wellies. You can see immediately what's in stock and they offer a speedy delivery service.

Prices:	Medium	Express Ship? (UK)	No but delivery is very fast
Delivers to:	UK	Gift Wrap?	No
Based:	UK		

www.shoestudio.com

The Shoe Studio Group is a multi-branded fashion footwear retailer on the UK high-street with brands such as Pied a Terre, Kenneth Cole, Bertie, Nine West and Principles. On the clearly photographed website you can buy from most of their modern and well-priced brands and find everything from day and evening heels to boots, holiday shoes and flats plus a very good range of handbags.

Prices:	Medium/Very Good Value	Express Ship? (UK)	No
Delivers to:	UK and Eire	Gift Wrap?	No
Based:	UK		

www.shudoo.co.uk

If you're a fan of the extraordinarily comfortable and popular Ugg boot from Australia then you'll need this website, which offers the full range of UGG Australia boots including the Classic short and tall versions and a choice of colours. They also sell baby Uggs, Snow Joggers, Love from Australia, My Sweet Feet, Simple footwear and their own Ugs & Kisses brand.

Prices:	Medium	Express Ship? (UK)	No
Delivers to:	Worldwide	Gift Wrap?	No
Based:	UK		

Shade Shop

I'm not going to pretend that buying a new pair of sunglasses online is easy – you really do need to have a good idea of the shape/designer/style you like for this to work really well. The fact that this is such a popular area for online sale must mean that lots of people do and in many cases the prices are better than you'll find in the stores. If for any reason you're not sure, don't buy – go for the Miu Miu handbag instead.

If I haven't yet succeeded in putting you off (which was not my intention, I just wanted to be realistic), many of the shade stores online have good 'buy to fit your face shape' areas, which you can check out. They're also extremely good at telling you what Victoria Beckham, Cameron Diaz and Jessica Alba (et al) were last seen wearing, so be warned, this is not necessarily the helpful temptation you need.

www.shadestation.co.uk

For the cooler end of the market have a look round here, where the emphasis is on young, modern styles from brands such as Prada, Police, D & G, Diesel, Gucci and Armani and you'll find watches by some of these names as well. They stock the complete Oakley brand including glasses, accessories, goggles and watches plus replacement lenses and sunglass cases.

Prices:	Luxury/Medium	Express Ship? (UK)	Yes
Delivers to:	UK	Gift Wrap?	No
Based:	UK		

www.sunglasses-shop.co.uk

The Sunglasses Shop offers you free express UK delivery and you can choose from designer brands Prada, Gucci, Chanel, Versace, Dolce & Gabbana, Dior and many more. They have a comprehensive and modern range and if you click on the pair you like you not only get a close-up but also detailed pictures showing you what the side hinges and nose piece look like.

Prices:	Luxury/Medium	Express Ship? (UK)	Yes
Delivers to:	UK	Gift Wrap?	No
Based:	UK		

www.sunglassesuk.co.uk

Just about every brand of sunglasses is available from this UK site including Gucci, Chloe, Dolce & Gabbana, Moschino, Bolle and Prada. You can check out their bestsellers or buy the same pair of sunglasses your favourite celebrity is wearing this year. It's a fun site with lots to see. They don't carry every style in stock and it's best to call them if you find something you really like to make sure it's available now.

Prices:	Luxury/Medium	Express Ship? (UK)	No
Delivers to:	UK	Gift Wrap?	No
Based:	UK		

www.unitedshades.com

Choose from Versace, Armani, Ferragamo, Givenchy, Gucci, Yves St Laurent and many more here and with over 25 brands on offer you're sure to find something you like. Delivery is free for most countries – check their Shipping Tariff form to make sure that yours is on there.

Prices:	Luxury/Medium	Express Ship? (UK)	Yes
Delivers to:	Worldwide	Gift Wrap?	No
Based:	EU/US		

All That Glitters

Buying jewels online is just too easy. The online stores are beautifully designed, the range as luxe and sparkling as you want it to be and the choice simply endless. Although I've been told that some are spending huge sums of money for quite large diamonds online (and I do believe my source, he's a diamond dealer and entirely reliable), I would advise caution. With diamonds you always get what you pay for and you need to know exactly what you're doing before shelling out (or getting him to shell out). If you want the contact details for my diamond expert friend just send me an email to phd@thesiteguide.com and I'll be delighted to tell you.

For expensive jewellery you have the choice of talking to and buying from major brands such as Tiffany, Boodles, Asprey and Cartier (where you will pay more for the stones but you get their gorgeous designs as well) or through a smaller jeweller where you can have more input into the design yourself. I would be careful though – know exactly what you want and you'll be OK but I personally would always rather choose from a specific range so I know for sure that I won't be disappointed at the end of the day.

Designer Jewels

www.astleyclarke.com

Luxury online jewellery boutique Astley Clarke carries exquisite contemporary fine and designer jewellery collections from all over the world. This is the perfect place to find romantic jewellery gifts or something special for your own jewellery box. With a strong base of celebrity customers including Nicole Kidman, Julia Roberts and Christie Turlington and a gorgeous, modern range this online shop is not to be missed.

Prices:	Luxury/Medium	Express Ship? (UK)	Yes
Delivers to:	Worldwide	Gift Wrap?	Yes
Based:	UK		

www.boucheron.com

Luxury French jewellery house Boucheron offers a beautiful, grown-up array of jewellery and watches at their e-boutique. You can expect to spend several thousands of pounds here whatever you choose and even if you're not of a mind to buy right now this is a gorgeous place to have a browse (and add to your wish list, of course).

Prices:	Luxury	Express Ship? (UK)	No
Delivers to:	EU this site	Gift Wrap?	No
Based:	France		

www.mikimoto-store.co.uk

Mikimoto is a name synonymous with beautiful and luxurious pearls (they've been in business for over 100 years) and you can buy a selection of their bestselling jewellery online. Prices start at around £120 for a pair of timeless pearl studs and go up to around £2000 for their Tahitian pearl, and pink sapphire pendants and earrings.

Prices:	Luxury/Medium	Express Ship? (UK)	Yes
Delivers to:	Worldwide	Gift Wrap?	Yes
Based:	UK		

www.theofennell.com

Theo Fennell's modern diamond-studded crosses and keys are recognised the world over, together with his solid silver Marmite lids and Worcester sauce bottle holders. Nothing on this website is inexpensive but you'll find some extremely beautiful and unique designs and if you buy anything you can be sure it will be exquisitely presented.

Prices:	Luxury	Express Ship? (UK)	No
Delivers to:	Worldwide	Gift Wrap?	Yes
Based:	UK		

www.tiffany.com

Anything in the signature Tiffany blue box is sure to make a perfect present, from a contemporary piece of Elsa Peretti, Frank Gehry or Paloma Picasso jewellery to wonderful classic diamonds and pearls. Beautiful Tiffany glass candlesticks, bowls and stemware, the Tiffany fragrance in its lovely glass bottle or christening gifts for a new baby are all available here.

Prices:	Luxury	Express Ship? (UK)	Yes
Delivers to:	UK and USA	Gift Wrap?	Yes/Automatic
Based:	UK		

Gorgeous and Accessible

www.avasia.com

Avasia offers lovely and unusual jewellery sourced from around the world, using semi-precious stones such as African amethyst, black onyx, Dalmation jasper and moonstone. In their 'About Us' section you can learn about all the stones used, where they originate and the legends behind them.

Prices:	Medium	Express Ship? (UK)	No
Delivers to:	Worldwide	Gift Wrap?	Free
Based:	UK		

www.blaguette.com

If you missed this retailer in the press recently then here's your chance to take a close-up look at a small collection of fab jewels from new jewellery kid on the block Blaguette. Reasonably priced and exceptionally modern and pretty, there's temptation here from dangly earrings to sparkling bangles you almost certainly won't be able to resist - I couldn't!

Prices:	Luxury/Medium	Express Ship? (UK)	No
Delivers to:	UK	Gift Wrap?	No
Based:	UK		

www.byelise.com

There are so many places you can buy jewellery online but often it's difficult to find something unique. At By Elise you can discover glamorous and contemporary necklaces, bracelets and earrings, handcrafted, individually designed and incorporating freshwater pearls, coloured, faceted stones and semi-precious jewels such as citrine and smoky quartz. This is an excellent place to find dramatic and different jewellery and well worth a visit. Prepare to be tempted.

Prices:	Luxury/Medium	Express Ship? (UK)	Yes
Delivers to:	Worldwide	Gift Wrap?	No
Based:	UK		

www.chapmansjewellery.co.uk

This is quite an unusual collection of reasonably priced jewellery, most of which is designed in-house and includes contemporary pieces such as the silver ball on leather strand necklace and mother of pearl flower earrings. They also offer designer jewels by Vivienne Westwood, Shaun Leane and Kit Heath, with a designer list that changes regularly.

Prices:	Medium	Express Ship? (UK)	No
Delivers to:	UK	Gift Wrap?	No
Based:	UK		

www.dinnyhall.com

Here you can see beautifully designed, well-priced modern jewellery from one of Britain's foremost jewellery designers. Every piece is handcrafted using traditional jewellery making techniques with high-quality silver, gold and precious and semi-precious stones. If you haven't discovered her work up until now then this is the time to start collecting.

Prices:	Medium	Express Ship? (UK)	No
Delivers to:	Worldwide	Gift Wrap?	Yes
Based:	UK		

www.emmachapmanjewels.com

Emma Chapman is a London-based jewellery designer who creates beautiful and glamorous designer gemstone jewellery which is exotic with a contemporary edge. It's a covetable collection grouped by descriptions such as Beach Babe, Baroque Goddess and Indian Princess.

Prices:	Medium	Express Ship? (UK)	No
Delivers to:	Worldwide	Gift Wrap?	No
Based:	UK		

www.fameo.co.uk

The jewellery at Fameo is really beautiful, and from the glamorous green amethyst faceted drops to the unique, contemporary platinum and yellow gold 'Tangled Swirl' pendant there's a magical mix of classic, modern and whimsical design. Although this is very much a 'fine jewellery' retailer, there are plenty of reasonably priced ideas here as well including diamond or ruby heart pendants for Valentines Day – worth a few hints, perhaps?

Prices:	Luxury/Medium	Express Ship? (UK)	Yes
Delivers to:	Worldwide	Gift Wrap?	Yes
Based:	UK		

www.green-frederick.co.uk

If you love beautiful jewellery and the sparkle of diamonds but the real thing is slightly out of your range you'll need to spend some time on this website where there are 18ct gold necklaces, bracelets and earrings set with glittering hand cut cubic zirconias plus a wide range of real pearl jewellery. No one but you will know they're not real.

Prices:	Medium	Express Ship? (UK)	Yes
Delivers to:	Worldwide	Gift Wrap?	No
Based:	UK		

www.harriet-whinney.co.uk

Harriet Whinney specialises in pearl jewellery – made-to-order and beautiful timeless pearl earrings, necklaces and bracelets. You can select from her ready made range or choose the quality of the pearl you want for your piece of jewellery and then select the type of clasp. If you're looking for something unique you can call her and she will make it for you.

Prices:	Luxury/Medium	Express Ship? (UK)	No
Delivers to:	UK	Gift Wrap?	No
Based:	UK		

www.icecool.co.uk

At Ice Cool you can select from a range of modern and classic well-priced jewels, including diamond studs, tennis bracelets, pendants and rings, mostly set in 18ct gold with diamonds. Prices start at around £100 and they offer a bespoke service as well if you want something unique.

Prices:	Medium	Express Ship? (UK)	No
Delivers to:	Worldwide	Gift Wrap?	No
Based:	UK		

www.kabiri.co.uk

Kabiri is a jewellery shop on London's Marylebone High Street, carrying a range of modern, international designers. Collections range from exclusive luxury fine jewellers Ana de Costa and Roberto Marroni, through to classic designers Amfitheatrof King and Me & Ro and the fashionista's darlings of the moment Tom Binns and Johanne Mills.

Prices:	Luxury/Medium	Express Ship? (UK)	No
Delivers to:	Worldwide	Gift Wrap?	No
Based:	UK		

www.linksoflondon.com

Links of London are well known for an eclectic mix of jewellery in sterling silver and 18ct gold, charms and charm bracelets, cufflinks, gorgeous gifts and leather and silver accessories for your home. Each season they design a new collection of totally desirable pieces so it's well worth checking back to see what you can discover.

Prices:	Luxury/Medium	Express Ship? (UK)	Yes
Delivers to:	Worldwide	Gift Wrap?	Yes
Based:	UK		

www.manjoh.com

Manjoh.com offers contemporary designer jewellery by designers such as Izabel Camille, Benedicte Mouret, Vinnie Day and Scott Wilson and the list is regularly being added to. This is a sophisticated one-stop shop showcasing the crème de la crème of cutting edge designer jewellery from around the world and where you can also find monthly features, exclusive interviews with designers and ideas on how to wear the latest trends in jewellery.

Prices:	Medium	Express Ship? (UK)	Yes
Delivers to:	Worldwide	Gift Wrap?	Yes
Based:	UK		

www.pascal-jewellery.com

Here's a collection of timeless stylish jewellery from a retailer that was originally established in Liberty of London about 25 years ago. As members of the National Association of Gold-smiths you can be sure that you're buying real quality. The collection is updated at least four times a year so you can be tempted regularly and prices start at around £50 (and average about £300).

Prices:	Luxury/Medium	Express Ship? (UK)	No
Delivers to:	Worldwide	Gift Wrap?	Yes
Based:	UK		

www.pebblelondon.com

The Pebble collections include metals, stones, wood, glass, coral and amber, sourced from countries such as India, China, Africa, Thailand and Nepal. This is a beautiful, wearable, contemporary collection as you would expect from a company that has worked with designers such as John Galliano and Roberto Cavalli. Expect a fascinating, colourful range of unique jewellery and a wide range of prices.

Prices:	Medium	Express Ship? (UK)	Yes
Delivers to:	Worldwide	Gift Wrap?	Yes
Based:	UK		

www.reglisse.co.uk

For those of you who are looking for something different and unusual take a look round here. This collection of accessories and jewellery, created by an eclectic group of modern luxury designers, includes some really beautiful pieces with a wide collection of jewellery and unique items such as lizard-embossed calfskin passport covers and assymetric wine carafes.

Prices:	Luxury/Medium	Express Ship? (UK)	Yes
Delivers to:	Worldwide	Gift Wrap?	Yes
Based:	UK		

www.swarovski.com

Swarovski are still famous for their sparkling figurines and collectibles. However, the jewellery collection is now one of the best around at a reasonable price, offering a wide range from beautiful and simple contemporary pieces to unmissable statement jewels. They also have clever ideas such as crystal-encrusted headphones and flash drives, watches and small leather goods.

Prices:	Medium	Express Ship? (UK)	No
Delivers to:	Worldwide	Gift Wrap?	Yes
Based:	Germany		

Fashion Rocks

www.accessoriesonline.co.uk

Here's modern designer jewellery by Les Nereides, Butler and Wilson, Lola Rose, Kenneth Jay Lane, Angie Gooderham (and more), with a varied and attractive range. Click here when you want your next fashion jewellery fix or when you're looking for a treat for a friend and you'll not be disappointed. Many of the pieces here are really unusual and pretty, not necessarily inexpensive but always in line with the season.

Prices:	Medium/Very Good Value	Express Ship? (UK)	No
Delivers to:	Worldwide	Gift Wrap?	No
Based:	UK		

www.accessorize.co.uk

Accessorize is the essential destination if you're looking for up-to-the-minute and extremely well-priced accessories including a wide range of jewellery. It's also an excellent place for a gift for an older child or if your early teen and upwards hankers after a new pair of earrings, flip-flops, party slip-on shoes, scarf or bag.

Prices:	Very Good Value	Express Ship? (UK)	No
Delivers to:	UK	Gift Wrap?	No
Based:	UK		

www.butlerandwilson.co.uk

Famous for their signature sometimes whimsical sometimes totally in your face fashion jewellery you can choose here from a glamorous and well-priced online range of necklaces, bracelets, earrings and brooches. Costume jewellery and jewellery using semi-precious stones such as rose quartz, agate, amber and jade; the collection of very pretty printed and beaded handbags plus bridal jewellery and accessories are all available as well.

Prices:	Medium	Express Ship? (UK)	No
Delivers to:	Worldwide	Gift Wrap?	No but everything is beautifully packaged
Based:	UK		

www.lolarose.co.uk

This is an unusually designed website where you see all the products as on the pages of a book. However, it's clever as well, as you can not only see everything very clearly but also view all the different colourways of the necklaces and bracelets made with rose quartz, white jade, green aventurine, mother of pearl and black agate.

Prices:	Medium	Express Ship? (UK)	No
Delivers to:	Worldwide	Gift Wrap?	No
Based:	UK		

www.mikeyjewellery.co.uk

Mikey is an excellent contemporary jewellery designer, whose collections are always moving forward and in tune with what's going on in fashion. Make a note here – if you have a daughter who loves to collect accessories (preferably that you've paid for) you may want to look at this website at dead of night just before Christmas or a birthday as otherwise you'll almost certainly be spending more than you intend.

Prices:	Very Good Value	Express Ship? (UK)	No
Delivers to:	UK	Gift Wrap?	No
Based:	UK		

www.treasurebox.co.uk

Here you'll find a wealth of costume jewellery from Butler and Wilson, Tarina Tarantino, Angie Gooderham, Juicy Couture, Barbara Easton and Les Nereides with the emphasis on what's in fashion right now. You can select your jewellery to go with each new season's look and they're adding in new designers all the time.

Prices:	Medium	Express Ship? (UK)	Yes
Delivers to:	Worldwide	Gift Wrap?	Yes
Based:	UK		

Tic Toc

www.ernestjones.co.uk

Ernest Jones have a really well-designed website where you can buy watches by a wide range of premium designers such as TAG Heuer, Gucci, Longines and Rado. The advantage of buying here is that if you have any problems you can choose to visit one of their 190 UK-based stores or use the online address.

Prices:	Luxury/Medium	Express Ship? (UK)	Yes
Delivers to:	UK	Gift Wrap?	Yes
Based:	UK		

www.goldsmiths.co.uk

Here's another well-known offline chain of jewellery stores offering a wide range of its products online on a well-designed and easy-to-navigate website. Alongside the jewellery ranges where there's an excellent choice they also have watches by Seiko, Tissot, Longines and Citizen plus fashion brands Gucci, DKNY, Armani, Versace and Burberry. Expect delivery within three days.

Prices:	Medium	Express Ship? (UK)	No
Delivers to:	UK	Gift Wrap?	No
Based:	UK		

www.thewatchhut.co.uk

Buy your next watch from thewatchhut.co.uk and you'll know that you're buying from an authorised dealer with the full manufacturer's guarantee. On some of the watches there are excellent discounts so it's worth having a good look through the brands on offer such as Ebel, Accurist, Breil, Diesel and Fossil.

Prices:	Medium	Express Ship? (UK)	Yes
Delivers to:	UK	Gift Wrap?	No
Based:	UK		

www.watchshopuk.com

The Watch Shop offers watches by Tissot, Seiko, DKNY, Rotary and many other reasonably priced brands. This is one of the most well-designed watch websites and although you should use a shopping comparison website once you've made your choice just to make sure you're getting the best price, you may well want to shop here.

Prices:	Medium	Express Ship? (UK)	Yes
Delivers to:	UK	Gift Wrap?	No
Based:	UK		

Wraps and More

www.black.co.uk

If you're not a black and neutral person you won't like this website. However, if, like me, you're known for being a black addict you should have a browse through this collection offering beautiful – and beautifully photographed – accessories such as shawls and scarves, gloves, bags, jewellery and belts in (you guessed it) black, grey, cream and beige. This may not be the most sophisticated website but the collection of cashmere scarves is the best.

Prices:	Luxury/Medium	Express Ship? (UK)	Yes
Delivers to:	Worldwide	Gift Wrap?	Yes
Based:	UK		

www.jobuckler.com

If you're one of those people who is always looking for the perfect scarf or shawl to add the finishing touch, you should take a look at this small but beautiful collection of scarves and wraps in pleated chiffon. These are very much statement pieces and are available in different sizes and a very good range of colours from neutrals to brights. Delivery is free in the UK.

Prices:	Medium	Express Ship? (UK)	Yes
Delivers to:	Worldwide	Gift Wrap?	No
Based:	UK		

www.samanthaholmes.com

This is an exclusive collection of handcrafted luxury alpaca gifts, comprising fashion accessories, babywear and homeware, so don't be surprised to find cobweb knit scarves and shawls in a gorgeous range of colours, baby beanies and pixi hats and beautiful satin-edged blankets here plus cushion covers and leg warmers (and much more).

Prices:	Medium	Express Ship? (UK)	Yes
Delivers to:	EU	Gift Wrap?	Yes
Based:	UK		

www.sophiec.co.uk

At SophieC you can buy superb quality cashmere scarves, shawls, throws and blankets and a luxurious collection of scarves for men. For each there's a choice of gorgeous colours with names such as chilli, marshmallow, morello and lupin. This is a beautifully designed website with clear pictures of all the products on offer.

Prices:	Luxury/Medium	Express Ship? (UK)	Yes
Delivers to:	Worldwide	Gift Wrap?	No
Based:	UK		

www.thetravelwrapcompany.com

The Scottish cashmere Travelwrap comes in a range of unique colours and is particularly perfect for anyone who spends time jetting around the world. Whether you're one of the lucky ones who sits up front or not, one of these beautiful soft cashmere wraps will help to create a glamorous aura and keep you snug at the same time. Buy one for yourself or give them as gifts and use yours at home or away. You can never have too much cashmere.

Prices:	Luxury/Medium	Express Ship? (UK)	Yes
Delivers to:	Worldwide	Gift Wrap?	Yes
Based:	UK		

www.trehearneandbrar.com

This must surely be the most beautiful collection of pashminas and shawls available. Don't expect cheap prices here and don't expect to be able to see the full range online, either. Having said that, you can clearly see each item by using their enlarged view, then either email them or call through with your order or any queries. Their collection includes plain, dyed-to-order, lined and reversible shawls.

Prices:	Luxury	Express Ship? (UK)	No
Delivers to:	Worldwide	Gift Wrap?	No
Based:	UK		

Also take a look at www.pickett.co.uk.

Gloved and Waisted

It's rare to see people wearing gloves unless the cold demands it, or you're going to a really (really) dressy function, but as soon as the chill is in the air I'm always hunting for mine. Having left my favourite pair behind in Canada last year I'll be on the hunt this autumn for the simplest pair of black sheepskin lined gloves to keep me warm for the season. There aren't a lot of dedicated glove stores other than in the US and as well as here you should check out www.pickett.co.uk, www.celtic-sheepskin.co.uk and www.ewenique.co.uk.

www.corneliajames.com

Long-standing glove maker Cornelia James has now expanded their range to include fashion accessories such as faux fur wraps and gilets, stoles and silk scarves. There's a small but very special selection of gloves to buy online, including leather, snaffled trimmed gloves, sexy lace mittens, opera-length satin gloves trimmed with boa feathers and long and short velvet leopard print gloves perfect for Christmas.

Prices:	Luxury/Medium	Express Ship? (UK)	No
Delivers to:	Worldwide	Gift Wrap?	No
Based:	UK		

www.elliotrhodes.com

The minute you arrive at this website you know you're going to be seriously tempted. It's not just that it's gorgeous to look at, but the belts and buckles on offer are all seriously beautiful and not so overpriced that you're not inspired to dive in and buy. Choose the style of belt you want first, and then you can select your colour, width and buckle.

Prices:	Luxury/Medium	Express Ship? (UK)	Yes
Delivers to:	Worldwide	Gift Wrap?	Automatic
Based:	UK		

www.rodeobelts.co.uk

It was a real toss-up whether to put this online belt retailer in the jeans section or not as these are the perfect belts for anyone who likes to dress up their jeans with heels and something gorgeous, glittery and quite over the top round their waist. If that's you then you'll feel totally at home here. This is a small but superb range.

Prices:	Luxury/Medium	Express Ship? (UK)	Yes
Delivers to:	Worldwide	Gift Wrap?	No
Based:	UK		

Small Accessory Store

Some people carry just about everything in their handbags and don't really care when they haul that battered old purse out of their Prada bag. I have to confess that I do – it may not be something that other people notice but for me, to have smart small accessories matters quite a lot. So get rid of that tatty diary and scuffed cosmetic bag and feast yourself here on beautiful, high-quality leathers and quirky designs. Then when you drop your bag and everything falls out you can feel pleased with yourself that your elegant image is still maintained.

www.aspinaloflondon.com

If you're looking for top-quality leather and British craftsmanship then take a look at this beautifully designed and photographed website where the product range is growing all the time and now includes chic handbags for day and evening, luxurious travel bags and accessories such as wallets and purses, gloves, cosmetic cases, jewellery rolls and make-up brush sets.

Prices:	Luxury/Medium	Express Ship? (UK)	Yes
Delivers to:	Worldwide	Gift Wrap?	Yes
Based:	UK		

www.heroshop.co.uk

There are lots of places you can buy leather goods online, but very few that offer the quality and service you'll find here. It's not a huge range but a selection of classic luggage and weekenders, photo albums, home accessories, document wallets, jewellery boxes and cosmetic bags for her, wet packs for him plus shooting accessories and luxury dog leads, collars and baskets.

Prices:	Medium	Express Ship? (UK)	No
Delivers to:	Worldwide	Gift Wrap?	Yes
Based:	UK		

www.julieslaterandson.co.uk

Everything on this website is beautifully pictured so you'll know exactly what you're ordering and there's a very good choice of leather purses, gifts and travel accessories using interesting and unusual colours (which include pistachio, pale blue, meadow green, hot pink, carnation and royal blue) and occasionally whimsical designs.

Prices:	Medium	Express Ship? (UK)	Yes
Delivers to:	Worldwide	Gift Wrap?	Yes
Based:	UK		

www.knomobags.com

The idea behind Knomo was to design a range of laptop bags for both men and women that look totally different to everyone else's, so yours will never be picked up by someone by mistake again. The collection includes laptop bags and sleeves and ipod cases and there are lots of detailed views for each so that you can see exactly what you're ordering.

Prices:	Medium	Express Ship? (UK)	No
Delivers to:	Worldwide	Gift Wrap?	Yes
Based:	UK		

www.violetmaylondon.com

Violet May's aim is to create beautiful and stylish business accessories for women that you won't find anywhere else, so ditch that boring laptop bag you've been carrying around for soooo long, get out your credit card and prepare to spend. Everything here, whether it's the clever and roomy Blackberry purse, snake effect card cases or glamorous, satin-lined laptop bags is cleverly styled and beautifully made.

Prices:	Luxury	Express Ship? (UK)	Yes
Delivers to:	Worldwide	Gift Wrap?	Yes
Based:	UK		

Also take a look at:

www.pickett.co.uk
www.cross.com
www.smythson.com
www.forzieri.com

Section 4
Beauty Stop

So what can I tempt you with first? I suppose it really depends on what state of mind you're in. If you're reading this at the end of the day, just imagining some of the amazing products here landing at your door will make you feel better – a Tocca candle perhaps, a magical shower gel by Guerlain or revitalising Beauty Flash Balm by Clarins.

If you're thinking about what to add into your existing beauty regimen I suggest you check out the Philosophy range of daily peeling cleansers, a helpful lift from LiftFusion or Champneys' collagen mask. Then again you may be looking for a gift, and what better place to stop by? From luxurious fragrance to organic body polishers and perfect pedicures absolutely everything's on offer here plus all the men's ranges as well.

Imagine this as your personal beauty hall, but one where you don't have to jostle through the crowds and queue to pay but somewhere you can relax and browse at the same time. You really couldn't ask for more than that. I've said enough, I'll let you look for yourselves.

Superbrands Online

I'm sure that you've known for quite a while that you can buy your Lancôme, Arden, YSL and Chanel beauty products online from one or two select retailers such as www.boots.com. Now many of them have launched their own dedicated websites, and the main difference from buying from their sites rather than elsewhere is that you can find out more about the products, where there are special offers offline and if they have a promotion or gift online. If you're a dedicated follower of a specific brand you'll be really pleased to use these websites, and more are launching all the time.

www.biotherm.co.uk

World-famous brand Biotherm offers a complete range of skincare and cosmetics, plus a men's line, for all skin types, incorporating the extracts of thermal plankton which make it unique. Every product was formulated to work perfectly with the skin's natural processes to renew, restore and rejuvenate and there are specialist treatments as well for sensitive skin and anti-aging.

Prices:	Medium	Express Ship? (UK)	Yes
Delivers to:	Worldwide	Gift Wrap?	Yes
Based:	UK		

www.bobbibrown.co.uk

Bobbi Brown has the some of the best colours and tools you can find and (unfortunately for my bank balance) they seem to manage to create something I really can't resist each season. If you haven't yet tried this excellent all-American cosmetics and skincare company I suggest you get going as you've been missing some of the best products available anywhere.

Prices:	Medium	Express Ship? (UK)	Yes
Delivers to:	UK this website	Gift Wrap?	No
Based:	UK		

www.clarins.co.uk

If you're a Clarins wearer then this is the website for you, as not only can you buy all your favourite products here but you can immediately discover what's new, what's going on in which stores (i.e. where there are special offers and gifts), as well as special promotions online. You can also set up your profile so that they can recommend which products are best for your age and skin type.

Prices:	Medium	Express Ship? (UK)	No
Delivers to:	UK this website	Gift Wrap?	No
Based:	UK		

www.clinique.co.uk

Here not only can you purchase replacements for all your favourite Clinique products but you can also read all about what's new, visit their Gift Centre to order special sets and accessory kits and join Club Clinique, where you can register for fast checkout, free samples with your orders, 'Beauty Scoops' and expert advice. Delivery is to the UK only but there's an express service and gift-wrap option.

Prices:	Medium	Express Ship? (UK)	Yes
Delivers to:	UK	Gift Wrap?	Yes
Based:	UK		

www.cremedelamer.co.uk

You've no doubt read about Creme de la Mer and seen their products in the stores, and now they're available to buy online – from the incredibly popular (and expensive) moisturising cream to the new range of skin and body treatments, foundations and powders. These products are all at the luxury end of the market; however, when you take a look at them you're sure to be tempted. You have been warned.

Prices:	Luxury	Express Ship? (UK)	Yes
Delivers to:	UK	Gift Wrap?	No
Based:	UK		

www.esteelauder.co.uk

As you'd expect, Estée Lauder have a really beautiful website and although you can buy their products from other online retailers here, there are lots of extra goodies, such as information on the latest products and best-sellers and where you can find (offline, of course) their free gifts and brow bars around the country. They offer express and Saturday delivery services plus gift wrapping.

Prices:	Luxury/Medium	Express Ship? (UK)	Yes
Delivers to:	Worldwide	Gift Wrap?	Yes
Based:	UK		

www.lancôme.co.uk

You can buy all the products from this world famous skincare and cosmetics company online from other retailers, and now you can buy them directly from Lancôme on their clear, stylish website. If you're a Lancôme addict this is surely the site to visit as you can immediately find out about the latest products, take a look at their best-sellers and find out about gifts and special events taking place offline.

Prices:	Luxury/Medium	Express Ship? (UK)	Yes
Delivers to:	UK	Gift Wrap?	No
Based:	UK		

www.narscosmetics.co.uk

On the gorgeously black-based new Nars website you can find out about and order all the NARS products which include the famous range of cosmetics (try the excellent creme blush), make-up brushes and sets. Then there's the shimmering bronzing glow and powder, NARSskin beauty products and the full range of palettes which contain up to ten eye, cheek and lip colours.

Prices:	Medium	Express Ship? (UK)	No
Delivers to:	UK	Gift Wrap?	No
Based:	UK		

Fabulous Fragrance

From classic brands such as Chanel No 5 and Diorissimo to the more contemporary Miller Harris and Ormonde Jayne you can find just about every fragrance online, and sometimes at very reasonable prices. Don't expect the retailers here to offer you scents for less unless they're having a sale, the best place to go to check up if your favourite is on offer is the Beauty for Less section below. Here you can find out about and order for gifts and for treats, take advantage of the gorgeous packaging and often ask for samples to be sent out before you invest heavily.

www.escentual.co.uk

Escentual carry what is probably the widest range of fragrance for men and women in the UK. Choose a fragrance or fragrance linked bath and body product and then search for it on this site – you're almost certain to find it. Bath and body products include Burberry, Bvlgari, Calvin Klein, Gucci, Guerlain, Rochas and Versace plus Crabtree and Evelyn, Tisserand and I Coloniali.

Prices:	Luxury/Medium/Very Good Value	Express Ship? (UK)	Yes
Delivers to:	Worldwide	Gift Wrap?	Yes
Based:	UK		

www.florislondon.com

Here's one of the oldest and most traditional perfumers, having been established originally in 1730. You'll find favourites Lavender, China Rose, Gardenia and Stephanotis and more modern fragrances Night Scented Jasmin, Bouquet de la Reine and No 89. The updated packaging is lovely and for each fragrance there's a full range of bath and body products plus special wrapped sets for Christmas.

Prices:	Luxury/Medium	Express Ship? (UK)	Yes
Delivers to:	Worldwide	Gift Wrap?	Yes
Based:	UK		

www.jomalone.co.uk

This has to be one of my personal favourites, where you can buy Jo Malone's beautifully packaged range of luxurious fragrances plus bath and body products with names like Pomegranate Noir and Blue Agava and Cacao. You'll also find her cleansers, serums and moisturisers, facial finishers such as mascara and lip gloss and irresistible travel sets.

Prices:	Luxury	Express Ship? (UK)	Yes
Delivers to:	Worldwide	Gift Wrap?	Yes
Based:	UK		

www.kennethturner.com

White Flowers, Wild Garden, Magnolia Grandiflora and Rose (plus his Original fragrance) are some of the fragrances you'll find on this pretty website, presented as candles, tea lights, shower gel and body lotions, room colognes and pot pourri. His packaging, in flower-printed blue-and-white boxes, turns his products into perfect gifts and you'll find travel sets and prepared gift boxes here as well.

Prices:	Luxury/Medium	Express Ship? (UK)	Yes
Delivers to:	Worldwide	Gift Wrap?	Yes
Based:	UK		

www.laboutiquedelartisanparfumeur.com

If you're not already aware of this gorgeous collection of French fragrance and bath and body products by L'Artisan Parfumeur, with names such as Mure et Musc (blackberry and musk), Figuier and Orchidee Blanche, then now's the time to discover a new beautifully presented range and order it online.

Prices:	Luxury	Express Ship? (UK)	Yes
Delivers to:	Worldwide	Gift Wrap?	Automatic
Based:	UK		

www.lessenteurs.com

Les Senteurs is a famous perfumery based in London, offering different and unusual fragrance and bath and body products and an excellent service. Brands they offer are Creed, Annick Goutal, Diptyque, E Coudray, Serge Lutens, Caron and Parfums Historique to name but a few. The ranges are split into categories, such as fragrance, bath and body or fragrance notes, such as citrus, oriental or fruity.

Prices:	Luxury/Medium	Express Ship? (UK)	No
Delivers to:	Worldwide	Gift Wrap?	Yes
Based:	UK		

www.millerharris.com

If you'd like to give someone a gorgeous fragrance or bath and body product which is not so well known, then Miller Harris may have the answer. This is a small, independent company which specialises in blending its own fragrances, with enticing names such as Tangerine Vert, Fleur Oriental and Terre de Bois. In each one you'll find not only the Eau de Parfum but bath and body products and candles as well.

Prices:	Luxury/Medium	Express Ship? (UK)	Yes
Delivers to:	Worldwide	Gift Wrap?	Yes
Based:	UK		

www.ormondejayne.com

This is a wonderful London-based perfumery where you can find a range of fragrance, candles, bath and body products that you may well not have heard of before. Everything is totally luxurious and beautifully presented with a unique range of fragrances such as the citrussy Osmanthus and floral Champaca. Try their velvet and satin pouched sample programme before you splash out on a large bottle or give one away as a gift.

Prices:	Luxury	Express Ship? (UK)	Yes
Delivers to:	Worldwide	Gift Wrap?	Yes
Based:	UK		

www.parfumsdorsay.co.uk

Here you'll find a very small, beautifully photographed range of fragrances, soaps and scented candles from long established fragrance house Parfums d'Orsay of France. If you already know the fragrances you'll be delighted that they're now available here and if you haven't tried them before, email and ask for the sample of your choice – you'll find they're very special.

Prices:	Luxury/Medium	Express Ship? (UK)	Yes – call
Delivers to:	UK	Gift Wrap?	No
Based:	UK		

www.penhaligons.co.uk

Penhaligons offers fragrance, candles and bath and body products for perfect and luxurious gifts for men and women. Choose from classics Lily of the Valley, Elizabethan Rose or Blue-bell or the more modern and spicy Malabah, Artemesia or LP No 9. Each fragrance is matched up to its own shower gel, soap, body lotion and candle.

Prices:	Luxury	Express Ship? (UK)	Yes
Delivers to:	Worldwide	Gift Wrap?	Automatic
Based:	UK		

Perfect Pampering

It seems to me that everyone's definition of 'pampering' is different. Mine is of the 'time to myself with a massage thrown in' variety and it can be anywhere in the world. For most of us who are busy all the time, with work, kids, dogs, entertaining and more, that short time when no one can interrupt my world is truly marvellous and absolutely essential. So take some time when no one can call you, you don't have to answer questions or solve anyone else's problems, and enjoy. You'll feel so much better afterwards.

Here you'll find information on where to find spas anywhere in the world and also wonderful products for relaxing moments, preferably when you have the house to yourself.

www.bathandunwind.com

Bath & Unwind specialise in luxury products that help you to relax (and unwind) after a hard day's work. They offer brands such as Aromatherapy Associates, Korres, Nougat, Burt's Bees and Jane Packer. Delivery is free (UK) provided you spend over a certain amount and they'll ship to you anywhere in the world. They also have a gift selector and an express service for the next time you forget that special present.

Prices:	Medium	Express Ship? (UK)	Yes
Delivers to:	Worldwide	Gift Wrap?	No
Based:	UK		

www.blisslondon.co.uk

Sign up for Bliss Beut e-mails and stay in the 'Glow'. Does that give you some idea of the tone from beauty online from New York and London's hottest spa? If you don't have the time to visit the spas themselves you can at least now buy the products online and relax at home with your own treatments, shower gels and shampoos with simple names like Body Butter, Rosy Toes and Glamour Glove Gel.

Prices:	Medium	Express Ship? (UK)	Yes
Delivers to:	Worldwide	Gift Wrap?	No
Based:	UK		

www.comptoir-sud-pacifique.com

Comptoir Sud Pacifique is a brand synonymous with escape, exoticism and sun, so if you feel the need for an exotic change of scenery just click through here and let your senses take you away. Choose from Vanilla, Spicy, Fruity, Woody, Floral and Fresh Waters fragrances and candles such as Muscade Orange, Vanille Apricot and Aqua Motu. You can order as you go round the website or from a list by clicking on Buy Online. All prices are in euros.

Prices:	Medium	Express Ship? (UK)	No
Delivers to:	France	Gift Wrap?	No
Based:	UK		

www.cowshedonline.com

Recognised for their fun, quirky, bovine-inspired names such as Dirty Cow Hand Wash, Until the Cows Come Home Gift Set, and Grumpy Cow Uplifting Candle (so you really do need to know who you're giving them to), Cowshed products contain theraputic blends of herbal infusions and high-quality pure essential oils from around the world. The names derive from the original Cowshed spa at Babington House in Somerset.

Prices:	Medium	Express Ship? (UK)	Yes if you ask them
Delivers to:	UK and USA (separate site)	Gift Wrap?	No
Based:	UK		

www.crabtree-evelyn.co.uk

Well known and sold throughout the world, Crabtree & Evelyn offer a wide range of bath, body and spa products from classic fragrances such as Lily of the Valley to the ultra modern La Source and brand new India Hicks' Island Living collection. Everything is cleverly and attractively packaged and offered here on their well-designed and easy-to-use website.

Prices:	Medium	Express Ship? (UK)	No
Delivers to:	Worldwide	Gift Wrap?	No
Based:	UK		

www.lush.co.uk

This is a 'very interesting' website, and without a doubt if you haven't already visited you should do so now, it'll lift your spirits almost immediately. Products include such items as Ibiza Party Shampoo, Sweetie Pie Shower Jelly and Frosty Glitter Bubble Bars and if those don't make you want to take a peek this is probably not the site for you. Lush make all their products by hand and believe in 'long candlelit baths ... and filling the world with perfume'. Don't we all?

Prices:	Medium	Express Ship? (UK)	Yes
Delivers to:	Worldwide	Gift Wrap?	No
Based:	UK		

www.moltonbrown.co.uk

As a Molton Brown addict I can tell you that the range is wonderful to use, reasonably priced and every time they launch a new product I'm there, ready, willing and able to give it a try without the guilt that comes of investing in some of the more expensive brands. The cosmetics and skincare ranges are also growing rapidly so you need to keep checking back.

Prices:	Medium	Express Ship? (UK)	No
Delivers to:	Worldwide	Gift Wrap?	Yes
Based:	UK		

www.savonneriesoap.com

This is a beautiful website with an extremely luxurious feel where you can buy exquisitely packaged handmade soaps (think Flower Garden and Honey Cake), bath and body products such as Geranium and Bergamot Oil, perfect gift boxes and The Naughty Weekend Kit – take a look and you'll find out. Be warned, the photography alone makes you want to buy something immediately.

Prices:	Luxury/Medium	Express Ship? (UK)	No
Delivers to:	Worldwide	Gift Wrap?	No
Based:	UK		

www.therenovationstore.co.uk

Don't be confused by the name here – this website is about beautiful pampering products by brands such as Nougat, Gianna Rose Atelier, Abahna and Lothantique, then there are wonderful slippers by CicciaBella, The Laundress New York luxury detergents, accessories for everywhere in your home and pretty nursery ideas.

Prices:	Medium	Express Ship? (UK)	No
Delivers to:	Worldwide	Gift Wrap?	Yes, free
Based:	UK		

www.thesanctuary.co.uk

Just looking at this spa website makes you feel more relaxed, with its shades of blue and white and the attractive, simple packaging of pampering products such as Sanctuary Salt Soak, Body Polisher and Body Moisture Spray. You can buy the full range of Sanctuary products here plus gift vouchers and information on treatments at the Covent Garden spa.

Prices:	Medium/Very Good Value	Express Ship? (UK)	Yes
Delivers to:	Worldwide	Gift Wrap?	Yes
Based:	UK		

Hair and Nail Salon

Your favourite hair products may be by Nexxus, Paul Mitchell, Frederic Fekkai or Aveda. You may use Seche Vite wonder dry when you do your manicure at home, like Opi lacquers and Jessica foot spa products – whatever you like to use, you can buy them online. So no more trips back from the salon loaded with heavy bottles, or even worse, where you've bought a smaller, more expensive quantity in order not to have to carry too much. Now you can find your products in bulk or whatever quantity you prefer, take advantage of free delivery offers and have everything delivered to your door frequently even at a discounted price – what more could you ask for?

www.hqhair.com

It's quite hard to define this marvellous online retailer from whom I have ordered many times, as they do offer an incredible range of hair products, but they've also moved on to contemporary skincare and cosmetics, essential high-quality accessories and gorgeous fragrance. Brands include Paul Mitchell, Philosophy, Johnny Loves Rosie, Benefit and Fusion Beauty. This is one of the all-time greats.

Prices:	Luxury/Medium	Express Ship? (UK)	Most orders take
Delivers to:	Worldwide		24–48 hours
Based:	UK	Gift Wrap?	Yes

www.justbeautifully.co.uk

This is a recent addition to the hair care online retailers list and a really great website, offering the full range of my favourite hair dryers by Parlux – which come in colours such as pink, red and chocolate as well as black, of course – straighteners by Coriolis, T3 and Kodo Creative, manicure and pedicure tools and lots of other beauty treats.

Prices:	Medium	Express Ship? (UK)	No
Delivers to:	UK	Gift Wrap?	No
Based:	UK		

www.lenawhite.co.uk

Green Tea Massage, Espresso Scrub and the MicroWrap Emergency Nail Repair Kit are just some of the products you can find here alongside Ink, Amethyst and Makes Men Blush nail lacquers on this excellent salon online store. When they talk about the Coconut Melon Juicie I have to say I thought we'd moved over to food and drink but no, everything here is gorgeously beauty related and you should take a look.

Prices:	Medium	Express Ship? (UK)	Yes
Delivers to:	UK	Gift Wrap?	No
Based:	UK		

www.lookfantastic.com

Here's a marvellous selection of hair care products from well-known brands such as Kerastase, Paul Mitchell, Tigi and Redken, plus nailcare by Essie, Opi, Jessica and Nailtiques. In the Beauty Accessories section they offer straighteners, dryers, brushes and clippers by GHD, Babyliss, T3 and Icon and if you haven't discovered ghd ceramic brushes yet you can order them here. Try them, they're excellent.

Prices:	Medium/Very Good Value	Express Ship? (UK)	Yes
Delivers to:	Worldwide	Gift Wrap?	No
Based:	UK		

www.nailsbymail.co.uk

Calling themselves 'The UK's leading nail boutique' Nails by Mail offer products by Essie and Seche (and if you haven't yet tried the truly marvellous Seche Vite quick dry yet you should) together with colours, treatments, files and buffers making this is an excellent well-priced site for all the elements necessary for keeping your nails in top shape.

Prices:	Medium	Express Ship? (UK)	No
Delivers to:	UK	Gift Wrap?	No
Based:	UK		

www.saloneasy.com

This is the place to find your professional standard hairdryer, hair straighteners and stylers by GHD and Babyliss and a wide range of hair brushes. This site is aimed at the professional so there are a wide range of salon products that you probably won't be interested in but the choice and prices for the dryers and brushes are some of the best you'll find and the service is extremely speedy.

Prices:	Medium	Express Ship? (UK)	No
Delivers to:	Worldwide	Gift Wrap?	No
Based:	UK		

Play with Colour

This is another area where it's very hard to choose – nearly all the brands are online, many with their own dedicated sites just waiting to tempt you with the latest totally irresistible products for the season. My advice is to be very careful buying colour online. Yes I know that the colour reproduction is so much better than a few years ago but I stick to the same thing I said then. If you know the colour of the foundation, powder or concealer you need then buy it online of course. If you're not sure then choose the right colour in the stores (and near to daylight) then stock up online afterwards. You need really good light to find the right colour for you and it's hard enough in the artificial light of many of the shops – it's totally impossible from a screen.

www.beccacosmetics.com

If you haven't yet discovered modern cosmetics and skincare brand Becca watch out when you visit their website – undoubtedly you're going to be tempted here, from the 34 different shades of concealer to the Brazilian bronzing sheen and luminous skin colour.

Prices:	Medium	Express Ship? (UK)	Yes
Delivers to:	Worldwide	Gift Wrap?	No
Based:	UK		

www.benefitcosmetics.co.uk

You can find Benefit cosmetics in the major stores but you'll be hard put to see this complete range anywhere else online, and with tempting products such as Benetint, Lip Plump, Super Strength Blemish Blaster and Ooh La Lift how can you resist buying from this veritable candy store for the face?

Prices:	Medium	Express Ship? (UK)	Yes
Delivers to:	Worldwide	Gift Wrap?	Yes
Based:	UK		

www.boots.com

Not only can you buy your basic bathroom cupboard items here, plus fragrance from most of the major brands, but from their Brand Boutique you can also buy the full ranges from Chanel, Clarins, Clinique, Dior, Estée Lauder, Elizabeth Arden and Lancôme plus ultra modern brands Ruby and Millie, Urban Decay and Benefit. Delivery is free when you spend £40 and returns are free too.

Prices:	Luxury/Medium/Very Good Value	Express Ship? (UK)	Yes
Delivers to:	UK	Gift Wrap?	Yes
Based:	UK		

www.eyeslipsface.co.uk

Eyes Lips Face, the beauty brand that's hot in the USA, has launched its website in the UK with a line of simple, luxurious, problem-solving and extremely well-priced cosmetics and accessories. With everything here priced at £1.50 or less (excluding kits) you can afford to play. Click through to the Elements section to design your own compact or choose from their pre-selected colour combinations.

Prices:	Very Good Value	Express Ship? (UK)	Yes
Delivers to:	UK	Gift Wrap?	No
Based:	UK		

www.justbeautydirect.co.uk

If you haven't come across this website yet you need to take a look now, particularly as they're currently the only online retailer in the UK offering cult US brand Smashbox online, alongside Philosophy, Bare Escentuals and other brands you may not have heard of. The site is certainly not the most sophisticated to look at although it's very easy to navigate, and having bought from them more than once myself I can tell you that the service is excellent.

Prices:	Medium/Very Good Value	Express Ship? (UK)	Call them
Delivers to:	Worldwide excluding US and Canada	Gift Wrap?	No
Based:	UK		

www.maccosmetics.co.uk

Shop here by category – lips, eyes, nails, skincare, etc. – or from one of their collections, with names such as Viva Glam, Barbie Loves Mac, Untamed, Rockocco or Technacolour – and these change each season. Click on 'What's New' to discover the latest treats and tips or go through to 'Looks' to discover how they're created (and buy the products, of course). Be warned, it's extremely hard to leave without buying.

Prices:	Medium	Express Ship? (UK)	Yes
Delivers to:	UK	Gift Wrap?	No
Based:	UK		

www.pixibeauty.com

Pixi is an independent British beauty company consisting of cosmetics and skincare ranges and beauty accessories. It was started by three sisters, two of whom are make-up artists and the third a skin therapist, so you know you're in the hands of experts. In their words the range is 'magical, individual, feminine, small, cute, playful, free spirited, mischievous, friendly, colourful, cheeky, unique, illusive and tempting'. Irresistible (my word).

Prices:	Medium	Express Ship? (UK)	No
Delivers to:	Worldwide	Gift Wrap?	No
Based:	UK		

www.screenface.com

The next time you want to buy a new set of cosmetic brushes have a good look here before you rush off and spend hundreds of pounds on some of the major brands. The selection is huge and very well priced and you can also buy make-up bags and cases, professional make-up and Tweezerman products. Some of the pictures are not very clear (if they're there at all) but you can send off for their catalogue.

Prices:	Very Good Value	Express Ship? (UK)	No
Delivers to:	UK	Gift Wrap?	No
Based:	UK		

www.spacenk.co.uk

Nars, Stila, Shu Uemura, Rodial, Darphin, Laura Mercier, Eve Lom, Diptyque, Frederic Fekkai and Dr Sebagh are just some of the 60-plus brands offered on the website of this retailer, famous for bringing unusual and hard to find products to the UK. They're updating their product list all the time and if you're anything like me you'll be tempted to spend a small fortune trying new 'miracle workers' as often as you can.

Prices:	Luxury/Medium	Express Ship? (UK)	Yes
Delivers to:	Worldwide	Gift Wrap?	Yes
Based:	UK		

Natural Skincare

Natural, organic and eco-friendly are words that are used a great deal at the moment, and this is set to increase. But what do they really mean? There are companies that use totally (or at least 95%) organic ingredients which gives them a clear place in the Greener Beauty section below. There are some that probably are properly organic but do not have the accreditation, and others which are probably not but say that they are. Then there are those offering a mix of organic and 'natural' products which you'll find below.

Don't allow yourselves to be confused and only buy from companies which do not make their degree of 'organicness' absolutely clear if you really love what they offer and you're not too worried about the percentage of organic ingredients.

www.aromatherapyassociates.com

You may well have heard of this company, as their products are now sold in over 20 countries worldwide at exclusive hotels, spas and retail outlets. You can also buy them elsewhere on-line, however the dedicated site is so clear, informative and easy to use I thought you should be able to click straight to the beautifully packaged bath, body and skincare collections for yourselves.

Prices:	Medium	Express Ship? (UK)	Yes
Delivers to:	UK	Gift Wrap?	No
Based:	UK		

www.balanceme.co.uk

Here's a range created by a team of experts who are passionate about natural aromatherapy products and who believe that everyone deserves a little bit of luxury in their everyday lives. The collection contains pure essential oils, with body washes, creams and lotions, candles, balms and polishes being just a small selection of what you can buy here. There are travel-sized products as well.

Prices:	Medium	Express Ship? (UK)	No
Delivers to:	Worldwide	Gift Wrap?	No
Based:	UK		

www.beautyicon.co.uk

There are some products here that I have no doubt you're going to find hard to resist, such as Bella Lucce's Vanilla-Coconut Whipped Shea and Peruvian Chocolate Scrub, Rodial's Glam Balm and This Works' In the Zone bath and shower gel. Many of the brands are hard to find elsewhere and bringing them all together here on this easy-to-navigate and attractive natural beauty website is simply inspired.

Prices:	Medium	Express Ship? (UK)	Yes
Delivers to:	UK	Gift Wrap?	No
Based:	UK		

www.beautynaturals.com

This is a family-run business offering a comprehensive and affordable collection of high-quality, natural health and beauty products, inspired by Martha Hill, who launched her herbal-based, cruelty-free skincare products over 30 years ago. The collection encompasses all aspects of natural beauty and includes skincare, cosmetics, hand and nail care and bath and body products.

Prices:	Medium	Express Ship? (UK)	Yes
Delivers to:	UK	Gift Wrap?	No
Based:	UK		

www.bodyshop.co.uk

Alongside all the gorgeous luxury skincare and cosmetic brands you can now find online there's The Body Shop, well known for so many years and now with a beautifully laid out, fun to use website offering all their well-priced ranges of skincare, bath and body products and cosmetics, such as their Ultra Smooth Foundation, Aloe Soothing Night Cream and Relaxing Lavender Massage Oil.

Prices:	Very Good Value	Based:	UK
Delivers to:	UK but there are overseas	Express Ship? (UK)	Yes
	transactional websites	Gift Wrap?	No

www.caudalie.com

You can find Caudalie products to buy on other health and beauty websites but I don't think you get the full feel of the products and what they are aiming to achieve, other than here. So have a good read about Vinotherapy, the basis for this range of skin and hair care and then buy products with names such as Crushed Cabernet Scrub, Vinoperfect Radiance Serum and Merlot Shower Gel, all reasonably priced.

Prices:	Medium	Express Ship? (UK)	No
Delivers to:	Worldwide	Gift Wrap?	No
Based:	UK		

www.fushi.co.uk

Fushi was established just over four years ago as a lifestyle brand of holistic health and beauty products. Expanding on the philosophy that inner health promotes outer well-being, Fushi have developed a range of natural products including herbal remedies, cosmetic ranges and aromatherapy oils, most of which are organic. Use their product finder to treat specific ailments or select by product range. There's lots of information so be prepared to spend some time.

Prices:	Medium	Express Ship? (UK)	No
Delivers to:	Worldwide	Gift Wrap?	No
Based:	UK		

www.loccitane.com

L'Occitane is another brand you're sure to have heard of, offering everything from personal care to home fragrance and all manufactured in traditional ways using natural ingredients, primarily from Provence. The range includes fragrance, body and hand care, bath and shower products, skincare, hair care and home fragrance.

Prices:	Medium	Express Ship? (UK)	Yes
Delivers to:	Worldwide	Gift Wrap?	Yes
Based:	UK		

www.musthave.co.uk

Musthave offers the best in natural and organic skincare, bodycare, fragrance and cosmetics sourced from suppliers around the world. You'll find REN, Paul & Joe, Anthony Logistics, Cowshed, Jo Wood Organics, Headonism Organic Haircare, Living Nature and Abahna, alongside brands you probably already know such as Nailtiques, Phyto and Caudalie.

Prices:	Medium	Express Ship? (UK)	Yes
Delivers to:	Worldwide	Gift Wrap?	Yes
Based:	UK		

www.mysanatural.com

Quite a lot of online retailers offering natural and environmentally friendly products think that we want to see them looking as natural as possible. Personally I don't think we do – buying lotions and potions online should always be a treat. Here at Mysa both the natural and treat elements meet beautifully, think Pink Grapefruit Hand and Body Lotion, Ginger Loofah Soap or Sweet Jasmine Body Scrub and you'll get the idea.

Prices:	Medium	Express Ship? (UK)	Yes
Delivers to:	Worldwide	Gift Wrap?	No
Based:	UK		

www.origins.co.uk

You may well have heard of Origins, specialists in natural skincare using aromatic plants, earth and sea substances and other resources to produce products as close to nature as they can be. Now you can buy the full range online, including their luxurious Ginger Soufle Whipped Body Cream, Jump Start Body Wash and Pomegranate Wash cleanser. You really do want to try them all.

Prices:	Medium	Express Ship? (UK)	Yes
Delivers to:	UK	Gift Wrap?	No
Based:	UK		

www.planetbotanic.com

Founded in 2000 as a herbal apothecary, Planet Botanic is dedicated to natural healthcare and wellbeing and offers a lovely collection of soothing, calming oils, lotions and luxuries.

These include Diptique candles, Badger Balms, Claus Porto body washes and Creed fragrance as well as their own comprehensive range of essential oils.

Prices:	Medium	Express Ship? (UK)	No
Delivers to:	Worldwide	Gift Wrap?	Yes
Based:	UK		

www.potions.co.uk

Potions & Possibilities produce natural toiletries and aromatherapy products, ranging from soaps and bath oils to restorative balms and creams. Everything is blended and created using the highest-quality essential oils, and you can find their award-winning products in Bloomingdales (in the USA) and Fenwicks in the UK among other stores and, of course, online.

Prices:	Medium	Express Ship? (UK)	Yes
Delivers to:	Worldwide	Gift Wrap?	No
Based:	UK		

www.puresha.com

This is a gorgeously designed website with lovely photographs of luxurious natural beauty products you're bound to want to buy, such as Patyka, Chocolate Sun, Ginger & Smart, Hamadi and Perfect Organics plus REN, l'Artisan Parfumeur and Mama Mio. The site is extremely quick to get round and not over busy so it's a pleasure to browse. Delivery is to UK, Ireland, Australia and the USA.

Prices:	Luxury/Medium	Express Ship? (UK)	Yes
Delivers to:	Worldwide	Gift Wrap?	Yes
Based:	UK		

www.urbanapothecary.co.uk

Whether you're looking for a pampering gift or something for yourself you'll almost certainly like this website which is easy to use and well photographed. Choose from Beauty, Skincare, Hair Care, Candles and Home Fragrance or Gifts and Accessories from brands such as Korres, Sohum or This Works. Alternatively shop by brand or by scent, check out their recommendations or take advantage of free gifts and special offers.

Prices:	Medium	Express Ship? (UK)	Yes
Delivers to:	UK	Gift Wrap?	No
Based:	UK		

Greener Beauty

As we become more and more concerned about what we put into our bodies, onto our skin and how we treat the planet, organic beauty is becoming one of the fastest growing areas of the beauty industry. To be truly described as organic, produce has to have been grown without the use of any artificial fertilisers, pesticides or ingredients that have been genetically modified.

Because European law on organic produce only covers food, The Soil Association and Organic Food Federation have created their own rules pertaining to health and beauty products. Where a product is approved under these rules you'll find their symbols, or the letters UKROFS followed by a number.

For a product to be truly organic, it must contain at least 95% of naturally grown ingredients. If the description is 'made with organic ingredients' it must contain over 70%.

Neal's Yard Remedies, Aveda and Spiezia Organics are two of the best know organic brands that manage to combine gorgeous packaging with beautifully scented products. There are lots more below.

www.aveda.co.uk

Award-winning Aveda was founded in 1978 with the aim of providing beauty professionals with high performance, botanically based products that would be more beneficial to their clients and also for the planet. You'll find their famous plant-based hair care, skincare, cosmetics, fragrance and lifestyle products here for both men and women, most of which are very reasonably priced.

Prices:	Medium	Express Ship? (UK)	Yes
Delivers to:	UK this site – also www.aveda.com	Gift Wrap?	No
Based:	UK		

www.baldwins.co.uk

G. Baldwin & Co is London's oldest and most established Herbalist and if you pay a visit to the shop you'll find that it still has a nostalgic atmosphere of stepping back in time. You can shop online from the complete ranges of both Bach Flower Remedies and the Australian Bush Flower Essences, their own brand aromatherapy oils, natural soaps, creams and bath accessories and herbs, seeds, roots and dried flowers.

Prices:	Medium	Express Ship? (UK)	Yes
Delivers to:	Worldwide	Gift Wrap?	No
Based:	UK		

www.barefoot-botanicals.com

The name, Barefoot Botanicals, was inspired by the ancient Chinese tradition of barefoot doctors who travelled from village to village without shoes, dispensing wisdom and remedies. It consists of a range of natural remedies and organic skin and hair care products which include Rescue Me face and body cream, Hair Repair masque and Intensive Eye Serum. The packaging is pretty but simple and everything is reasonably priced.

Prices:	Medium	Express Ship? (UK)	Yes
Delivers to:	Worldwide	Gift Wrap?	No
Based:	UK		

www.circaroma.com

Soil Association Certified Circaroma offers organic standard skincare incorporating rose otto, jojoba berry, ylang ylang, wild frankincense and bergamot amongst their ingredients. Products include cleansing balms, skin serums and body butters and this is a seriously good place to shop if you want to move to a totally natural regimen. Every product is clearly described and attractively, but simply packaged.

Prices:	Medium	Express Ship? (UK)	No
Delivers to:	Worldwide	Gift Wrap?	No
Based:	UK		

www.johnmasters.co.uk

Here you'll find an excellent range of organic hair care (and skincare) from Lavender and Rosemary or Honey and Hibiscus shampoo to Rosemary and Peppermint Detangler and Bourbon, Vanilla and Tangerine Hair Texturizer. His range of skincare includes face washes and cleansers, serums and body milks with fragrances such as Blood Orange and Vanilla, Lavender, and Green Tea and Rose.

Prices:	Medium	Express Ship? (UK)	No
Delivers to:	Worldwide	Gift Wrap?	No
Based:	UK		

www.jowoodorganics.com

Jo Wood offers a range that contains the highest possible percentage of organic ingredients from accredited sources. You'll find bath oils, body lotions and soaps plus natural soy wax candles all exquisitely presented in glass bottles and jars. Note that because of the lack of chemical ingredients here your products need to be stored out of sunlight and to be used within nine months.

Prices:	Luxury/Medium	Express Ship? (UK)	No
Delivers to:	Worldwide	Gift Wrap?	Gift boxes
Based:	UK		

www.jurlique.co.uk

Jurlique has been developing biodynamic beauty products since 1985 and every product here begins with a Jurlique biodynamic blend, with plants and flowers from the founders' farms in South Australia. Order their beautifully packaged cleansers, moisturisers, treatments and lotions and know that everything you buy here is designed to leave the smallest possible footprint on the planet.

Prices:	Medium	Express Ship? (UK)	Yes
Delivers to:	Worldwide	Gift Wrap?	No
Based:	UK		

www.lovelula.com

There's a huge amount of information available here on Love Lula's organic apothecary website – from which natural products to buy for stress, acne, chapped lips and stretch marks to the online skincare consultation and 'Ask Lula' email option. There are lots of products to choose from, including gifts and special ranges for mother and baby and everything's very clear and easy to see.

Prices:	Medium	Express Ship? (UK)	Yes
Delivers to:	Worldwide	Gift Wrap?	No
Based:	UK		

www.mandala-aroma.com

Mandala Aroma is a luxury organic Aromatherapy company set up by ex-fashion buyer and qualified aromatherapist Gillian Kavanagh. Here you'll discover bath oils, body treatment oils and aromatherapy candles all under the headings of Wisdom, Love, Courage and Strength. Click on the item of your choice and you'll find out more about its ingredients and benefits.

Prices:	Medium	Express Ship? (UK)	No
Delivers to:	Worldwide	Gift Wrap?	No
Based:	UK		

www.naturalcollection.com

All the products on this website are seriously natural, from fairly traded laundry baskets to organic cotton bed linen. They also have a Personal Care selection which includes brands such as Organic Options (natural soaps), Faith in Nature (aromatherapy body care) Barefoot Botanicals (skin and body care) plus lots of natural pampering products and gift ideas. In their Wellbeing section you'll find Sage Organics vitamins and minerals and Bath Indulgence Spa sets.

Prices:	Medium	Express Ship? (UK)	Yes
Delivers to:	Worldwide	Gift Wrap?	No
Based:	UK		

www.nealsyardremedies.com

This is probably one aromatherapy and herbal remedy retailer you have heard of. From the first shop located in Neal's Yard in the heart of London's Covent Garden, Neal's Yard Remedies has grown into one of the country's leading natural health retailers. On their attractive website you can buy a wide range of their products, from aromatherapy, body care, luxurious bath products and homeopathic remedies plus attractively packaged gift sets.

Prices:	Medium	Express Ship? (UK)	Yes
Delivers to:	Worldwide	Gift Wrap?	No
Based:	UK		

www.soorganic.com

All the products you'll find here have been tested by the team at So Organic, so they're not going to recommend anything to you they haven't enjoyed using themselves. There's a wide range of beauty and everyday organic products here, from brands which include Badger Balm, Earth Friendly Kids, John Masters and Spiezia Organics and there's something for every member of the family plus excellent gift ideas.

Prices:	Medium	Express Ship? (UK)	No
Delivers to:	EU	Gift Wrap?	No
Based:	UK		

www.spieziaorganics.com

Using only organic ingredients, Spiezia combines the latest scientific knowledge with sound environmental values. You'll find such products as Organic Body Firming Oil, Restorative Body Balm, body scrubs and guest soaps with lemongrass, lavender and coconut oil being some of the ingredients. Everything here is beautifully packaged in signature blue glass bottles and is made on the Lizard Peninsular, in Cornwall.

Prices:	Medium	Express Ship? (UK)	No
Delivers to:	Worldwide	Gift Wrap?	Gift boxes
Based:	UK		

www.theorganicpharmacy.com

The Organic Pharmacy is dedicated to health and beauty using organic products and treatments and specialise in herbs, homeopathy and organic skincare. They promise no artificial preservatives, colourings or fragrances and everything they offer is handmade in small batches. Look for their Organic Glam cosmetics, skincare and gorgeously fragranced candles here plus mother and baby care.

Prices:	Luxury/Medium	Express Ship? (UK)	No
Delivers to:	Worldwide	Gift Wrap?	No
Based:	UK		

www.theorganicsalon.com

TheOrganicSalon.com is a new company aiming to supply only the highest-quality products derived from an ethical and safe source. Many of these are at the forefront in the development of certified organic face, body, hair and cosmetic products and they promise that almost all are choc full of ingredients that are actually beneficial to your health. Brands include Barefoot Botanicals, Figs and Rouge, and Spiezia.

Prices:	Medium	Express Ship? (UK)	Yes
Delivers to:	Worldwide	Gift Wrap?	Yes
Based:	UK		

www.willowbeautyproducts.co.uk

Described by Normandie Keith in the *Mail on Sunday*'s *You* magazine as 'luxurious, organic and delicious', this company must be worth a look at if you're seriously into organic beauty products. There's a full range from scented candles in fragrances such as Jasmine and Geranium to bath and shower gels, exfoliating soaps and salt scrubs and everything is beautifully packaged.

Prices:	Medium	Express Ship? (UK)	Yes
Delivers to:	UK	Gift Wrap?	Yes
Based:	UK		

Skin Deep

Specialist skincare from a great number of brands who you may or may not have heard of are what you'll find here, so if you're in the mood to try something new, or you're tired of your usual regimen and want a complete change, then you're in the right place. Many of these products are expensive so I would just say that before you really splash out you should call and ask for any extra advice and information you might like and also ask for samples to try first. You should be able to try the products for free and if they want you to pay for samples, you should get your money back from your next purchase.

www.amandalacey.com

Amanda Lacey is known for her luxurious facials, using the purest most special oils. Known as 'The English rose of skincare' and fast becoming a firm favourite among stars of stage and screen, you can buy into her skincare regimen online, which includes her classic Cleansing Pomade and Oils of Provence, Protecting Day Moisturiser and Restoring Mandarin Mask.

Prices:	Medium	Express Ship? (UK)	No
Delivers to:	Worldwide Most Countries	Gift Wrap?	No
Based:	UK		

www.beautique.com

Beautique is an excellent beauty and hair website divided into three sections: Learn, where you can find tips and advice written by industry experts in all areas of beauty and hair, Buy, where you can order all the products offered, and Experience, showcasing treatments, spas and salons in the UK and around the world. Brands include Aveda, Bumble and Bumble, Carole Franck, Rodial, Guerlain, La Prairie and J C Brosseau.

Prices:	Luxury/Medium	Express Ship? (UK)	Yes
Delivers to:	UK	Gift Wrap?	No
Based:	UK		

www.beautyexpert.co.uk

Here you'll find one of the best collections of beauty products online including treatments and general skincare by brands such as Caudalie, Aromatherapy Associates, Fudge, L'Occitane, NV Perricone, Phytomer and Ren. Many of these are exclusive salon and spa products that you'll be hard put to find in the shops. There's specialist help on the Advice Line run by beauty therapists if you should have a query.

Prices:	Medium	Express Ship? (UK)	Yes
Delivers to:	Worldwide	Gift Wrap?	Yes
Based:	UK		

www.beautyflash.co.uk

Beauty Flash offers the full range from Dermalogica, including masques and moisturisers, specialist treatments and treatment foundations (although you really need to know your colour before you buy these) spa body products and sun care. They have the Skin Doctors range of professional strength skincare, Fake Bake and St Tropez tanning products, Air Stockings and Dermablend Cover Crème plus Decleor, GHD, Fudge and more.

Prices:	Medium	Express Ship? (UK)	Yes
Delivers to:	UK	Gift Wrap?	Yes
Based:	UK		

www.champneys.co.uk

Forget about thinking about Champneys as just a group of spas – their range of skincare, from scrubs and masks to cleansers and anti-aging treatments is totally excellent (and I can say this having tried some of them) and also surprisingly reasonably priced. Start with their wonderful Collagen Enriched Face Mask, Super Cooling Eye Rescue Gel and Aqua Therapy Recharging Bath Tonic and go on from there.

Prices:	Medium/Very Good Value	Express Ship? (UK)	Yes
Delivers to:	UK	Gift Wrap?	Yes
Based:	UK		

www.drhauschka.co.uk

You may well have read about Dr Hauschka's natural skincare products through its press celebrity connections. When you look at the products online you'll find that they're not overpriced and there's lots of information about each one, not just what it's for, but also how to use it, plus a full list of ingredients. When you find something you like, check to see if a trial/travel size is offered before you splash out.

Prices:	Medium	Based:	UK
Delivers to:	UK but there are international websites	Express Ship? (UK)	Yes
		Gift Wrap?	Yes

www.espaonline.com

ESPA was created to bring together the best of ancient and modern therapies with the finest quality ingredients and skincare advances. This is a lovely light and modern website offering their famous range of aromatherapy products from specific beauty treatments to bath and body products and luxury gifts, with everything formulated from the highest quality organically grown plants. So if you're feeling stressed, this would be a good place to start.

Prices:	Medium	Express Ship? (UK)	No
Delivers to:	Worldwide	Gift Wrap?	No but there are special gift sets
Based:	UK		

www.evelom.co.uk

This is surely one of the most famous names in modern skincare, based on Eve Lom's belief that the best skincare is quite simply total cleansing using natural products and her famous polishing cloth. You may not be able to get to her for a personal facial but at least now you can find her products to buy online. The range is small and not inexpensive but you can be sure that you're buying the very best.

Prices:	Luxury	Express Ship? (UK)	Yes
Delivers to:	Worldwide	Gift Wrap?	No
Based:	UK		

www.garden.co.uk

The Garden Pharmacy's list of top brands seems to be growing by the day. Here you'll find Chanel, Elizabeth Arden, Lancôme, Revlon, Clinique and Clarins online together with Vichy, Avene, Caudalie and Roc and spa products by I Coloniali, L'Occitane, Roger et Gallet and Segreti Mediterranei (and no doubt a few more will have appeared by the time you read this). The list of fragrances they offer is huge.

Prices:	Luxury/Medium/Very Good Value	Express Ship? (UK)	Yes
Delivers to:	Worldwide	Gift Wrap?	Yes
Based:	UK		

www.karinherzog.co.uk

'We didn't just jump on the oxygen band wagon we created it', they say here,where you can order from this range of oxygen skincare from Switzerland. If you're not quite sure (and the products aren't cheap), go for one of their trial packs and kits, such as the Congestion Charge, which aims to help skins with acne and dull, excessively oily skin or the energising Detox in a Box. There's a lot to read here and you may well be tempted.

Prices:	Luxury	Express Ship? (UK)	No
Delivers to:	UK	Gift Wrap?	No
Based:	UK		

www.kornerskincare.com

Created by Australian Rebecca Korner, Korner Skincare is a product range formulated in Paris, using rare plant, marine and mineral extracts with cell restructuring and regenerating properties sourced from around the world. The range includes Radiate Presence day cream, Look Famous purifying mask and Seem a Dream cleansing wash and for each product there's plenty of seductive information to make you want to give them a go.

Prices:	Medium	Express Ship? (UK)	No
Delivers to:	Worldwide	Gift Wrap?	No
Based:	UK		

www.lizearle.com

Liz Earle has a beautiful website offering her 'Naturally Active Skincare' – a pampering range of skin, body and sun care products. She's particularly well known for her cleanse and polish hot cloth cleanser and well-priced but excellent special treatments and moisturisers. Shimmer products for body and lips, Vital Aromatherapy Oils and travel mini-kits from the wide range are just some of the temptations on offer and the lovely packaging is an extra bonus.

Prices:	Very Good Value	Express Ship? (UK)	Yes
Delivers to:	Worldwide	Gift Wrap?	Yes, everything is beautifully packaged
Based:	UK		

www.panachecosmetics.com

This is a really beautifully designed website calling itself 'the world's premier luxury skincare E-boutique.' They offer premium skincare and anti-aging brands Natura Bisse of Barcelona, skincare to the stars Sjal and Steven Victor MD. There are, in fact (at time of writing), no cosmetics here at all, just a group of cult products clearly described, which frankly sound quite miraculous and so they should do – nothing here is inexpensive.

Prices:	Luxury	Express Ship? (UK)	Yes
Delivers to:	Worldwide	Gift Wrap?	Yes, everything is beautifully packaged
Based:	UK		

www.salonskincare.com

Some of the brands you'll find here such as Elemis, Decleor, Gatineau and Phytomer are not hard to find on the web and others, such as luxury skincare brand Carita, Baxter of California, Max Benjamin (candles) and MD Formulations are not readily available. You can also buy

Dermalogica, Fake Bake, Molton Brown and Nailtiques plus Klein-Becker Strivectin SD, the stretch mark turned anti-wrinkle wonder cream.

Prices:	Luxury/Medium	Express Ship? (UK)	Yes
Delivers to:	Worldwide	Gift Wrap?	No
Based:	UK		

www.skinlight.co.uk

If this is the moment when you think you'd like to add a new luxurious treatment into your skincare regimen then take a look here, where you'll find a range of specialist products, particularly good for anti-aging and radiance boosting (although there are a lot of other categories as well). Do make sure that you know exactly what you're buying before you invest – you can spend a fortune here.

Prices:	Luxury/Medium	Express Ship? (UK)	No
Delivers to:	EU	Gift Wrap?	No
Based:	UK		

www.skinstore.com

What's great about this website, offering the latest anti-aging treatments and innovative skin and body products such as StriVectin, MD Skincare, Rodan and Fields and Sovage, is that you can access their online chat facility and 'talk' to an expert before you buy to help to make sure that what you're buying will be right for you. There's a huge range here plus lots of information, so if anti-aging is what you're after, you should have a look.

Prices:	Luxury/Medium	Express Ship? (UK)	No
Delivers to:	EU	Gift Wrap?	No
Based:	UK		

www.thebeautyroom.co.uk

You may already have come across the French salon brands Gatineau, Phytomer and Mary Cohr, and on this website you can order from their full ranges of skincare including anti-aging creams, cleansers, toners, moisturisers and exfoliators, plus the Mary Cohr/Masters Colours extensive collection of cosmetics.

Prices:	Medium	Express Ship? (UK)	Yes
Delivers to:	No	Gift Wrap?	No
Based:	UK		

www.thisworks.com

Here you'll find soothing, natural and gently scented products for bath and body with unusual names such as Energy Bank or Deep Calm Bath and Shower Oil, Muscle Therapy and Enjoy Really Rich Lotion or Hot Stone Essences, and all have been created by Vogue beauty expert Kathy Phillips to high acclaim. The collection also includes bath and shower gels, moisturisers, lovely gift ideas and irresistible travel kits.

Prices:	Medium	Express Ship? (UK)	No
Delivers to:	Worldwide	Gift Wrap?	Yes
Based:	UK		

www.timetospa.com

Time to Spa offers Elemis face and body products, La Therapie solutions for acne, scarring and hyper-pigmentation, and Steiner Haircare. This is not a retailer so much as a beauty salon, where you can register with them for an online consultation by one of their team of therapists on your beauty regimen, find out about food and fitness for health and have your beauty questions answered.

Prices:	Luxury/Medium	Express Ship? (UK)	Yes
Delivers to:	Worldwide	Gift Wrap?	Yes
Based:	UK		

www.zelens.co.uk

You may not have heard of this line of hi-tech skincare products: Zelens is a very small, expensive and specialist range of day, night and eye creams, formulated by leading skin aging and cancer specialist, Dr Marko Lens. They have two ranges – Skin Science, which is a natural cellular protector and rejuvenation cream, and Fullerene C60, an extremely potent antioxidant.

Prices:	Luxury	Express Ship? (UK)	No
Delivers to:	Worldwide	Gift Wrap?	No
Based:	UK		

Beauty for Less

Here you can really have fun. Find the online retailers who stock your favourite product and then be amazed and delighted at how much you can save. Also take into account how much is being charged for postage – some of the websites here offer excellent discounts and very reasonable postage wherever you are in the world. Take advantage of the savings you can make here and then go and splurge somewhere else.

www.beautybay.com

This is a beautifully laid-out website offering just about every fragrance with bath and body products to match and a small range of cosmetics and skincare, plus jewellery and fragrance giftsets (excellent for presents) Delivery is free on orders over £30, they'll ship to just about anywhere in the world and offer a next day service as well.

Prices:	Luxury/Medium/Very Good Value	Express Ship? (UK)	Yes
Delivers to:	Worldwide	Gift Wrap?	No
Based:	UK		

www.cheapsmells.co.uk

This Guernsey-based fragrance, skincare and cosmetic company offers a wide range of well-known brand products and some very good discounts. Having tried and tested them myself I can tell you that the service is good and the savings well worth having. You won't find the full ranges from any of the brands but if they stock your favourite you'll want to buy from them.

Prices:	Very Good Value	Express Ship? (UK)	Yes
Delivers to:	Worldwide	Gift Wrap?	No
Based:	UK		

www.feelunique.com

If you haven't yet discovered this great website then you should have a look round now. You won't find the full collection of all the major brands such as Dior and Lancôme but if they stock your cleanser, moisturiser, foundation or fragrance you'll probably find that it's a great deal less expensive than anywhere else. Delivery is £1 wherever you are in the world.

Prices:	Medium/Very Good Value	Express Ship? (UK)	No
Delivers to:	Worldwide	Gift Wrap?	Yes
Based:	UK		

www.powderpuff.net

Next time you go looking to buy one of your regular beauty essentials have a look at this website, offering free delivery in the UK and a huge selection of products. It's been called 'The Daddy of all Beauty Sites' and you'd find it hard to disagree. You'll find brand names such as Lancôme, Clarins, Clinique and YSL plus GHD, Kinerase and Fudge, together with skincare, cosmetics and fragrance and mostly at very good prices. They'll also deliver worldwide.

Prices:	Medium/Very Good Value	Express Ship? (UK)	Yes
Delivers to:	Worldwide	Gift Wrap?	Yes
Based:	UK		

www.scentstore.co.uk

This website is a good place to check out if you know exactly which fragrance you want to buy as you can find some excellent discounts. So although you won't find every product in each range, it's a good idea to have a look here in case your favourite is on offer. Brands for men include Lacoste, Hugo Boss, Burberry and Tommy Hilfiger and for women Gucci, Ralph Lauren and Issey Miyake.

Prices:	Medium/Very Good Value	Express Ship? (UK)	Yes
Delivers to:	Worldwide	Gift Wrap?	No
Based:	UK		

www.strawberrynet.com

Check to see if your favourite product is available on this Hong Kong-based website where shipping is free and most products are discounted. There's a really huge range of designers, so big it's not worth trying to list. To be clear, as this site is based overseas you may well get charged duty; however, delivery to anywhere in the world is free of charge and the discounts can be very good.

Prices:	Medium/Very Good Value	Express Ship? (UK)	No
Delivers to:	Worldwide	Gift Wrap?	Yes
Based:	Hong Kong		

Section 5
Men Only

W hether you're shopping for the man in your life or you're a man shopping for yourself you'll be happy to know that in the past year or so it's become even easier to find everything online. So from shirts and ties, belts and shoes to formal tailoring, toiletries and essential gadgets there's a wealth of choice to browse through.

You probably won't want to buy your next dinner jacket online (although you could if you needed to), but if you're someone who's always short of time, maybe dislikes the high street intensely and would rather do almost anything than shop, the internet is your true friend.

There are countless online retailers now specialising in clothing and accessories for men, but you won't find them all here. The shops you can browse through below are, in my opinion, the best. Some are beautifully designed, stocked with an amazing choice, and offer you everything from delivery anywhere in the world, gift wrapping and even bespoke tailoring. Others may not be quite so well laid out but just have that extra something that meant I felt you should know about them.

There's a wide range of prices as many of the shops here are designer stores (but frequently have excellent discount sections) and others are high street brands, where the overall pricing is lower. The choice is entirely yours.

Shirts and Ties, etc.

Is there a shirt maker who now isn't online? Maybe one or two but certainly most of them are and the best are here. There's a wide range of prices, from bespoke totally made-for-you shirts to high quality, off the peg and reasonably priced. Be aware that if you're buying bespoke you won't be able to send it back unless it's faulty, so take care when ordering and particularly if you're ordering for someone else. If I ever thought that Jermyn Street and Savile Row would be slow to join the online rush I got it totally wrong. They're all here now, waiting for you.

www.40savilerow.co.uk

The Savile Row Company have been in the business of creating made-to-measure shirts (and tailoring) since 1939. If you want to order a suit from them you need to pay them a visit, however for a luxury shirt just click through to 'Start Creating a New Shirt,' to choose your fabric, then use their style customiser to select fit, collar, cuffs, back style, buttons and pockets.

Prices:	Luxury	Express Ship? (UK)	No
Delivers to:	Worldwide	Gift Wrap?	No
Based:	UK		

www.blackstonelewis.co.uk

Blackstone Lewis offers you the facility of designing a bespoke shirt online. It's a cleverly laid-out site with one simple 'multiple choice' page where you choose your fabric and then select the style for your collar, cuff, pocket and fit. They're certainly not cheap but they make the whole process so quick and easy so that you end up with exactly what you want that I'd recommend you give them a try.

Prices:	Luxury/Medium	Express Ship? (UK)	No
Delivers to:	Worldwide	Gift Wrap?	No
Based:	UK		

www.ctshirts.co.uk

Charles Tyrwhitt are well known for their colourful and well laid out catalogues, and their website is also extremely attractive, easy to navigate and the service offered is excellent. There's a good selection of casual shirts and knitwear, tailoring, ladies shirts, cashmere knits and accessories and 'Tiny Tyrwhitt' clothing too plus excellent discounts at sale time.

Prices:	Medium	Express Ship? (UK)	Yes	
Delivers to:	Worldwide	Gift Wrap?	Yes	
Based:	UK			

www.emmawillis.com

Bespoke shirt maker Emma Willis trained at the Slade School of Art before starting her business in 1987. Her philosophy is the highest quality make, keeping to the original traditions of English shirt making and using luxurious Italian and Swiss cottons, silks and linens, many of which are exclusive to her collections. Nominated in *GQ Style* magazine as London's best bespoke shirt maker, if you're seeking the ultimate shirt, this is the place to visit.

Prices:	Luxury	Express Ship? (UK)	No
Delivers to:	Worldwide	Gift Wrap?	No
Based:	UK		

www.gievesandhawkes.com

Situated at Number 1 Savile Row, London and established in 1785, Gieves and Hawkes have always stood for the very best in men's tailoring whether for formal eveningwear, suiting or casualwear. On their website you can now not only find out a great deal about the brand, but also choose from their high-quality range of shirts, belts and braces, cufflinks, shoes and ties.

Prices:	Luxury/Medium	Express Ship? (UK)	No
Delivers to:	EU	Gift Wrap?	Yes
Based:	UK		

www.hawesandcurtis.com

Hawes and Curtis were established in 1913 and are famous for being the creators of the backless waistcoat, which was originally worn under a tailcoat and was renowned for its comfort. Now on their excellently designed website you can choose from their range of classic and fashion shirts, ties, cufflinks, silk knots and boxer shorts. They also offer a range of women's classic, high-quality shirts in three different styles.

Prices:	Medium	Express Ship? (UK)	No
Delivers to:	Worldwide	Gift Wrap?	Yes
Based:	UK		

www.hilditchandkey.co.uk

Recognised as one of the longest-established Jermyn Street retailers of mens shirts and accessories (as well as some women's shirts), Hilditch manage to give you a top-of-the-range shopping experience without you having to leave home. Their shirts are not the cheapest but if you order from them you can be absolutely certain that you'll get the high quality you're paying for. They also offer silk ties and some clothing.

Prices:	Luxury	Express Ship? (UK)	No
Delivers to:	Worldwide	Gift Wrap?	No
Based:	UK		

www.josephturner.co.uk

Joseph Turner offers men's shirts, ties, cufflinks, sweaters, shoes (made by Loake) and accessories with a wide choice in all areas. There's much more information than usual on sizing than at a lot of men's online retailers and they also offer an alterations service. As with all the men's clothing websites they're extremely keen to offer something extra so you'll find cashmere sweaters, socks and belts here as well.

Prices:	Medium	Express Ship? (UK)	No
Delivers to:	UK	Gift Wrap?	No
Based:	UK		

www.kilgour.eu

Exclusive Savile Row 'shirtmaker to the stars' Kilgour is becoming known now not just for its beautifully made shirts but also as a luxury accessories retailer for items such as scarves, ties, cufflinks and wallets. The prices are quite frightening, the quality marvellous, but when you consider the famous names who have bought before you such as Jude Law and Daniel Craig, you'll know they're worth the extra.

Prices:	Luxury	Express Ship? (UK)	No
Delivers to:	EU	Gift Wrap?	No
Based:	UK		

www.thomaspink.co.uk

There's an enormous amount of detail available for every product offered here plus very clear pictures and a speedy search facility by pattern, style and finish. You can also buy scarves, knitwear, accessories and nightwear and you can always be sure that what you receive will be a very high-quality product, extremely well made and beautifully packaged.

Prices:	Luxury	Express Ship? (UK)	Yes
Delivers to:	Worldwide	Gift Wrap?	Yes
Based:	UK		

www.tjholland.co.uk

You'll find excellent quality of fabric and make here as you'd expect at these mid-to-high prices but then as well – and this is what makes them special – you can order your plain blue, pink or white Sea Island quality classic shirt with contrasting collars and cuffs. Wear them turned down in the boardroom then make a statement later on. There's a unique selection of ties, cufflinks and socks here too.

Prices:	Medium	Express Ship? (UK)	Yes
Delivers to:	UK	Gift Wrap?	No
Based:	UK		

www.woodsofshropshire.co.uk

This is a shirt retailer with a difference, offering you high-quality, mid-priced shirts, free and easy returns, worldwide delivery, extra collar stiffeners with every shirt plus complimentary silk knots with double cuff shirts. Roll your mouse over the shirt and tie pics and home right in on the fabrics. You can buy large size shirts here too up to a collar size 20.

Prices:	Medium	Express Ship? (UK)	No
Delivers to:	Worldwide	Gift Wrap?	No
Based:	UK		

Suits Him

Are suits any more difficult to buy online than women's clothing? I suspect that they are. Having said that, there are now a number of retailers offering to make you a totally bespoke suit from the measurements you supply. I think this is quite a difficult area and recommend that if at all possible you should go and have your measurements taken by the tailor if made to measure is what you're after and from then on they should be able to get it right every time.

If you're used to buying a certain brand of suit then this is much easier, find someone who's selling it, choose your cloth and select your size and you're away.

www.austinreed.co.uk

Austin Reed offers an extremely good range of clothing online, right through from tailoring and evening dress to casual jackets, shirts and jeans. This is an easy website to navigate and once you click on a product you can see immediately if your size is in stock. The signature collection is slightly more expensive than the main line, with higher quality fabrics and hand finishing. There's very good women's careerwear here as well.

Prices:	Medium	Express Ship? (UK)	Yes
Delivers to:	UK	Gift Wrap?	No
Based:	UK		

www.brooktaverner.co.uk

Brook Taverner has been in the business of classic men's tailoring since 1912, producing suits, jackets, trousers and overcoats from premium cloths sourced from around the world. One of the advantages here is that suit jacket and trouser sizes can be mixed and matched offering numerous size and length options and their suit trousers also have a hidden stretch waistband.

Prices:	Medium	Express Ship? (UK)	Yes
Delivers to:	UK and call for overseas	Gift Wrap?	No
Based:	UK		

www.crombie.co.uk

The Crombie name has been synonymous with high-quality, hard-wearing cloth for over 200 years and while that continues the Crombie brand has been developed into an excellent collection of clothing for men and women, much of which you can find online. There's an extensive range for men including the famous Crombie coat and for women there's a smaller range including dresses, separates, leather and suede.

Prices:	Luxury/Medium	Express Ship? (UK)	No
Delivers to:	Worldwide	Gift Wrap?	No
Based:	UK		

www.favourbrook.com

Jermyn Street-based Favourbrook have created a unique collection of menswear based on a contemporary take on 300 years of elegant British dress. Their hand-tailored styles include frock-coats, Nehru jackets, high-cut four-button single-breasted jackets, morning-suit tails and wonderful, eye-catching waistcoats and cravats. Not everything is available to order online.

Prices:	Luxury/Medium	Express Ship? (UK)	Yes
Delivers to:	Worldwide	Gift Wrap?	No
Based:	UK		

www.menalamode.com

Men a la Mode offer you the chance to order from the current season's collections of labels such as Paul and Joe, Joseph, Westwood, Nicole Farhi and Ungaro. They have a well-designed website, where you can easily select by garment or by your favourite designer, and in each category there's a good range to choose from. Get ready for your other half to have a hissy fit when she realises that you can buy your Joseph trousers online and she can't yet.

Prices:	Luxury/Medium	Express Ship? (UK)	Yes
Delivers to:	Worldwide	Gift Wrap?	No
Based:	UK		

www.mossdirect.co.uk

No, this is not the place you can hire your dinner jacket, but an offshoot of the famous brand (and men's hire shop) retailing Moss Bros's own brand, plus Savoy Tailors Guild, De Havilland, Pierre Cardin and Baumler. You won't find an enormous range but a well-designed website with some very good special offers and particularly good dress shirts (which is one of the things they're famous for, after all). Delivery is UK only and you need to allow ten days.

Prices:	Medium	Express Ship? (UK)	No
Delivers to:	UK	Gift Wrap?	No
Based:	UK		

www.oliverbrown.org.uk

OK, I have to admit it now, men's fashion websites are officially getting as good as those for us girls (well, almost, anyway). Here's an excellent example, with a full collection of high-quality clothes and accessories from city suits, formalwear and overcoats to huntin', shootin' and fishin' essentials, Barbour, waistcoats, collarless shirts, stiff collars and even top hats. Yes and shoes, links, belts, braces and wallets. It's a great site. I'll say no more.

Prices:	Luxury/Medium	Express Ship? (UK)	No
Delivers to:	Worldwide	Gift Wrap?	No
Based:	UK		

www.pakeman.co.uk

Here's an extensive range of high-quality, reasonably priced classic clothing for men and women. For men you can choose from black tie tailoring, suits, flannels, cords, jeans, shirts and ties, belts, shoes, cufflinks and underwear. The women's range has very good occasion-wear which brings all the elements, from hats to dresses and jackets, together in the same place.

Prices:	Medium	Express Ship? (UK)	Yes
Delivers to:	Worldwide	Gift Wrap?	No
Based:	UK		

www.racinggreen.co.uk

Famous for its well-priced men's and ladies' wear for several years, Racing Green has now relaunched its website with a good range of menswear including shirts, tailoring, dinner jackets, dress shirts, shoes and accessories. It's a very easy site to get round and much more classic than it used to be, with smart pictures of a wide range of products. The prices are reasonable and the branding is classy, so give it a try.

Prices:	Medium/Very Good Value	Express Ship? (UK)	Yes
Delivers to:	UK	Gift Wrap?	No
Based:	UK		

www.reubenalexander.com

This is without doubt the luxury end of the online tailoring market, where a suit will set you back something in the region of £1000. However, having said that, what you're buying here is the highest-quality, handmade tailoring using premium cloth. These are modern versions of classic and vintage designs, woven at the family mill Charles Clayton Ltd in Yorkshire. They offer a range of Superfine wools in qualities of Super 180s, Super 150s and Super 120s.

Prices:	Luxury	Express Ship? (UK)	No
Delivers to:	Worldwide	Gift Wrap?	No
Based:	UK		

www.savilerowco.com

This is a really good and fast-developing range of menswear with everything you could possibly need, including tailoring (and dinner jackets) a wide range of formal shirts, casual shirts, trousers and sweaters plus a full collection of accessories. The site is very clearly photographed and the order system is really easy. There are also some men's gift ideas here such as cashmere scarves and cufflinks.

Prices:	Medium	Express Ship? (UK)	Yes
Delivers to:	Worldwide	Gift Wrap?	No
Based:	UK		

www.tmlewin.co.uk

T M Lewin have one of the easiest sites to get round, with simple drop-down menus and clear pictures. They also frequently have some very good special offers. You can buy almost everything here, from formal tailoring to casual trousers, a good selection of accessories and there's a wide range of striped, check and solid coloured shirts with simple size and length options.

Prices:	Medium	Express Ship? (UK)	Yes
Delivers to:	Worldwide	Gift Wrap?	No
Based:	UK		

Casual Collections

In my view casual clothing falls into two groups, whether it's contemporary or not – it's either the kind you want to relax in at the weekend and includes sporty t-shirts and hoodies, chinos and cords, or it's the sort you want to wear to go huntin', shootin,' fishin' or walking the moors in. Now you might say to me that in that case it should be classified as sportswear, but who hasn't thrown their Barbour jacket over their casual shirt, polo or cords for a walk in the country or a day at the races? This type of clothing is hard working and does double duty for both the real sports enthusiast and everyone else as well, which is why you'll find it all here.

Classic Casual

www.barbourbymail.co.uk

Yes, this is just exactly what you'd expect, the full range of Barbour (for men, women and kids) with everything available online. What makes it different from anywhere else you can buy Barbour are the atmospheric main category pictures and the huge range and the excellent and clear information about every product, whether it's just a simple fleece or a high-tech 'Endurance' jacket.

Prices:	Medium	Express Ship? (UK)	Yes but you need to call them. Items in stock only.
Delivers to:	UK this site		
Based:	UK	Gift Wrap?	No

www.cordings.co.uk

Quintessentially British, Cordings was established in the Strand in 1839 and in 1860 an advertisement appeared which described them as 'nautical and sporting waterproofers and tailors'. Everything at Cordings is made to exclusive specifications from materials tradition-ally found in the UK, and the range includes covert coats and field clothing, rainwear, cotton poplin and Tattersall check shirts plus one of the best selections of classic casual trousers to be found anywhere.

Prices:	Medium	Express Ship? (UK)	No
Delivers to:	Worldwide	Gift Wrap?	No
Based:	UK		

www.farlows.co.uk

Long-established Royal warrant holders Farlows are, in their own words, 'a Mecca for fishing enthusiasts' and offer fly-fishing and shooting equipment plus contemporary performance clothing and luxury accessories. On their well-designed website you can buy everything from breeks and garters to Chasseur boots, ear defenders, cartridge bags and those heavy wool socks that (in my house, anyway) always get shrunk in the wash.

Prices:	Medium	Express Ship? (UK)	No
Delivers to:	Worldwide	Gift Wrap?	No
Based:	UK		

www.hackett.co.uk

Hackett have an atmospheric website offering their well-known, high-quality sportswear, tailoring, shirts and ties, knitwear and outerwear online. In the Rugby Shop you can choose from very good range of striped rugby shirts and you can also visit the Aston Martin Shop, with 'Aston Martin Racing by Hackett' clothing and the Army Polo collection.

Prices:	Medium	Express Ship? (UK)	2 working days
Delivers to:	UK	Gift Wrap?	No
Based:	UK		

www.mainlinemenswear.co.uk

Hackett, Lyle and Scott, Diesel, D & G and Boss are just a few of the brands offered here. This is an extremely busy, though attractive website with an enormous range, information on the latest arrivals on the left-hand side and a constantly changing and updating range. I'll be honest; the photographs aren't wonderful, but they're perfectly clear and the sheer choice makes this one of the best menswear sites to check out.

Prices:	Luxury/Medium	Express Ship? (UK)	No
Delivers to:	Worldwide	Gift Wrap?	No
Based:	UK		

www.ptarmiganclothing.com

This is another well-designed website aimed at the outdoor enthusiast and they travel the world to bring you a highly crafted selection, which includes bags by Sandstorm, boots and moleskin trousers by R M Williams, accessories by Digeridoonas and Beretta shooting jackets and trousers. This is a seriously good selection by people who obviously know what they're doing and if you have any queries about what you might need just give them a call.

Prices:	Luxury/Medium	Express Ship? (UK)	No
Delivers to:	Worldwide	Gift Wrap?	No
Based:	UK		

Contemporary Casual

www.extremepie.com

There are enough casual/sportswear brands here to answer anyone's needs from famous brands such as O'Neill, Quiksilver, Animal, Vans, Billabong, RipCurl, Addict, Extreme and Reef, plus loads more that you may not have heard of. This is a very good site for anyone who's addicted to sport or just wants the sporty look (and for gifts for sporty people).

Prices:	Medium	Express Ship? (UK)	Yes
Delivers to:	Worldwide	Gift Wrap?	No
Based:	UK		

www.fatface.com

When you first take a look at the fatface.com website you may be a little disconcerted. It's certainly not like most others, with pictures and type all being used to reinforce Fatface's idiosyncratic 'cool' active style. But it works together. You'll find a wide selection of tops and t-shirts, jackets and fleece, denim and sweats, all in unique fabrics and style and their more often than not muted colour palette.

Prices:	Medium	Express Ship? (UK)	Yes
Delivers to:	Worldwide	Gift Wrap?	No
Based:	UK		

www.milanclothing.com

At Milan Clothing you'll find casual clothing from brands such as Fake London, Paul Smith, Pringle and Paul and Shark. There's a wide selection so you'll no doubt want to take advantage of the speedy search facility where you can search by brand, or type of clothing, or both. The pictures are very simple indeed because the range is changing all the time. However, this is a clear and easy-to-navigate website and one of the best for casualwear.

Prices:	Medium	Express Ship? (UK)	Yes
Delivers to:	Worldwide	Gift Wrap?	No
Based:	UK		

www.oki-ni.com

Oki-ni has moved on from its 'designer special' roots to become one of the best men's lifestyle clothing stores. You'll find brands (from their huge list) such as Acne, Rick Owens, Alexander McQueen and Lacoste with a wide range of products which sit beside Levi Vintage, Puma Bespoke and Evisu Heritage plus some of the exclusives that they specialised in before. Visit here for a really contemporary online shopping experience.

Prices:	Luxury/Medium	Express Ship? (UK)	No
Delivers to:	Worldwide	Gift Wrap?	No
Based:	UK		

www.routeone.co.uk

Route One is a young, independent and immensely busy online store aimed at inline skate and skateboard riders, but having such a large selection of shoes, clothing and accessories by brands such as Converse, Atticus, Fenchurch, Billabong and Carhatt (and, I have to confess, loads of others I haven't heard of) it's bound to appeal to anyone who likes a contemporary, sporty look. The service is speedy and reliable.

Prices:	Medium	Express Ship? (UK)	Yes
Delivers to:	Worldwide	Gift Wrap?	No
Based:	UK		

www.stoneisland.co.uk

Trendy, relaxed and well photographed, this website offers Stone Island and CP Company casualwear (and some more formal jackets) plus outerwear, jeans, shirts, knitwear and accessories. Then there is CP Company Donna, Stone Island Junior and CP Under-Sixteens. This is an extremely fast and attractive website to look round offering contemporary designer casualwear and a brand that is growing at speed.

Prices:	Luxury/Medium	Express Ship? (UK)	No
Delivers to:	UK	Gift Wrap?	No
Based:	UK		

www.tedbaker.co.uk

Expanding global brand Ted Baker offers well-made and innovative clothing on this modern, well-photographed and easy-to-navigate website, for men, women and kids. Don't expect cheap here, you won't find it. What you will find is up-to-the-minute, mainly understated fashion, totally in line with each season's trends. Also swimwear, underwear, watches, accessories and fragrance.

Prices:	Medium	Express Ship? (UK)	No but UK delivery is very fast
Delivers to:	Worldwide	Gift Wrap?	No
Based:	UK		

www.theclothesstore.com

The Clothes Store has a very good range of brands for both men and women including collections by Polo Ralph Lauren, Burberry London, Nigel Hall, Lacoste, Puma, One True Saxon and 'Urban Menswear' by Fred Perry, Ben Sherman, Wrangler and Edge. The designer ranges are changing all the time so check back to see who's listed each season. They also offer a good footwear collection from Converse, Sketchers and Kickers.

Prices:	Medium	Express Ship? (UK)	No
Delivers to:	Worldwide	Gift Wrap?	No
Based:	Channel Islands		

www.w1style.co.uk

This is an excellent website offering new and current brands such as Quiksilver, Roxy, O'Neill, Bench, Billabong, Diesel and FCUK in an easy-to-view format. Although most of the items offered are brand new, current season's stock (and new stock is regularly being added to the site), there are also some very good reductions. They will ship to North America as well as Europe and all items are shipped from Gibralter.

Prices:	Medium	Express Ship? (UK)	Yes
Delivers to:	EU and North America	Gift Wrap?	Yes
Based:	Gibralter		

Also take a look at the following for designer menswear:
www.julesb.co.uk
www.shoptommy.co.uk
www.matchesfashion.com
www.jaeger.co.uk
www.paulsmith.co.uk
www.cruiseclothing.co.uk

Feet First

I'm always surprised how many people still think that it must be difficult to buy shoes online. Truly it isn't. Your feet tend, unlike your clothes, to stay the same size and particularly if you like a specific brand it's incredibly easy to buy online. You're also helped by the fact that the photographs are usually excellent, with several views of each product. If you're not absolutely sure what size you should take then check it up offline, but you most likely have been wearing the same size for years so take advantage of the choice and discounts available online.

International shoe size conversions										
UK	7	7.5	8	8.5	9	9.5	10	10.5	11	11.5	12
EU	40.5	41	42	42.5	43	44	44.5	45	46	46.5	47
US	7.5	8	8.5	9	9.5	10	10.5	11	11.5	12 12.5

www.andersonsofdurham.co.uk

Trickers, Sebago, Loake and Mephisto are some of the shoe brands offered here on this well-designed and easy-on-the-eye website. They don't hold stock of everything but the range and the website are so comprehensive that it'll be worth waiting the 3–4 days for delivery (of most items) particularly bearing in mind that delivery within the UK is free of charge.

Prices:	Luxury/Medium	Express Ship? (UK)	No
Delivers to:	Worldwide	Gift Wrap?	No
Based:	UK		

www.bexley.com

This is a French-based website offering excellent shoes and accessories for men. Clearly and attractively photographed and easy to navigate, you can buy socks, formal and casual shoes, ties, shoe trees, polishing kits, belts and gloves at reasonable prices. Average shipping time for Europe is roughly one week and up to two weeks for the rest of the world.

Prices:	Medium	Express Ship? (UK)	No
Delivers to:	Worldwide	Gift Wrap?	No
Based:	France		

www.herringshoes.co.uk

Church's, Loake, Timberland, Cheaney and their own brand are some of the collections you will find here at this family shoe store offering top quality shoes and excellent service. Obviously with these brands you won't be expecting footwear for less but they do have special offers and sale areas so you can check out what's available in your size.

Prices:	Medium	Express Ship? (UK)	No
Delivers to:	Worldwide	Gift Wrap?	No
Based:	UK		

www.oliversweeney.com

Oliver Sweeney is best known for his high-quality 'classic with a twist' and fashion-forward footwear which you can order online here. Alongside these and in the same mode, there are leather wallets and key holders, gloves and belts, edgy attache cases and weekenders plus a small range of outerwear. If the man in your life is a true traditionalist this is probably not the place, but if he's into modern menswear take a look.

Prices:	Luxury/Medium	Express Ship? (UK)	No
Delivers to:	Worldwide	Gift Wrap?	No
Based:	UK		

www.samuel-windsor.co.uk

Here you'll find an excellent range of handcrafted shoes, with everything from classic brogues to driving shoes and loafers. They frequently have special offers such as two for the price of one which makes everything here extremely good value, particularly bearing in mind the quality you're buying. Choose your next pair (or pairs) by style or colour and then you can take a look at the shirt and tie collection as well for which, again, there are often gifts and offers.

Prices:	Medium	Express Ship? (UK)	Yes
Delivers to:	UK	Gift Wrap?	No
Based:	UK		

www.shiptonandheneage.co.uk

Shipton and Heneage have been trading for over 12 years and offer a high-quality collection of over 120 styles of shoe. You choose first from different types such as brogues, country shoes, town shoes, Oxfords, extra wide and loafers and then make your choice from the selection of each that rapidly appears. They also have a range of sailing shoes, plus slippers, socks and accessories.

Prices:	Medium	Express Ship? (UK)	Yes
Delivers to:	Worldwide	Gift Wrap?	No
Based:	UK		

www.shoesdirect.co.uk

For reasonably priced smart and casual shoes stop here, where you'll find Loake, Rockport, Gregson, Ecco, Clarks and Barker. Everything is very clearly shown and they couldn't make the order process easier. Some of their shoes go up to a UK size 16 which is really large and if you're in doubt about which size to use their shoe size conversion chart is always available. They'll also tell you which shoes have extra width.

Prices:	Medium	Express Ship? (UK)	No
Delivers to:	UK	Gift Wrap?	No
Based:	UK		

www.wellie-web.co.uk

Here's a website with a name that you won't forget quickly but if you're someone who spends a lot of time outdoors, particularly in wet weather, you'll find it indispensible. You can buy a cheap pair of wellies here with prices starting at £22 and you'll also find some with flowers all over them (er, maybe not). However, this website specialises in the quality end of the market where a top-notch pair of boots can set you back up to £200.

Prices:	Luxury/Medium	Express Ship? (UK)	Yes
Delivers to:	UK	Gift Wrap?	No
Based:	UK		

Grooming Greats

Men's grooming is very much like women's beauty, if you know what I mean: it's all available online. There are now some really well-designed and attractive men's grooming product online retailers where it's a pleasure to browse, and they frequently offer discounts, gift wrapping, express delivery and reasonable worldwide shipping. Many of the large fragrance retailers in the Fabulous Fragrance section also offer products for men so check there as well.

www.adonisgrooming.com

The first thing you think (or at least, I thought of) when you come across this website is just how easy on the eye it is. Not only that, but Adonis offers an excellent range of grooming products for men, from shaving, hair care and bodycare from brands such as Dermalogica, Clarins for Men and Jose Eisenberg to gifts and accessories; travel kits by California North, Jack Black and 4V00, D R Harris fragrances and Zirh products.

Prices:	Medium	Express Ship? (UK)	Yes
Delivers to:	Worldwide	Gift Wrap?	Yes
Based:	UK		

www.carterandbond.com

Carter and Bond was established in 2002 to bring together the very finest male grooming products around. The simple to use secure website is home to over 600 products from more than 40 brands including Molton Brown, American Crew, Baxter of California, Geo F Trumper and Proraso. Whether you're looking for skincare, hair care, fragrance, shaving products or gift ideas you'll find it all here.

Prices:	Medium	Express Ship? (UK)	Yes
Delivers to:	Worldwide	Gift Wrap?	Yes
Based:	UK		

www.hqman.com

If you've spent any time at all at thesiteguide.com you (hopefully) will already have come across wonderful hair and accessories website hqhair.com. Well now they've launched a website specifically for men and excellent it is too. Check out brands such as 4V00, Anthony Logistics, Calmia, Decleor Men, Malin+Goetz, Comptoir-sud-Pacifique and Fred Bennett, plus lots more and expect to find the full ranges across body, bath, skincare, hair care and accessories.

Prices:	Luxury/Medium	Express Ship? (UK)	No
Delivers to:	Worldwide	Gift Wrap?	No
Based:	UK		

www.jasonshankey.co.uk

If you're a fan of Tigi, Fudge, NV Perricone, Skin Doctors or Dermalogica products this could well be the place for you and there are lots of other brands as well. The range includes everything from hair and nail care to hair appliances, slimming products, men's grooming and slimming products and you can expect an extremely speedy and efficient service.

Prices:	Medium	Express Ship? (UK)	Yes
Delivers to:	Worldwide	Gift Wrap?	Yes
Based:	UK		

www.mankind.co.uk

This is one of the best men's websites. It's modern, easy to use and has a great range of products, showcasing the very best and most innovative shaving, skin and hair care brands made for men such as Lab Series, Nickel and K2 and offering them in a way that makes buying simple, fast and fun. There are shaving products, skin basics and problem-skin solutions as well as gift ideas here.

Prices:	Medium	Express Ship? (UK)	Yes
Delivers to:	Worldwide	Gift Wrap?	Yes
Based:	UK		

www.murdocklondon.com

Murdock London is a modern men's grooming product retailer with a slick, easy-to-navigate website offering brands such as D R Harris, Caron, Malin+Goetz and Kevin Murphy plus aromatic candles and room scents by Mariage Freres. In their Gift Box section you'll find an excellent selection of pampering and beautifully presented hampers by Edwin Jagger and Santa Maria Novella ranging from around £40 to over £100.

Prices:	Luxury/Medium	Express Ship? (UK)	Yes
Delivers to:	Worldwide	Gift Wrap?	No, but beautifully wrapped gift boxes
Based:	UK		

www.theenglishshavingcompany.co.uk

At The English Shaving Company you'll find the highest quality handcrafted razors and shaving sets plus travel sets, soaps, brushes and aftershaves from Geo Trumper, Edwin Jagger, D R Harris and Molton Brown. You can read their 'shaving tutorial' in Useful Information plus razor shaving tips, so if you're tired of using your electric razor and want to turn traditional you'll need this site.

Prices:	Luxury/Medium	Express Ship? (UK)	No
Delivers to:	Worldwide	Gift Wrap?	Yes
Based:	UK		

www.trumpers.com

Established in 1875 in Curzon Street, Mayfair, this famous traditional London barber is well known for superb exclusive men's fragrances and grooming products. Think of fragrances such as Sandalwood, Bay Rum and Spanish Leather, which all have matching soaps and body washes. Now you can buy the full range online plus an exclusive collection of ties and cufflinks and they'll be delighted to ship to you anywhere in the world.

Prices:	Luxury/Medium	Express Ship? (UK)	Yes
Delivers to:	Worldwide	Gift Wrap?	Yes
Based:	UK		

www.wholeman.co.uk

This is a relatively new, contemporary, multi-channel business offering a whole range of treatments and products for men and including brands such as Acca Kappa, Baxter of California, Edwin Jagger and Murad. They've made it extremely easy for you to find what you're looking for – as well as their suggestions you can shop by brand or type of product and you can immediately see all the relevant items on one page.

Prices:	Medium	Express Ship? (UK)	Yes
Delivers to:	UK	Gift Wrap?	Yes
Based:	UK		

Accessory Heaven

Here you'll find everything from beautiful quality leather wallets and belts to your next Montblanc pen, so this is an excellent area for updating what you carry around with you and also for gifts. Also check out the websites in the shirts and ties section. Many of them offer far more than just shirts and ties (although some do not) and you'll find cufflinks, belts, socks, small leathers, underwear and nightwear as well. It's worth getting to know them all as they all often have seasonal sales and many have sale areas available all year round.

www.dalvey.com

Dalvey of Scotland have created a range of elegant and useful gifts which are attractively displayed on their extremely well laid out website. Suggestions such as beautifully made leather travel clocks and business card cases, cufflinks and cufflink cases, hipflasks and binoculars are all luxuriously presented and would make really lovely gifts.

Prices:	Luxury	Express Ship? (UK)	No
Delivers to:	Worldwide	Gift Wrap?	No
Based:	UK		

www.dunhill.com

The first Alfred Dunhill collection included car horns and lamps, leather overcoats, goggles, picnic sets and timepieces. Over 100 years later Dunhill is one of the leading makers of English luxury accessories for men and here you can choose from their range which includes luggage, briefcases, washbags, wallets, diaries and belts, ties and cufflinks.

Prices:	Luxury	Express Ship? (UK)	No
Delivers to:	UK	Gift Wrap?	No
Based:	UK		

www.filofax.co.uk

Your Filofax is now available in many different colours, sizes and styles, including mini, pocket, A5 and A4, black, red, pink, purple, pale blue and denim and on this website you can see each and every one, plus all the refills and accessories such as calculators and pens. Together with this you can download their address software and also buy the luxury range of Yard-O-Led pens.

Prices:	Medium	Express Ship? (UK)	Yes
Delivers to:	Worldwide	Gift Wrap?	No
Based:	UK		

www.h-s.co.uk

This is a name you may well never have heard of, but Harrison and Simmonds have been in business since 1928 offering pipes, cigar humidors and accessories and luxury gifts from companies such as Dalvey. There's also a wide range of Mont Blanc pens and accessories which you need to call them to order, plus chess sets, Hunter pocket watches and umbrella shooting sticks.

Prices:	Luxury/Medium	Express Ship? (UK)	Yes
Delivers to:	Worldwide	Gift Wrap?	No
Based:	UK		

www.kjbeckett.com

K J Beckett have a really good selection of branded accessories, including Regent Belt Company belts, cufflinks by Simon Carter, Ian Flaherty and Veritas, silk ties, cummerbunds, wallets and handkerchiefs – and that's just a few of the many items they offer. They'll deliver almost anywhere in the world using their priority service and UK delivery is free of charge.

Prices:	Luxury/Medium	Express Ship? (UK)	Yes
Delivers to:	Worldwide	Gift Wrap?	Yes
Based:	UK		

www.old.co.uk

Robert Old has a really attractive and easy-to-navigate website, offering a high-quality range of men's gifts and accessories including cashmere sweaters and scarves, leather gifts from cufflink boxes to travel alarm clocks, classic English briefcases and weekenders and shoes by Crockett and Jones. There's lots of clear information about each item and although standard delivery is the norm, they switch to express delivery towards Christmas.

Prices:	Medium	Express Ship? (UK)	Yes
Delivers to:	Worldwide	Gift Wrap?	No
Based:	UK		

www.pickett.co.uk

Gloves, wallets, umbrellas, belts, briefcases and stud boxes are just some of the high-quality, beautifully made men's accessories available on Pickett's website. If you've ever visited one of their shops you'll know that everything is the best you can buy and most items will last a long while. For women there are handbags, small leathers, gloves, jewels, scarves and shawls.

Prices:	Luxury/Medium	Express Ship? (UK)	No
Delivers to:	Worldwide	Gift Wrap?	No, but luxury packaging
Based:	UK		is standard

www.swaineadeney.co.uk

If you know London well you're bound to have passed the elegant Swaine Adeney Brigg store at 54, St James's Street. Well known as purveyors of the highest-quality gentlemen's accessories such as umbrellas with unique handles, wallets, attaché and document cases in a variety of styles and leathers plus wonderful (and wonderfully priced) leather luggage.

Prices:	Luxury	Express Ship? (UK)	No
Delivers to:	Worldwide	Gift Wrap?	No
Based:	UK		

Also take a look at www.aspinaloflondon.com.

Pens, etc.

www.cross.com

Established in 1846, Cross is one of the oldest manufacturers of fine writing instruments. Since then it has grown into a luxury brand offering not just fountain pens and pencils, but also watches, high-quality leather accessories, diaries, desk essentials and beautifully designed laptop bags for girls. The website is really excellent and well worth a browse.

Prices:	Luxury/Medium	Express Ship? (UK)	Yes
Delivers to:	Worldwide	Gift Wrap?	Yes
Based:	UK		

www.deskstore.com

This is a Swedish-based online retailer offering an excellent range of contemporary office tools and gifts and shipping worldwide. You'll find pens and pencils, stationery, desk sets and clever ideas such as the Pen Clip, which enables you to attach your pen to whatever notebook you might be using, and the MoMA Spiky USB hub – take a look and see for yourself.

Prices:	Luxury/Medium	Express Ship? (UK)	No
Delivers to:	Worldwide	Gift Wrap?	No
Based:	UK		

www.penandpaper.co.uk

The Pen and Paper Company are based in the Royal Arcade, Cardiff and offer a very good selection of brands from Cross, Yard-o-Led, Waterman and Parker to Visconti and Yoro. They also have left-handed pens and bottled inks plus an excellent technical drawing implement section. If you have a query you should call them, you're likely to get an extremely personal service here.

Prices:	Luxury/Medium	Express Ship? (UK)	No
Delivers to:	Worldwide	Gift Wrap?	No
Based:	UK		

www.penshop.co.uk

This is a really attractive website offering one of the best selections of luxury pens including Yard-O-Led's beautiful sterling silver fountain pens, ballpoints and pencils, Faber Castell pens in wood and silver, Mont Blanc (which you need to phone to order), and Porsche Design steel pens. They also offer Lamy, Rotring, Sheaffer and Waterman, aim to send out the day you order and they'll deliver worldwide. There's a repairs service as well.

Prices:	Luxury/Medium	Express Ship? (UK)	Yes
Delivers to:	Worldwide	Gift Wrap?	No
Based:	UK		

www.thepencompany.co.uk

Here you can order brands such as Lamy, Faber-Castell, Ducati, Lalex and Porsch, so not your usual selection of pens but hard to find, different and sometimes limited edition fountain pens, ball points and pencils which would make excellent gifts. They also have a choice of non-standard nibs for which you need to email them to order and diaries, inkwells and pen cases too

Prices:	Luxury/Medium	Express Ship? (UK)	No
Delivers to:	UK	Gift Wrap?	No
Based:	UK		

www.websterspenshop.co.uk

Webster's Pen Shop is a long established business with an excellent website. Brands of writing instruments include Mont Blanc, Cartier, Faber-Castell and Dunhill at the luxury end plus Cross, Lamy, Parker and many more. As well as pens, Webster's offers desk and leather business accessories, Filofax, gift ideas, and refills for all the brands stocked.

Prices:	Luxury/Medium	Express Ship? (UK)	Yes
Delivers to:	Most worldwide	Gift Wrap?	No
Based:	UK		

Gadget Land

So why is this here, do I hear you ask? Well, it's because these are not all silly gadgets as such (although you can find those here as well), but the clever, useful type, such as computers, Sat-Nav systems, mobiles and more. There are so many stores now offering these online that it's important to find a way through the choice. One way of doing this is to buy from a retailer/manufacturer you already know and trust such as Sony or John Lewis, but if you want to find the best price you're just going to have to choose your make and model and price compare. There are lots of price comparison websites, all of which have financial relationships with the retailers they propose, but you can frequently find some amazing price differentials between stores. Just make sure you check out the retailer if you haven't bought from them before.

Clever and Useful

www.applestore.co.uk

Yes, you can buy everything Apple at lots of online stores, but only here can you find the full range, all the Mac Books, iMacs, Nanos, Shuffles, iPod Touch, iPhone and Apple TV plus every accessory – speakers, headphones, games, cases and more – that you could possibly need. You may find cheaper prices elsewhere but always click here first to decide on what you want to buy and you'll probably be tempted by the sheer choice and slick site.

Prices:	Luxury/Medium	Express Ship? (UK)	No
Delivers to:	UK	Gift Wrap?	No
Based:	UK		

www.expansys.co.uk

This website, specialising in wireless technology, is an excellent place to find out about the latest mobile phones, smartphones, laptops and pocket PCs plus digital cameras and GPS navigation systems. In all the departments you can immediately see the best-sellers (and how long you'll have to wait for delivery) then browse their list which is clearly sub-sectioned by brand. Brands include Sony, Apple, Asus, Blackberry, Palm and far too many more to list here.

Prices:	Luxury/Medium	Express Ship? (UK)	Yes
Delivers to:	Worldwide	Gift Wrap?	No
Based:	UK		

www.microanvica.com

Here's an online site with an offline presence in Tottenham Court Road and Selfridges, offering the latest in computers, cameras and audio equipment including iPod and all the accessories. Expect a very good choice and excellent service – they do know what they're talking about and really want to help. Being a slightly less well-known retailer Micro Anvika is a very good place to look if you're trying to buy that hot new product just before Christmas.

Prices:	Medium	Express Ship? (UK)	Yes
Delivers to:	Worldwide	Gift Wrap?	No
Based:	UK		

www.oregonscientific.co.uk

Oregon Scientific, established in the USA in 1989, creates electronic products for modern lifestyles. Its innovative range is the combination of cutting-edge US technology and chic European design. You've no doubt seen their stylish wireless weather stations and thermometers but there are lots of other clever ideas as well.

Prices:	Luxury/Medium	Express Ship? (UK)	Yes
Delivers to:	UK	Gift Wrap?	No
Based:	UK		

www.sonystyle.co.uk

Here you can see all those gorgeously slim, modern laptops with VAIO on the front which come in red, indigo blue, gold and luxury pink (plus black, of course) or the latest mega-mega pixel digital cameras, micro hi-fi and headphones. Sony not only produces equipment that's functional and longlasting but manages to include an element of sexy design that places it ahead of the rest.

Prices:	Luxury/Medium	Express Ship? (UK)	Yes
Delivers to:	UK	Gift Wrap?	No
Based:	UK		

http://eurostore.palm.com

At this worldwide specialist in hand-held computers you can purchase a wide range of products from the newest state-of-the-art compact models to all the essential accessories to link your hand-held to your PC. As the world of hand-held computers seems to develop by the day you'll need all the excellent information they give you here. GPS solutions and SmartPhones are available as well.

Prices:	Luxury/Medium	Express Ship? (UK)	Yes
Delivers to:	Worldwide	Gift Wrap?	No
Based:	UK		

Clever and Sometimes Daft

www.addonsworld.co.uk

Having bought from this company several times I thought it only fair that you should know about them too. This is a totally different gadget shop offering useful and daft 'add-on' ideas which are all nearly always extremely clever, such as the Power Monkey emergency charger, triple cigarette lighter adaptor and tiny powerful Minimax speakers. All products you'll want for yourself but which make great gifts as well. Whatever mobile phone you use they'll have lots of accessories for that as well.

Prices:	Medium	Express Ship? (UK)	Yes
Delivers to:	Most worldwide	Gift Wrap?	No
Based:	UK		

www.firebox.com

From silly gadgets, chilli peanuts and scorpion vodka, to tech toys they'll actually keep and use such as digital photo frames, sleek 8 in 1 remote controls and The Bevy – an all in one iPod shuffle, keyring and bottle opener – you can find everything here and a wide range of prices. The Firebox website is extremely easy to get round and you'll be amazed at how much you can spend in an extraordinarily short space of time.

Prices:	Medium	Express Ship? (UK)	Yes
Delivers to:	Worldwide	Gift Wrap?	No
Based:	UK		

www.iwantoneofthose.co.uk

An irresistible (and very cleverly designed) gift and gadget shop with a huge choice and a very well-designed website. You can search by price or product type and there's a wide range of all levels. With excellent animation for most products you can choose from gadgets for garden, kitchen and office plus the inevitable toys and games. They offer sameday delivery, free standard delivery on orders over £50 and are happy to ship to you anywhere in the world.

Prices:	Medium/Very Good Value	Express Ship? (UK)	Yes
Delivers to:	Worldwide	Gift Wrap?	Yes
Based:	UK		

www.paramountzone.com

Paramount Zone offers an extensive and carefully selected choice of gadgets, games, boys' toys, bar items, sports gadgets (a good selection), mp3 players, executive items/toys, bachelor pad stuff, gift ideas, and lifestyle accessories – and these are just some of the items you'll find. The majority of UK address orders are despatched the same day for 1–2 day delivery and they're happy to deliver worldwide.

Prices:	Luxury/Medium	Express Ship? (UK)	Yes
Delivers to:	Worldwide	Gift Wrap?	No
Based:	UK		

www.thegadgetshop.com

Browse their online catalogue for some of the funniest, coolest gadgets you can buy, with everything from the frivolous to the functional, the digital to the downright silly. You'll find Big Boy's Toys, Retro Toys, Fun Stuff, Star Wars and iPod accessories here too. They'll ship all over the world, and offer an express delivery service in the UK. This is a particularly good website for mid-to-late teenagers so if you've one of those to buy for, take a good look round.

Prices:	Medium/Very Good Value	Express Ship? (UK)	Yes
Delivers to:	Worldwide	Gift Wrap?	Yes
Based:	UK		

www.thesharperedge.co.uk

Originally in the mobile phone industry, this retailer branched out into up-to-the-minute gadgets and gifts several years ago and specialises in keeping you up to date with the latest ideas on the market. It's an excellent store offering you clever and unusual suggestions plus innovative household accessories. It's a good place to look if you need a last-minute present as they despatch aiming for next-day delivery and offer to wrap your present as well.

Prices:	Medium	Express Ship? (UK)	Yes
Delivers to:	Worldwide	Gift Wrap?	Yes
Based:	UK		

Section 6
Babes, Kids and Mums-to-be

What I'm going to say now may sound a bit harsh, which will probably surprise you as I'm very complimentary about the websites I include, and before I start please don't get me wrong: all the ones below are lovely. The ones that aren't here probably number up into the thousands, and that's my problem – there are so many people trying to jump on the baby, toddler and children's product bandwagon. I'm well aware that there are loads of kids about – I have three of my own, don't I? Having said that, I don't believe that should mean that we need quite so many, often really badly designed, badly photographed and difficult-to-navigate websites.

Having written a complete book about baby goods online I have thoroughly trawled cyberspace for you to look out the best sites and here are some of them. The rest you will find in my mother and baby online shopping guide.

To anyone who is thinking of starting a new kids' kit webstore, or who has just started one and is wondering why it isn't working, please hear this. There are some wonderful websites to follow, with a great range of products, excellent usability, pretty pictures and intelligent writing, so use them as your examples. Don't try to re-invent the wheel, it won't work, and if you're even thinking of going the 'design your own' route, 'we can take our own pictures of little Tommy' route, 'it's bound to work, it's the world wide web' route, forget it. You can take it from me, it won't. Sorry, but it needs to be said.

The Boutiques

Baby and childrenswear stores should be beautiful to look at and a pleasure to browse and buy from. The same is true for the ones online and I have to say that there are some lovely places here for all ages, from newborn babes to older kids. Some of these stores offer clothes up to age 14 which, speaking from experience, was an age when you couldn't drag any of mine into a children's shop and they really wanted to start to choose 'grown-up' clothes for themselves. However, maybe you still have control. In which case, congratulations, lucky you, I lost it years ago.

www.alexandalexa.com

Alex and Alexa is an upmarket online baby, toddler and child boutique for 0–5 year olds, which launched in Autumn 07. Designers include Album Di Famiglia, Cacharel, Paul & Joe, Ralph Lauren and Roberto Cavalli. You'll find the latest collections from their designers beautifully photographed and easy to buy from on this well-designed site.

Prices:	Luxury/Medium	Express Ship? (UK)	Yes
Delivers to:	Worldwide	Gift Wrap?	Yes
Based:	UK		

www.balloonsweb.co.uk

Balloons offers designer childrenswear from 0–16 years, with brands including Catimini, Replay, Miss Sixty, Kenzo, Timberland and Ted Baker. They're adding new designers each season such as Energie for boys and Oilily for girls so keep checking back to see what's on offer.

Prices:	Luxury/Medium	Express Ship? (UK)	No
Delivers to:	Worldwide	Gift Wrap?	No
Based:	UK		

www.caramel-shop.co.uk

If you're looking for childrenswear you must take a look here, as Caramel have one of the most attractive websites and best collections around. The clothes are designed for babies, and children aged 2–12, and you can also buy shoes, boots and socks. Each part of the range is divided into themes so you can clearly see what works together.

Prices:	Luxury/Medium	Express Ship? (UK)	Yes
Delivers to:	Worldwide	Gift Wrap?	Yes
Based:	UK		

www.childrenssalon.co.uk

This is a family-run childrenswear company offering designer children's clothes from 0–12 years from labels such as Oilily, Bengh Per Principesse, Oxbow, Gabrielle, Elle, Cacharel, Kenzo, Dior and loads more (and I mean loads). They also have the Petit Bateau range of underwear for boys and girls, nightwear and dressing-up clothes, plus christening gowns and accessories.

Prices:	Luxury/Medium	Express Ship? (UK)	Yes
Delivers to:	Worldwide	Gift Wrap?	No
Based:	UK		

www.cosyposy.co.uk

This well thought-out childrenswear website has gone straight into my list of favourites, as it's attractive to look at, easy to navigate and offers an original and reasonably priced range for boys and girls from 2–6 plus a separate babies' collection. Brands include Inch Blue, Cacharel, Elizabeth James and Butterscotch. There are also some very good gift ideas for new babies and children.

Prices:	Medium	Express Ship? (UK)	Yes
Delivers to:	Worldwide	Gift Wrap?	Yes
Based:	UK		

www.iglookids.co.uk

This is a fun, contemporary kids' boutique offering clothes and accessories from ages 0–8 years. Most of the clothing is well priced and by a range of brands from labels such as Cat-amini, and Imps and Elfs to many that are interesting and different and far less well known. As well as the clothing collections there are toiletries, bed and bath accessories, parenting and baby books and CDs.

Prices:	Medium	Express Ship? (UK)	Yes
Delivers to:	Worldwide	Gift Wrap?	Yes
Based:	UK		

www.kidscavern.co.uk

Kids Cavern is one of the top children's designer stores in the North West of England and their website covers childrenswear over three departments from newborn to 3 years, 4–10 years and 11–16 years. Designers offered include Timberland, Moschino, DKNY, Burberry, Armani, Miniman, Dior and many more and they'll ship worldwide although outside the UK and USA you need to email them to find out how much your postage will cost.

Prices:	Medium	Express Ship? (UK)	Yes
Delivers to:	Worldwide	Gift Wrap?	No
Based:	UK		

www.littlefashiongallery.com

Little Fashion Gallery is based in France and has a range of beautiful, luxury clothes and accessories for children aged 0–6. As well as offering brands such as American Apparel, Antik Batik, Caramel Baby and Child and Bonnie Baby, this is an excellent destination for gifts which they're happy to ship worldwide.

Prices:	Luxury	Express Ship? (UK)	No
Delivers to:	Worldwide	Gift Wrap?	No
Based:	France		

www.mariechantal.com

This is an exquisite collection of baby and childrenswear designed by Marie Chantal of Greece. As you would expect the prices are quite steep, but you'll be hard put to find this quality of fabric and modern use of colour and design in many other children's stores. The clothing is available in two sections; babies, and toddlers (although some of these go up to age 8). If you want something really special you should have a look here.

Prices:	Luxury/Medium	Express Ship? (UK)	No
Delivers to:	Worldwide	Gift Wrap?	No
Based:	UK		

www.bebeo.com

Bebeo is a new, seriously lovely baby clothing online retailer offering the collections of designers such as Cavalli, Jean Bourget, Ikks, Kenzo, Armani and many more. It's exceptionally easy to navigate, and beautifully photographed. What more can I say? I'm sure you're going to love it as well. Bebeo is perfect for treats for your own baby and for special gifts as well.

Prices:	Luxury/Medium	Express Ship? (UK)	Worldwide express
Delivers to:	Worldwide	Gift Wrap?	Yes
Based:	France		

www.patriziawigan.com

This is not the place to expect to find that inexpensive off-the-peg number for your little one, but if you love pretty, beautifully made clothes such as hand-smocked dresses and special-occasion outfits, then this is a wonderful place to look. All the clothing is made to order so you will have to wait a while but you can be sure it'll be worth it. In the gift shop there are blankets, pretty children's china and soft toys.

Prices:	Luxury/Medium	Express Ship? (UK)	No
Delivers to:	Worldwide	Gift Wrap?	No
Based:	UK		

www.petitpatapon.com

I'm sure that my kids were never as well behaved as the ones in the pictures here, where delightful girls and boys in gorgeous clothes are happily playing and laughing and modelling. The range goes from newborn layettes to babies and then toddler boys and girls up to age 5. Finally there's a girls range up to age 14 and all the prices are reasonable. Remember to click on your currency first.

Prices:	Medium/Very Good Value	Express Ship? (UK)	No
Delivers to:	Worldwide	Gift Wrap?	No
Based:	Portugal/USA		

www.pleasemum.co.uk

This is a company that was established in London in 1971, aiming to provide fashionable, unique and high-quality children's clothing. They now offer their excellent own-brand collections online for children up to age 12/13, and there are some really gorgeous outfits here, particularly for girls, plus designer childrenswear by Moschino, D & G, Armani, Versace and Roberto Cavalli.

Prices:	Luxury/Medium	Express Ship? (UK)	No
Delivers to:	Worldwide	Gift Wrap?	No
Based:	UK		

www.rachelriley.com

The next time you're asked where someone could find a really special outfit for your little one, point them in the direction of Rachel Riley, where you'll discover a truly lovely collection for infants, teens and grown ups as well. Everything there is exquisite with a marvellous attention to style and detail and as you'd expect, nothing is inexpensive.

Prices:	Luxury	Express Ship? (UK)	Yes
Delivers to:	Worldwide	Gift Wrap?	No
Based:	UK		

www.thekidswindow.co.uk

The Kids Window is a real children's department store, offering children's clothing brands from designers such as Catfish, Inside Out, Marie Chantal and Budishh, a full range of baby equipment, activity toys such as trampolines, swings and slides and lots of toys and games. You can search on this website by age, gender, season and brand or click through to each section of the range.

Prices:	Luxury/Medium	Express Ship? (UK)	Yes
Delivers to:	Worldwide	Gift Wrap?	Yes
Based:	UK		

Bump Magic

Bumps have never been so fashionable. When I had my three (and I promise I'm only going to talk about this once) there was no internet you could buy from and the maternity clothes on offer were frequently horrendously expensive and, well ... just horrendous. Now there's a gorgeous contemporary choice of dresses and separates from totally casual to dressed up to the nines and at a wide range of prices as well. Whether you want a dress for the Oscars, something not so little and black for a night on the town or a great pair of designer jeans – it's all here waiting for you.

www.apeainthepod.com

This is without a doubt one of the most famous US-based maternity stores, offering both their own well-priced range plus designer selections by Tocca, Lily Pulizer, Juicy Couture, Diane von Furstenberg, Betsey Johnson and lots more plus premium denim brands such as Citizens of Humanity and Paige. Take a look at their Celebrity Red Carpet which includes actresses such as Holly Hunter and Maggie Gyllenhall then choose something for yourself.

Prices:	Luxury/Medium	Express Ship? (UK)	No
Delivers to:	Worldwide	Gift Wrap?	No
Based:	US		

www.bloomingmarvellous.co.uk

There's a wide choice of well-priced but good-quality clothes for expectant mothers and babies on this fun, colourful website. Whether you're looking for casualwear or city clothes you're sure to find something as they offer a wide range from sophisticated skirts and tops to lots of modern, casual options. There's also advice on how to dress with a bump and a monthly newsletter to sign up for.

Prices:	Medium/Very Good Value	Express Ship? (UK)	No
Delivers to:	Worldwide	Gift Wrap?	No
Based:	UK		

www.blossommotherandchild.com

Blossom caters for the fashion-conscious expectant mum, with a collection of glamorous dresses and separates which combine high-end fashion with comfort and functionality. You'll also find customised jeans by brands such as Rock and Republic and James. They use an assortment of luxurious fabrics such as silk-cashmere, voile and jersey, and they expand the collection continuously.

Prices:	Luxury/Medium	Express Ship? (UK)	Yes
Delivers to:	Worldwide	Gift Wrap?	No
Based:	UK		

www.cravematernity.co.uk

Crave Maternity have a well-designed, friendly and clearly photographed website offering well-cut and versatile separates and dresses in good fabrics and at reasonable prices. You'll find tailoring, eveningwear and casualwear all aimed at the busy woman who wants to carry on with her normal life and look smart throughout her pregnancy and afterwards.

Prices:	Medium	Express Ship? (UK)	No
Delivers to:	Worldwide	Gift Wrap?	No
Based:	UK		

www.formes.com

Formes is a French company offering beautifully styled 'designer' pregnancy wear and selling all over the world. You won't find their full collection but an edited range and it's well worth looking through. Unlike a lot of the maternity shops, here you'll find all the information you could possibly want, from complete product detailing to fabric content and full measurements plus very clear pictures.

Prices:	Medium	Express Ship? (UK)	No
Delivers to:	Worldwide	Gift Wrap?	No
Based:	UK		

www.fortyweeks.co.uk

The aim of maternity designer basics retailer Forty Weeks is to offer you contemporary, streamlined design combined with great fabrics to create a wardrobe that can be worn before, during and after pregnancy. There's a wide selection of colours and styles which would work perfectly with the more formal pieces of your new wardrobe and, unlike many things you buy now, you'll almost certainly want to wear them afterwards.

Prices:	Luxury/Medium	Express Ship? (UK)	No
Delivers to:	Worldwide	Gift Wrap?	No
Based:	UK		

www.isabellaoliver.com

Isabella Oliver is a maternity wear company for pregnant women who love clothes. Their sexy designs in soft jersey fabrics have signature style details like ruching and wrapping to flatter new curves and you can see each item as a model shot, drawing and also using their really clever and innovative catwalk animation. As well as day and evening separates you can buy lingerie, loungewear, sophisticated sleepwear, chic outerwear, sun and swimwear.

Prices:	Luxury/Medium	Express Ship? (UK)	Yes
Delivers to:	Worldwide	Gift Wrap?	Yes
Based:	UK		

www.jojomamanbebe.co.uk

This is a really pretty website offering a good choice for expectant mothers, babies and young children. The drop-down menus on the home page take you quickly and clearly to everything you might be looking for, whether it's maternity occasionwear or safety gates for young children. There's a range of underwear and swimwear as well.

Prices:	Medium	Express Ship? (UK)	No
Delivers to:	Worldwide	Gift Wrap?	No
Based:	UK		

www.mamalamode.co.uk

Mama La Mode offers the collections from designers such as Issa, Paul and Joe, Velvet, Paige Premium Denim and Rock and Republic to help you be stylishly pregnant whether you need red carpet glamour, working staples or trendy denim. Here you can also find lingerie, resortwear, accessories and beauty products plus gifts for babies and new mums and lots of helpful style advice, making this one of the best one-stop shops for mums to be.

Prices:	Luxury/Medium	Express Ship? (UK)	Yes
Delivers to:	Worldwide	Gift Wrap?	Yes
Based:	UK		

www.mamasandpapas.co.uk

This company combines great attention to detail, high-quality fabrics and pretty designs in their well-priced maternity section, covering everything from eveningwear and separates to sleepwear and swimwear. There's lovely clothing here as well for babies and toddlers plus a wide range of equipment and lots of present ideas. This is really a beautifully photographed website offering loads of advice on what to buy.

Prices:	Medium	Express Ship? (UK)	No
Delivers to:	UK but US site available	Gift Wrap?	No
Based:	UK		

www.seraphine.com

Find excellent maternitywear on this really attractive website where the collection is stylish and different and the prices reasonable. You can choose from the latest looks, maternity essentials and glamorous partywear and as well as all of this there's lingerie by Elle MacPherson, Nougatine and Canelle, gorgeous layettes for newborn babies and Tommy's Ts.

Prices:	Medium	Express Ship? (UK)	No
Delivers to:	Worldwide	Gift Wrap?	No
Based:	UK		

www.tiffanyrose.co.uk

Here you'll find smart and unusual maternitywear including dresses and chic separates. It's quite a small range but very stylish so if you're looking for something for a special occasion you should have a click around. There are also beautiful maternity wedding dresses and a sale area where there are usually some very good discounts.

Prices:	Luxury/Medium	Express Ship? (UK)	Yes
Delivers to:	Worldwide	Gift Wrap?	No
Based:	UK		

All the Essentials

And I mean *all* the essentials and more. You could really get carried away in these stores offering you everything from Moses baskets to strollers, prams, car seats and other equipment. I'm sure you know what I'm going to say – always price compare. Even if you're pretty sure you know where you want to buy that high-tech three-wheeler you should check the prices elsewhere to make sure you're getting the best deal. Online is a far better place to shop, in my opinion, for everything baby related – you can choose online, you don't have to haul it home and you'll get a much better price. What more could you want?

www.babeswithbabies.com

This is a lovely place to buy a gift for a new mum or baby or to find the coolest changing bags and essentials, with a range that you can't find anywhere else. There's a wide selection in each of the categories – they offer pretty polka dot mama and baby pyjamas, chic nursing tops, Superfluffy alpaca slippers and pampering gift sets as just some of their ideas. You can book baby portrait sessions and buy gift vouchers here as well.

Prices:	Medium	Express Ship? (UK)	Yes, but call to arrange
Delivers to:	Worldwide	Gift Wrap?	Automatic
Based:	UK		

www.babygurgles.co.uk

There's a really good choice here of baby items including some innovative items such as the Buggy Snuggle, Silly Billyz Bibs and HandySitt as well as lots of other ideas. Check out The Bug in a Rug baby wrap, Miracle swaddling blanket, Wheelie Bug toddler rides and lots of other basic and essential equipment.

Prices:	Medium	Express Ship? (UK)	No
Delivers to:	UK	Gift Wrap?	No
Based:	UK		

www.kiddicare.com

Kiddicare is a large independent retailer of baby and nursery equipment and nursery furniture and claims to keep everything in stock ready to send out to you. You can buy Avent sterilisers and feeding bottles, Grobags, buggies and travel cots, high chairs, rockers and baby swings plus equipment for the home including playpens, stair gates, cots, changing units and nursery furniture. Delivery is free to most of the UK and takes about four working days.

Prices:	Medium	Express Ship? (UK)	No
Delivers to:	UK	Gift Wrap?	No
Based:	UK		

www.kiddies-kingdom.com

This is a really well laid-out website which helps you get to the product you're looking for with no fuss. So you can choose from high chairs, prams and pushchairs, buggy boards and travel systems, Moses baskets, cots and cribs, furniture and monitors and much, much more.

Prices:	Luxury/Medium	Express Ship? (UK)	Yes, automatic
Delivers to:	UK	Gift Wrap?	No
Based:	UK		

www.preciouslittleone.com

Here's an excellent baby equipment website offering, among other things, footmuffs, push-chairs and accessories with plenty of details to help you choose. There are also car seats and a very good range for the nursery including the high-quality Saplings range of furniture, most of which will take your child from baby to older years. You can buy giant, themed sticker sets for room decorating here too.

Prices:	Medium	Express Ship? (UK)	No
Delivers to:	Worldwide	Gift Wrap?	No
Based:	UK		

www.thebaby.co.uk

Don't be put off by the tremendous range here, including Mountain Buggy Prams, Simon Horn and Wigwam Kids furniture, Stevenson Rocking Horses and so much more. Whatever you're looking for, for your baby or child, you'll probably find it, whether you need travel accessories, full room sets or baby accessories such as high chairs and monitors. They offer a next-day delivery service and will ship worldwide, although some items are restricted by weight.

Prices:	Luxury/Medium	Express Ship? (UK)	Yes
Delivers to:	Worldwide	Gift Wrap?	No
Based:	UK		

www.twoleftfeet.co.uk

This is a fantastic baby equipment website claiming to offer the largest selection in the UK. Browse through their sections offering cots and baby bedding, pushchairs, prams and the latest buggies, car seats, cribs and rocking horses and just about everything in between. Premium brands include Silver Cross, Bebe Confort, Chicco, Britax and Maclaren. You'll also find lovely children's furniture here.

Prices:	Medium	Express Ship? (UK)	Yes
Delivers to:	Most EU plus the USA	Gift Wrap?	No
Based:	UK		

Toys, Toys, Toys

If you're at that stage then there's nothing much I need to say here. Every brand and every type of toy is available online and unless you need a quick bribe (yes I did say that word) when you're out shopping and you have a noisy child, or worse, children, with you, then you're far better off choosing and buying in peace and quiet, particularly as many of the retailers here offer express delivery. Surely tomorrow is soon enough?

www.dollshouse.com

Whether you're new to the world of dolls' houses or a dedicated miniaturist, the Dolls' House Emporium should fill you with inspiration. The site features fully decorated dolls' houses and thousands of miniatures in colour co-ordinated room sets plus carpets and flooring, lighting and wallpapers. You can also see a selection of 1:12 scale dolls' houses shown open and fully furnished to give you ideas.

Prices:	Luxury/Medium	Express Ship? (UK)	No
Delivers to:	Worldwide	Gift Wrap?	No
Based:	UK		

www.elc.co.uk

The baby and toddler section at the Early Learning Centre's colourful website is well worth having a look round, as you'll find a wide range perfect for starting your baby off, including bath toys, Blossom Farm baby toys, buggy and cot toys and just about every other type of baby toy you can think of. They make it easy for you to choose because, as well as selecting by type of toy, you can choose by themes such as Action and Adventure, Art and Music.

Prices:	Medium/Very Good Value	Express Ship? (UK)	Yes
Delivers to:	UK	Gift Wrap?	No
Based:	UK		

www.gltc.co.uk

Here's a great range of ideas for babies and young children of all ages including Fairy Ballerina and Sports Champion duvet sets and accessories, reasonably priced traditional children's furniture, innovative storage ideas, playtables, bunk beds, baby and toddler sleeping bags and themed furniture. There's the Squishy, Squirty Bath Book, Jungle soft toy Bowling Set and Toy House Play Mat too, plus loads more clever suggestions.

Prices:	Medium	Express Ship? (UK)	Yes
Delivers to:	Worldwide	Gift Wrap?	No
Based:	UK		

www.hamleys.co.uk

If you've ever visited this world-famous Regent Street toy emporium (I hate the word but it's the only way to describe this store) you'll know that there's a huge range of gadgets, games, soft toys, puzzles, stocking fillers and every toy you can think of at all price levels and for all ages. In fact it's a disastrous place to take more than one child at a time as there's so much to see.

Prices:	Luxury/Medium	Express Ship? (UK)	No
Delivers to:	Worldwide	Gift Wrap?	No
Based:	UK		

www.lambstoys.co.uk

This is another of those toy websites that offers so many brands it's hard to know where to start. To help you I'll tell you that they have an excellent range of Meccano, Hornby and Scalextric, Lego, Schleich Models, Flashing Storm scooters and Power Rangers. Then for little girls there's Zapf Baby Annabel, Chou Chou and Colette plus Miss Milly and My Model make-up and hair styling sets (and lots more). Phew.

Prices:	Medium	Express Ship? (UK)	Yes
Delivers to:	Worldwide	Gift Wrap?	No
Based:	UK		

www.mailorderexpress.com

Mail Order Express claims to be the largest toy website in Europe and who am I to argue? It's a hugely busy site with loads of offers and pre-order invitations on the home page but where, thankfully, you can shop by categories such as Music, Gadgets, Party, Science, Toy Vehicle, Dolls and Accessories or by brand. Take a look for yourself.

Prices:	Medium/Very Good Value	Express Ship? (UK)	Yes
Delivers to:	Worldwide	Gift Wrap?	No
Based:	UK		

www.thetoyshop.com

This is one of the largest independent toy retailers in the UK, with a huge range and an excellent, easy-to-navigate website where you can search by brand, type of toy, age group or price. Once you've decided what you want to buy and registered both your address and any addresses where you want your orders despatched to, you simply select from the standard or express delivery services, give your payment details and you're done.

Prices:	Medium	Express Ship? (UK)	Yes
Delivers to:	Worldwide	Gift Wrap?	No
Based:	UK		

Time for Bed

When you start having children you want to have the perfect nursery, probably with matching curtains and borders, beautiful furniture and the highest-quality cot. Well, having had three children I'll definitely agree with the last one, provided it turns into a bed at the end of the day and so can continue to be used. Therein lies the key. Unless you really have money to burn, buy your children the highest quality you can afford that will last the longest time. I'm not talking about duvet covers and small accessories here, but where carpets, furniture, cots and beds are concerned make sure that they'll last you a) through several children and b) on through the years. You really won't regret it, I promise.

www.aspaceuk.com

At Aspace you can shop by range (Astor, Vermont, Porterhouse, Mill Tree, Key West, Captain's Girl, Boomsbury, Hudson) or by type of furniture, such as single or bunk beds, desks, wardrobes and chests, duvet sets, mattresses, sleeping bags, bean bags and cushions. In each section there's a great deal to see at a wide range of prices but there's also a lot of information and help on how to put ranges together.

Prices:	Luxury/Medium	Express Ship? (UK)	No
Delivers to:	UK	Gift Wrap?	No
Based:	UK		

www.dragonsofwaltonstreet.com

For unique handpainted children's furniture and perfect gifts and accessories this is a lovely place to shop. You can order everything from sleigh and bunk beds, tables and chairs and chests of drawers painted with flower fairies and soldiers to enchanting fabrics, artworks and other gift ideas. Nothing is inexpensive but anything you purchase here will almost certainly be treasured for years.

Prices:	Luxury/Medium	Express Ship? (UK)	No
Delivers to:	Worldwide	Gift Wrap?	No
Based:	UK		

www.kidsrooms.co.uk

Kids Rooms specialises in children's furniture and accessories for children's bedrooms, nurseries and playrooms. The range includes children's beds, wardrobes, chest of drawers, bedside cabinets, children's tables & chairs, toy boxes, bedding, bookends, height charts and much more. The website is attractive and easy to navigate and the product range is growing all the time.

Prices:	Medium	Express Ship? (UK)	No
Delivers to:	UK	Gift Wrap?	No
Based:	UK		

www.nurserywindow.co.uk

Once you arrive at this website you'll find it very hard to leave. There are some seriously lovely things here for children's rooms, from unusual bedding, Moses baskets and high-quality cots and furniture to gift baskets for new babies. Just click on the area of their online shop you're interested in, enter, and you'll certainly be hooked. You can also buy matching fabric to the bed linen. Nothing is cheap but it's all beautiful quality.

Prices:	Luxury/Medium	Express Ship? (UK)	No
Delivers to:	UK	Gift Wrap?	No
Based:	UK		

www.thechildrensfurniturecompany.co.uk

It's well worth having a good look round and investing here, as these are not children's things for the short term but pieces of furniture that will last and last, with childish accents that you can remove and change, such as bunks that can be debunked and safety rails removed, engraved panels which can be swapped for plain ones, and brightly-coloured panels which flip to reveal more muted tones.

Prices:	Luxury/Medium	Express Ship? (UK)	No
Delivers to:	UK	Gift Wrap?	No
Based:	UK		

www.tuttibambini.co.uk

Tutti Bambini offers a range of coordinating nursery furniture including cribs, cots, cot beds, wardrobes, dressers, toy boxes, shelves and cot top changers. They also sell glider chairs, wooden toys and quality mattresses which are available in four sizes. Their cot-top changers are designed to fit onto the top of a cot or cot bed and have raised sides and a padded, vinyl, wipe-clean surface.

Prices:	Luxury/Medium	Express Ship? (UK)	Yes, for some items
Delivers to:	UK	Gift Wrap?	No
Based:	UK		

www.vipkids.co.uk

VIP Kids specialises in the design, manufacture and import of high-quality, imaginative children's beds, chairs, bedroom furniture, toys, nursery furniture and accessories. You'll find collections featuring the 1930s reproduction Ferrari F2 Retro Racers. There's children's room lighting, handcrafted upholstered loose cover armchairs, fun light switch covers and wooden mobiles too.

Prices:	Luxury/Medium	Express Ship? (UK)	No
Delivers to:	UK	Gift Wrap?	No
Based:	UK		

www.hippins.co.uk

Here you can find a unique mix of traditional and modern children's and nursery furniture, baby bedding and nursery accessories such as bookshelves, hand-painted toy boxes, wooden height charts and lighting. There is a very wide choice with small pictures to start off with but it would be hard to come across such and extensive range anywhere else.

Prices:	Medium	Express Ship? (UK)	No
Delivers to:	EU most items	Gift Wrap?	Yes
Based:	UK		

Fun and Games

Where did you have to go before the advent of the web to see all this equipment? You could see brochures (and still can) at somewhere like John Lewis or you could travel as far as you needed to to the largest local garden centre where, if you were lucky, there would be some sort of choice.

Of course, now you can see and order everything online from a wide range of stores. Take a look at several before making your final decision to make sure you're getting it right and, particularly with trampolines, *please be careful*. They need to be totally supervised and with soft landings for tiny and medium-sized kids. Having spent nine hours in A&E with number two son and his fractured shoulder after he bounced off a friend's trampoline, I really do know about this.

www.adventuretoys.co.uk

Here you'll find a good range of climbing frames, trampolines and swing sets, and also lots of ride-on tractors and cars, sand and water tables, mini picnic tables, basketball sets, play houses, netball goals, practice tennis nets and trikes. Phew. Brands they carry include Brio, Little Tikes, TP Toys, Supertramp and Winther. This website is well worth having a good look round.

Prices:	Medium	Express Ship? (UK)	Yes
Delivers to:	UK	Gift Wrap?	No
Based:	UK		

www.airfix.com

Just about every boy has at some time made an Airfix model (or usually part made and left). The joy of opening all those tiny tins of paint and spending hours making a mess and sticking all those bits together seems totally irresistible. Well, here it all is online, on a simple site where you can order all the kits with just a few clicks. There's everything from a supercharged 1930 Bentley to a Tiger Moth, with clear details for them all.

Prices:	Luxury/Medium	Express Ship? (UK)	No
Delivers to:	Worldwide	Gift Wrap?	No
Based:	UK		

www.farscapegames.co.uk

You may be looking for a complete travel games compendium or just a new reasonably priced backgammon set and whether your favourite game is Mah Jong, dominoes, monopoly or bridge you're sure to find what you're seeking here. This without having to go to your local store and decide whether you should be in the children's section or somewhere else, then finding that, after all, there are only a couple of options for your chosen game.

Prices:	Medium	Express Ship? (UK)	Yes
Delivers to:	Worldwide	Gift Wrap?	No
Based:	UK		

www.gardengames.co.uk

Whether you're looking for trampolines, climbing frames, swings and slides, junior and full-sized croquet sets, snooker and pool tables, table tennis tables aqua slides or an old-fashioned wooden sledge you'll find everything on this friendly website. All the items are well photographed, the site offers speedy UK delivery and will also ship to the USA, Canada and Spain.

Prices:	Medium	Express Ship? (UK)	Yes
Delivers to:	UK, USA, Canada and Spain	Gift Wrap?	No
Based:	UK		

www.lego.com

Lego kits seem to have become more and more complicated and you practically need an engineering degree to build some of them (well I never was very good at that sort of thing). Let your son on this website if you dare. Everything is brilliantly shown, including Star Wars, Lego Sports, building sets, Robotics and the very latest editions. You can take the Club tour, order the magazine or click on to the Games Page.

Prices:	Medium	Express Ship? (UK)	Yes
Delivers to:	Worldwide	Gift Wrap?	No
Based:	UK		

www.slotcity.co.uk

Slot City is one the largest independent retailers of slot cars in the UK and Europe and you can only buy from them online. They offer the full range of Scalextric plus other brands such as Carrera from Germany and SCX for Spain – household names in their own countries but almost impossible to find here until now. You'll also find Hornby and Carrera model kits. Everything is ready for immediate delivery unless you're told otherwise on the website.

Prices:	Luxury/Medium	Express Ship? (UK)	No
Delivers to:	All EU countries and the USA	Gift Wrap?	No
Based:	UK		

Party Time

Theme-driven parties really seem to be the thing now and you can buy everything from goody bags to paper cups, napkins and plates and coordinating table cloths. You may, like me, find it all a bit much and prefer to let your food make the statement, but with all the competition from other kids' parties around it's very hard not to be drawn into trying to be the best. Thank goodness mine are now well beyond this stage, although they're now competing on cars and 21st birthdays. Oh dear, you simply can't win.

www.a2z-kids.co.uk

Choose from Historical Costumes, Girls Party Costumes, Books, Rhymes and Fairytales, Christmas and Nativity, Animals and Creatures such as Scooby Doo and Dinosaur, Superman Returns, Disney, and toddler and infant costumes. The menus here are particularly good and although you can find the same types of costumes elsewhere, you can narrow down your search on this website very fast.

Prices:	Medium	Express Ship? (UK)	Yes
Delivers to:	Worldwide	Gift Wrap?	No
Based:	UK		

www.greatlittleparties.co.uk

They've really made an effort here to get away from totally theme-driven party supplies (although ultimately it's best to do that here as well and yes there are lots to choose from, from Peter Pan and Noddy to Thomas the Tank, Fifi and the Flowerpots). Alongside these you can also order party music CDs, party games, books (party food recipes and planning a party), birthday cake candles and gift wrap.

Prices:	Medium	Express Ship? (UK)	Yes
Delivers to:	EU	Gift Wrap?	No
Based:	UK		

www.hopscotchdressingup.co.uk

Hopscotch have got the children's dressing-up market sewn up with their lovely, bright website full of dressing-up-box clothes for children from angels and fairies to witches and wizards, cowboys and indians to kings and queens and everything in between. There's no question that if your child has been asked to a fancy dress party and is determined to really look the part, you absolutely have to visit Hopscotch.

Prices:	Medium/Very Good Value	Express Ship? (UK)	Yes
Delivers to:	Worldwide	Gift Wrap?	No
Based:	UK		

www.partyark.co.uk

Let's move away for a moment from the huge, multi choice, online party retailers for everyone from 0–80 (although they are great) and settle here, on this prettily designed website just for tinies. You have the option of choosing each item to go with your theme, be it Dancing Fairies or Knights and Dragons or you can go straight to Party Packs where they've done it all for you. There are tips and advice, planning help and absolutely everything to make your life easier.

Prices:	Medium	Express Ship? (UK)	Yes
Delivers to:	Worldwide	Gift Wrap?	No
Based:	UK		

www.partypieces.co.uk

This is a really attractive children's party website where you can choose from totally themed children's accessories and gift boxes to games such as pass-the-parcel, Monster Hunt and Treasure Island. To make your life even easier there are lots of packs of invitations to buy which you can order first at their 'invitations only' first-class post rate, balloons and decorations, and gorgeous party clothes such as pirate outfits and ballet dresses.

Prices:	Medium	Express Ship? (UK)	Yes
Delivers to:	Worldwide	Gift Wrap?	No
Based:	UK		

For lots more places to shop for Mother and Child online order your copy of *The Shopaholic's Guide to Buying for Mother and Child Online* from www.amazon.co.uk.

Home is where the Heart is

I n my first *Shopaholic's Guide to Buying Online* I had very little for the home and was severely chastised by a well-known journalist who could see that my real loves were fashion and travel and so, she suggested, I obviously hadn't done enough research for the interiors addicts.

Well, I think you'll agree that I've made up for it now, with an amazing range of home stores offering everything from home fragrance to furniture, cookware, storage solutions and more, plus garden furniture and barbeques, flowers and the essentials for your pets.

There are some superb home stores online and it's well worth having a good look round to decide on your favourites which provide for your style, be it French, English contemporary or old style – and then you can really have fun.

The Home Stores

These are the online home retailers who offer something for every room in your house, from furniture to small accessories, so it's impossible to put them in any single section. They all, as I said above, have their own idiosyncratic style, so decide which is for you and then browse to your heart's content, from Heals' retro-contemporary chic to Dibor's pretty French look. These destinations are also excellent for wedding and other gifts.

www.dibor.co.uk

Dibor is an independent, UK-based company offering French style furniture, home accessories and gifts for every room including kitchen, dining, bed, bath, living and garden. There are also some very pretty ideas for children and a special Christmas department in season. The website is very easy to navigate and an extremely attractive place to browse, particularly as you'll find ideas here that aren't available anywhere else.

Prices:	Medium	Express Ship? (UK)	Yes
Delivers to:	Worldwide	Gift Wrap?	Yes
Based:	UK		

www.dotmaison.co.uk

This is a beautifully designed online home store, offering designer home furnishings and accessories by names such as Descamps, Lulu Guinness, Jasper Conran, Versace and Vera Wang. If that makes it sound more like a fashion boutique than a home store I can assure you that it isn't and you'll find Designers Guild, Eva Solo and Coalport here as well.

Prices:	Luxury/Medium	Express Ship? (UK)	No
Delivers to:	UK	Gift Wrap?	No
Based:	UK		

www.heals.co.uk

Heals offers contemporary styling and reasonable prices for major furniture items such as beds and sofas right through to lighting, small accessories, bed linen, towels and toiletries. Click through to their clear website and pay a visit to the room of your choice or check out their garden furniture and accessories and storage solutions. They also have a wedding list service, interior design, kitchen planning and much more.

Prices:	Medium	Express Ship? (UK)	Yes
Delivers to:	UK	Gift Wrap?	No
Based:	UK		

www.ikea.com

You will, I know, have heard of Ikea but you may have been put off from shopping there by the thought of all those crowds. Well now, depending on where you live, you can shop from this well-priced Swedish retail experience without setting foot outside your door, and choose from their wide range of well-designed, functional home furnishing products. Check to see if they deliver to you now.

Prices:	Very Good Value	Express Ship? (UK)	No
Delivers to:	Worldwide but UK this site	Gift Wrap?	No
Based:	UK		

www.muji.co.uk

Muji's products, whether for your home, office, school or travelling, are always well priced. That's not to say that you couldn't find the same goods at the same kind of price elsewhere, but when you couple what else Muji has to offer – chic, minimal styling, functional design and a wealth of ideas – with its excellent value this is a really good place to shop.

Prices:	Very Good Value	Express Ship? (UK)	No
Delivers to:	UK this site	Gift Wrap?	No
Based:	UK		

www.okadirect.com

Oka has a beautifully designed and photographed website where you'll find some inspirational ideas for your home and lovely gifts. Browse through their roomsets and pick out the individual items that would enhance your existing decor, or go for broke and buy them all. From throws, cushions, quilts and rugs to porcelain vases and elegant furniture there's a wealth of items to choose from.

Prices:	Medium	Express Ship? (UK)	Yes, for Central London only
Delivers to:	Worldwide	Gift Wrap?	No
Based:	UK		

Bed and Bath

For your next new hot tub or power jet bath please don't come here as you won't find what you're looking for. However, if you're after luxurious towels, robes and bed linen, gorgeous throws and other accessories then this is your place. You can even find bed linen for your new yacht here and have it personally piped and monogrammed to your specification.

www.armoirelinen.com

The next time you're buying bed linen for your yacht, stop off here and take a look (and yes I am being serious). Armoire have created a range of luxe bed linen specifically for yachts and five star hotels and now you can buy into their collection of pure linen and heirloom Egyptian cottons plus blankets, robes and towels.

Prices:	Luxury	Express Ship? (UK)	No
Delivers to:	Worldwide	Gift Wrap?	No
Based:	UK		

www.biju.co.uk

Luxurious bathrobes and towels, cashmere blankets and throws and a wonderful collection of table linen, Missoni tableware, mats and trays are just some of the items you can choose from on this treasure trove of a website where they offer enchanting children's bedding and bedroom accessories as well. They also offer a personalisation embroidery service on their bathrobes and towels to help you create totally individual gifts.

Prices:	Luxury/Medium	Express Ship? (UK)	No
Delivers to:	Worldwide	Gift Wrap?	No
Based:	UK		

www.cathkidston.co.uk

Cath Kidston started her company over ten years ago in a small shop in Notting Hill, selling second-hand furniture and vintage fabrics. She soon began to design her own fabric and wallpaper, creating signature floral prints which have come to stand for her unique look. On her colourful website you'll see some really pretty and different bed linen and bedspreads with pattern names such as 'New Bubbles' and 'Vintage Posy' plus crochet blankets and even sleeping bags.

Prices:	Medium	Express Ship? (UK)	Yes
Delivers to:	Worldwide	Gift Wrap?	Yes
Based:	UK		

www.christy-towels.com

The Christy at home website is really beautifully designed, clean, clear and modern and quickly makes you want to buy. Don't think of Christy just for towels, although there's a wide colour range to choose from, but look also at their high-quality bed linen in mostly neutral shades and cotton blends and other products including robes, cushions, throws and contemporary bathroom accessories.

Prices:	Medium	Express Ship? (UK)	No
Delivers to:	UK	Gift Wrap?	No
Based:	UK		

www.designersguild.com

You'll find Tricia Guild's gorgeously coloured bed linen here both for grown ups and children, plus very different towels, bedspreads and throws, small leather goods and Fragrant Home from Designers Guild – a beautiful collection of home fragrance and luxury body products. If you haven't come across Designers Guild until now but you like pretty, colourful designs then take a look here.

Prices:	Medium	Express Ship? (UK)	Yes
Delivers to:	UK	Gift Wrap?	Yes
Based:	UK		

www.egyptiancottonstore.com

If you like beautiful bed linen you'll love this attractively presented website, where you can buy top quality Egyptian Cotton (of course) duvet covers and sheets, goosedown and cotton duvets and pillows, nursery bedding, towels and bathrobes plus elegant table linen. Delivery is free in the UK and they'll ship worldwide. Everything here is expensive, but then for the quality you would expect it.

Prices:	Luxury	Express Ship? (UK)	Yes
Delivers to:	Worldwide	Gift Wrap?	Yes
Based:	UK		

www.kingofcotton.co.uk

If you haven't already come across this website you'll probably be delighted to do so now, particularly if you have several bedrooms in your house, like high-quality bed linen (and towels) but don't want to pay the earth – the best for less, as it were. At King of Cotton you'll find bed linen, duvets, pillows and mattress covers, towels and robes at really good prices and the service is excellent.

Prices:	Medium/Very Good Value	Express Ship? (UK)	No
Delivers to:	Worldwide	Gift Wrap?	No
Based:	UK		

www.lumadirect.com

If your preference for your bedroom is pretty colours and florals then don't shop here. If, however, you prefer soft stylish neutrals then this is an excellent website for you, where all the fabrics are luxurious organic cottons, environmentally friendly linens and silks and pure wools, including pashmina, merino and angora. Contact them for EU deliveries.

Prices:	Medium	Express Ship? (UK)	Yes
Delivers to:	EU	Gift Wrap?	No
Based:	UK		

www.maisoncollection.com

Maison offer a really pretty collection of plain and patterned high-quality and traditionally styled bed linen and bedspreads with detailing such as embroidery, hemstitching and lace edging. For some of the designs you'll find accessories such as lavender bags, tissue box holders and laundry bags. There's also a very feminine choice of gifts such as lace covered clothes hangers and fine linen guest towels plus lovely children's bed linen.

Prices:	Medium	Express Ship? (UK)	Yes
Delivers to:	Worldwide	Gift Wrap?	No
Based:	UK		

www.monogrammedlinenshop.co.uk

For the past 25 years The Monogrammed Linen Shop has provided classical and contemporary household linens to customers from all over the world. They only use the most beautiful laces and embroideries together with the finest cottons, linens, and silks to produce luxurious bed linen, table linen and nightwear. They also offer perfect ideas for gifts for all occasions and offer an exquisite babywear collection going up to age 4.

Prices:	Luxury/Medium	Express Ship? (UK)	No
Delivers to:	Worldwide	Gift Wrap?	No
Based:	UK		

www.thewhitecompany.com

The White Company offers a collection of beautifully made contemporary furniture, accessories, gifts and clothing in stylish neutrals, including luxurious bed linen, throws, towels, blankets, duvets and pillows, loungewear and clothing for tinies. Small accessories include vases, picture frames, rugs and mirrors and there's also a lovely gift-perfect collection of toiletries and candles.

Prices:	Medium	Express Ship? (UK)	Yes
Delivers to:	Worldwide	Gift Wrap?	Yes
Based:	UK		

www.volgalinen.co.uk

The Volga Linen Company is a family-run, British company that sells an exquisite collection of pure linen from Russia. The collection consists of table linen, bed linen, ready-to-hang curtains and a children's range and accessories. They produce plain weaves, fabric with drawn thread work embroidery, damasks, and richly coloured paisleys. Also take a look at their new clothing range online.

Prices:	Luxury	Express Ship? (UK)	No
Delivers to:	Worldwide	Gift Wrap?	Yes
Based:	UK		

Home Decor

For home decor read all those gorgeous accessories that come together to make your house your own and emphasise your style, whether it's the china, glass and cutlery you choose or just the pieces that you like to surround yourself with. Coming from an extremely untidy family (excluding me, of course) I'm always aiming for that perfect vase or bowl on a beautifully polished table in a perfectly tidied room and never, ever, succeed other than in a split second when everyone is out of the house. After which mayhem returns in every room. Still, as they say, you can't have it all.

Tableware and Table Linen

www.emmabridgewater.co.uk

Emma Bridgewater is well known for her high-quality pottery and clever and attractive designs such as Polka Dots, Hugs and Kisses and Hearts as well as her mug collections which include dogs, cats, birds and flowers. Every season she's bringing out new products, such as cutlery, glass, preserves and teas, all with her signature script. Almost every kitchen has one or two pieces of her pottery, the only question is, can you resist the urge to collect?

Prices:	Medium	Express Ship? (UK)	Yes
Delivers to:	Worldwide	Gift Wrap?	Yes
Based:	UK		

www.davidmellordesign.com

David Mellor, Royal Designer for Industry, has an international reputation as a designer, manufacturer and shopkeeper. Born in Sheffield, he has always specialised in metalwork and has often been described as 'the cutlery king.' On his website there's a selection of his modern stainless steel cutlery, plus contemporary glass and tableware, kitchen tools and equipment.

Prices:	Luxury/Medium	Express Ship? (UK)	Yes
Delivers to:	Worldwide	Gift Wrap?	Yes
Based:	UK		

www.dartington.co.uk

From bowls and vases to ice buckets, decanters, jugs and glassware, Dartington have created the modern options to match contemporary design in your home or to make excellent gifts (particularly for wedding presents). The prices are reasonable and you can be certain that anything you order will be very well made. They'll deliver to you anywhere in the world (7–14 days for overseas) and faster within the UK.

Prices:	Medium	Express Ship? (UK)	No
Delivers to:	Worldwide	Gift Wrap?	No
Based:	UK		

www.french-brand.com

This is a France-based retailer offering you all those home accessories you saw on your last trip but weren't able to sneak into your suitcase. Gorgeous and colourful table linen from Les Olivades and Jaquard Francais, quilted cushions by Souleido, and toiletries and home fragrance by Manuel Canovas and Jardin Secret are just some of the things you can order online. There's also a fantastic range of bed linen by designers such as Descamps and colourful beach towels as well.

Prices:	Luxury/Medium	Express Ship? (UK)	No
Delivers to:	Worldwide	Gift Wrap?	No
Based:	France		

www.purpleandfinelinen.co.uk

At Purple and Fine Linen their pure linen tablecloths, placemats, napkins and runners are designed to offer a look of timeless luxury and simple elegance. As well as traditional white and ivory you can also choose from their range in deep chilli red and damson (purple), which would be lovely for Christmas. These are investment table linens and very beautiful.

Prices:	Luxury/Medium	Express Ship? (UK)	Yes
Delivers to:	Worldwide	Gift Wrap?	No
Based:	UK		

www.smallislandtrader.com

Small Island Trader is an excellent company offering not only china and glass from a wide range of designers and manufacturers, but also kitchen equipment – from juicers and steamers to copper and Le Creuset pots and pans, Sabatier knives, baking trays, and the Eva Solo's range of kitchen and living products. Needless to say they can't carry everything they offer in stock and delivery time is very much dependent on what you order. Allow at least 28 days.

Prices:	Luxury/Medium	Express Ship? (UK)	No
Delivers to:	Worldwide	Gift Wrap?	No
Based:	UK		

www.thefrenchhouse.net

As you would expect, all the products here are from France, from tableware, linen and cutlery, to toiletries by Christian Lenart and Savon de Marseilles and elegant Anduze garden pots. Also a selection of pretty bed linen in traditional French designs such as Toile de Jouey, Fleurs de Champs and Monogram. The descriptions and information about every item are clear and well written and everything is beautifully photographed.

Prices:	Medium	Express Ship? (UK)	No
Delivers to:	UK	Gift Wrap?	No
Based:	UK		

www.welch.co.uk

Robert Welch trained as a Silversmith at Birmingham College of Art. He then moved to the Royal College of Art in 1952, where he specialised exclusively in stainless steel production design. In 1965 he was awarded Royal Designer for Industry. Together with his son, William, he has designed some unusual home accessories which you can buy from their website, including candlesticks, bathroom accessories, flatware and pewter.

Prices:	Luxury/Medium	Express Ship? (UK)	No
Delivers to:	Worldwide	Gift Wrap?	No
Based:	UK		

Decorative Accessories

www.alisonhenry.com

These are seriously gorgeous modern accessories, mainly in neutral colours, which would make superb gifts for weddings and other 'important' occasions, or when you feel in need of adding something really special to your home. There's a cut-crystal fragrance bottle filled with Alison's signature bath oil, pure cashmere cushions and double-sided throws, plus other beautifully photographed objects.

Prices:	Luxury/Medium	Express Ship? (UK)	No
Delivers to:	UK	Gift Wrap?	No
Based:	UK		

www.amara.co.uk

This is a lovely home accessories and gift website with some quite unusual products, such as the deliciously scented and beautifully packaged Gianna Rose Atelier soaps (robin's egg soaps in a porcelain dish, and ducks in a gift box are just two), Millefiori candles, Mulberry Home, de Le Cuona throws and shawls, Missoni tableware and lots of other ideas.

Prices:	Medium	Express Ship? (UK)	Yes
Delivers to:	Worldwide	Gift Wrap?	Yes
Based:	UK		

www.bodieandfou.com

The Bodie and Fou collection of European designer home accessories includes stylish, unique interior decor, kitchenware, lighting, babywear and gifts plus chic French homewares, luxurious bodycare and scented candles from Cote Bastide, Normann Copenhagen, Kathleen Hills, Flavia del Pra, MisseMai, Ole Jensen, Paulo Mendes da Rocha, Oromono, Menu and many more.

Prices:	Medium	Express Ship? (UK)	Yes
Delivers to:	Worldwide	Gift Wrap?	No
Based:	UK		

www.bombayduck.co.uk

This is a pretty home gifts and interiors website with a wide range of ideas, from their own beautifully packaged candles to candy coloured leather accessories, crystal glass chandeliers, vintage style bathroom accessories and printed cushions. There's a wealth of gift suggestions, some expensive – their gorgeous vintage-style chandelier at £275 – and others extremely reasonable. They also have a special Christmas area which you can browse in season.

Prices:	Luxury/Medium	Express Ship? (UK)	Yes
Delivers to:	Worldwide	Gift Wrap?	No
Based:	UK		

www.brissi.co.uk

Brissi began life as an interiors store in Marlborough, Wiltshire and has now grown up to have two stores in London plus an excellent online shopping facility. Although many of the products on offer have a retro feel the overall mood is chic and modern with beautifully clear photography and mainly neutral colours. The range includes crystal perfume bottles, black and white Limoges tableware and classic glass.

Prices:	Luxury/Medium	Express Ship? (UK)	Yes
Delivers to:	Worldwide	Gift Wrap?	No
Based:	UK		

www.casacopenhagen.com

Danish designer Theresa Bastrup Hasman has brought together a beautiful collection of cushions and soft furnishings grouped into categories with names such as Moroccan Nights, Indian Fairy Tales and Paisley Flowers. There's also a small section for children and they offer a bespoke service as well. Everything is made especially for you so you need to allow four weeks for delivery.

Prices:	Luxury/Medium	Express Ship? (UK)	No
Delivers to:	Worldwide	Gift Wrap?	No
Based:	UK		

www.coffeeandcream.co.uk

This is a beautifully calm website to visit, offering attractively photographed and unusual home accessories and a collection you won't find anywhere else. There are (at time of writing) scented candles, faux-fur throws, smoky glasses, almond-coloured velvet quilts, black ceramic canisters and pale French Provençal cushions. For anyone who likes natural colours and five-star chic in their home, this is the place to find it.

Prices:	Luxury/Medium	Express Ship? (UK)	No
Delivers to:	Worldwide	Gift Wrap?	Automatic
Based:	UK		

www.davidlinley.com

As you would expect, this is a really beautiful website offering you the opportunity to buy David Linley-designed accessories online including frames, vases, lamps, candlesticks, home fragrance, jewellery boxes and cushions. Everything is beautifully photographed and there are some gorgeous gift ideas here – just receiving one of his dark blue boxes makes you feel special straight away. Prices start at about £55 for his keyrings and head off upwards steeply.

Prices:	Luxury	Express Ship? (UK)	Yes
Delivers to:	Worldwide	Gift Wrap?	No, but packaging is lovely
Based:	UK		

www.decorativecountryliving.com

Decorative Country Living offers an excellent mix of antique, vintage and new items for the home and garden. The minute you arrive at this website you know you're in for a treat. From the pretty table lamps to timeless sofas and the antique collection which you can order online, everything is beautifully photographed and a treat to browse.

Prices:	Luxury	Based:	UK
Delivers to:	UK online and call for overseas deliveries	Express Ship? (UK)	No
		Gift Wrap?	No

www.dutchbydesign.com

Here you'll discover beautiful, modern home accessories from designers that Dutch by Design believe could become the interior design classics for tomorrow. Simplicity, clarity and often a sense of humour are the hallmarks of what they offer and the range includes mirrors, clocks, vases, throws and attractive lighting plus some very good gift ideas.

Prices:	Medium	Express Ship? (UK)	No
Delivers to:	Worldwide	Gift Wrap?	No
Based:	UK		

www.georgjensen.co.uk

Danish jewellery and silversmith Georg Jensen has always stood for a refined, timeless and elegantly simple design. He is considered to be one of the most influential silversmiths of the past century and part of the collection of jewellery, cutlery, home accessories and gifts (such as candlesticks and barware) can be ordered online.

Prices:	Medium	Express Ship? (UK)	No
Delivers to:	UK this site	Gift Wrap?	No, but packaging is lovely
Based:	UK		

www.grahamandgreen.co.uk

Graham & Green is a long-established retailer of home and lifestyle products including candles, tableware, silk cushions, pretty etched glasses and duvet covers and quilts. They're quite hard to really categorise as the products are so widespread, but if I tell you that some of their best-sellers are bevelled mirrors, Chinese lanterns, lavender scented bags and Penguin (as in the book) mugs, you'll probably get the idea.

Prices:	Medium	Express Ship? (UK)	Yes
Delivers to:	UK	Gift Wrap?	No
Based:	UK		

www.lavenderandsage.co.uk

Lavender & Sage offers a range of beautiful and well-made home accessories. Browse through this prettily designed website to find items such as embroidered cushions and organdie curtains, French tableware and 'Grand Hotel' luxury towels, traditional bed linen and unusual lanterns. You'll also discover the Senteurs du Sud home fragrance ranges.

Prices:	Medium	Express Ship? (UK)	No
Delivers to:	Worldwide	Gift Wrap?	No
Based:	UK		

www.lyttonandlily.co.uk

This is another wonderful home accessories website where there's so much to see you almost don't know where to start. For the kitchen there's colourful enamelware, Cath Kidston china and bistro cutlery. For the bathroom, Comptoire Grande towels and Branche d'Olive toiletries, and Monsoon Home and Comptoir bed linens and throws for the bedroom. Whilst there are candles, clocks and mirrors for your living room.

Prices:	Luxury/Medium	Based:	UK
Delivers to:	Worldwide, but you need to call or email	Express Ship? (UK)	Yes
		Gift Wrap?	No

www.ninacampbell.com

As you would expect, the website of interior designer Nina Campbell is beautifully designed. On it you can choose from a range of her home accessories, including glassware, linens, patterned lambswool throws, small items such as match strikers and pretty bonbon bowls. You can also order her stunningly packaged home-fragrance collection which includes candles and room sprays.

Prices:	Luxury/Medium	Express Ship? (UK)	No
Delivers to:	Worldwide	Gift Wrap?	No
Based:	UK		

www.objects-of-design.com

Here you'll find British designed and made gift and home accessory ideas, with everything either being made in small runs or specially for you. There's the Penguin collection of mugs, Emily Readett-Bayley bookends, wonderful Ferguson's Irish Linen and Phil Atrill crystal stemware and that's just a small selection to give you an idea. You can search by product type or by supplier and create a wish list as you go.

Prices:	Medium	Express Ship? (UK)	Yes
Delivers to:	Worldwide	Gift Wrap?	Yes
Based:	UK		

www.pier.co.uk

Based on the famous US furniture and accessories retailer Pier One Imports, everything here is attractive and well priced and you'll discover lovely gifts and accessories from all over the world. The range is very extensive: you could furnish an entire room in your house with their stylish, modern and traditional furniture or just choose from their wide selection of textiles, glassware and lighting.

Prices:	Medium	Express Ship? (UK)	No
Delivers to:	Worldwide	Gift Wrap?	No
Based:	UK		

www.reallylindabarker.co.uk

Click on any area of this busy website and you'll find a small but prettily edited range of home accessories, from small, stylish pieces of occasional furniture to vases, lamps and more. Everything is designed to work together in a very attractive, light and modern style which is 'reallylindabarker' and all in her chic, natural style. In the 'Living' section there are lamps, mirrors, cushions, clocks and storage ideas for the rest of your home.

Prices:	Medium	Based:	UK
Delivers to:	Worldwide, but phone if delivery is	Express Ship? (UK)	Yes
	for overseas	Gift Wrap?	No

Pots and Crocks

In my family there are three cooks (yes, one of them *is* me) and the amount of equipment we have is devastating, not to mention the number of cookery books. However, my advice here, as one who is far too happy to hand over the cooking duties and rush back to the sanctuary of my computer, is to say buy absolutely the best that you can and it will last for years, don't be tempted by all the latest gadgets you see on TV – they may work, but so, probably, will the one you bought last year. Also be very careful about giving cooking equipment as presents – you will almost certainly be frowned on.

Kitchen Equipment and Accessories

www.conran.com

Conran are famous for their modern, colourful and well-priced furniture and accessories which you can now buy online through their website. Discover their modern take on everything from kitchen accessories, candles and soft furnishings, lighting, clocks and gifts. Oh yes, and you can book your next Conran restaurant meal here as well.

Prices:	Medium/Very Good Value	Express Ship? (UK)	No
Delivers to:	Worldwide	Gift Wrap?	Yes
Based:	UK		

www.cooksknives.co.uk

Essential for any cooking enthusiast is a set of really good-quality sharp knives and you'll find a very good selection here. You can buy individual knives or sets by Global, Henckels, Sabatier, Haiku and Wusthof (and more), professional knife sharpeners and OXO 'good grip' tools. You will pay quite a lot for a really good set of knives and knife block but they will last you for years and be worth every penny.

Prices:	Luxury/Medium	Express Ship? (UK)	No
Delivers to:	EU	Gift Wrap?	No
Based:	UK		

www.cookware.co.uk

A same-day despatch online cook shop offering a wide range of high-quality items, including chopping boards, every kitchen utensil you can think of, pan racks and trolleys and clever storage solutions, plus bar accessories and everything for baking. There's also electrical equipment by Dualit, KitchenAid, Magimix and Krups. A great deal of care has gone into this website with lots of information and clear pictures.

Prices:	Medium	Express Ship? (UK)	Yes
Delivers to:	UK	Gift Wrap?	No
Based:	UK		

www.cucinadirect.co.uk

Here's another excellent retailer offering everything for the kitchen beautifully displayed, including knives, pots and pans, bar tools, glasses and serving dishes, picnic equipment, housekeeping items and a gift selection. You'll also find a small but very high-quality range of electrical appliances, with Dualit toasters and kettles and KitchenAid mixers just a couple of the items you can order to be shipped to anywhere in the world.

Prices:	Medium	Express Ship? (UK)	Yes
Delivers to:	Worldwide	Gift Wrap?	Yes
Based:	UK		

www.diningstore.co.uk

You'll find some quite different products on this website, such as the ZapCap bottle opener, Escali Cibo nutritional scale and CaddyO bottle chiller alongside their designer kitchen and tableware with collections from Eva Solo, Cuisinox Elysee, Le Creuset, Mauviel, Couzon and Jura. This is not the normal kitchen and cookware selection so have a look round, you're certain to discover something very different.

Prices:	Medium	Express Ship? (UK)	No
Delivers to:	Europe	Gift Wrap?	No
Based:	UK		

www.divertimenti.co.uk

This famous London-based cookery equipment site offers over 5000 items, from handpainted tableware – including decorated and coloured pottery from France – to a really comprehensive range of kitchen essentials including knives, boards and bakeware, Italian products such as parmesan graters and ravioli trays, copper bowls and pans and children's baking sets. There's also a wedding gift, knife sharpening and copper retinning service.

Prices:	Medium	Express Ship? (UK)	No
Delivers to:	Worldwide	Gift Wrap?	No
Based:	UK		

www.lakelandlimited.co.uk

You've probably already heard of this marvellous, colourful, fun and innovative kitchen collection. There's a huge range on offer, regularly updated, with something for just about every occasion and every room in the house. You'll find every kind of kitchen utensil plus boards and storage solutions, foils, cleaning products and waste bags and a whole host of other useful and original products.

Prices:	Medium/Very Good Value	Express Ship? (UK)	Yes
Delivers to:	UK	Gift Wrap?	No
Based:	UK		

www.saltandpepper.co.uk

For a really well-designed online cook store that doesn't try to bombard you with products but offers an excellent choice, have a browse here. There are some quite unusual brands alongside selections from the ranges by Nigella Lawson, AGA, Bialetti and Le Creuset and everything from bakeware and kitchen tools to pots, pans and small appliances.

Prices:	Medium	Express Ship? (UK)	No
Delivers to:	UK	Gift Wrap?	No
Based:	UK		

www.thecookingshop.co.uk

There are a lot of kitchen equipment shops online offering you every tool and gadget you can think of but this one is particularly well designed and easy to use. You can select from an excellent range of pots, pans, bakeware and other kitchen equipment plus some unusual tableware including an Eastern dining section with chopsticks, mats, bowls and accessories. They also offer recipe suggestions, household hints and tips and decorative ideas for the table.

Prices:	Medium	Express Ship? (UK)	No
Delivers to:	Worldwide	Gift Wrap?	No
Based:	UK		

www.thecookskitchen.com

A vast selection of products is available on this attractively designed site which promises to despatch just about all of its products to you anywhere in the world. Coffee makers, butchers blocks, knives, recipe books, saucepans and basic kitchenware are just a few of the items available. In their country kitchen department you'll find old-fashioned enamelware, farmhouse crockery and traditional style kettles to sit on your Aga.

Prices:	Medium	Express Ship? (UK)	No
Delivers to:	Worldwide	Gift Wrap?	Yes
Based:	UK		

Fragrant Home

Home fragrance is becoming big business, with everything from scented candles to diffusers and pomanders available from many brands. As one who loves to have her Essence of John Galliano candle by Diptyque to hand at all times (to just smell, not necessarily to light), I can understand totally why as I'm transported instantly into another, beautifully fragranced world.

You'll also find excellent home-fragrance products at some of the online retailers above such as Amara (Seda France, Linari, Lothantique and more), Dot Maison (Millefiori, Designers Guild and Jasper Contran) and The Renovation Store (Elizabeth W and Seda France). Check them out for yourself.

www.ancienneambiance.com

The Ancienne Ambiance concept of antiquity-inspired luxury goods has been designed and developed by Adriana Carlucci, a graduate of the London College of Fashion with a degree in product development. She began by creating a unique collection of six glass-encased candles, each featuring fragrances evocative of an ancient culture together with elegant handcrafted packaging.

Prices:	Medium	Express Ship? (UK)	Yes
Delivers to:	Worldwide	Gift Wrap?	Yes
Based:	UK		

www.cologneandcotton.com

This is a very special retailer offering some unusual and hard-to-find home fragrance, bath and body products and fragrance by Diptyque, Cath Collins, La Compagnie de Provence and Cote Bastide. There are also products by Annick Goutal, Coudray and Rosine. For the bathroom they have lovely fluffy towels and bathrobes and for the bedroom luxurious bed linen and throws.

Prices:	Luxury/Medium	Express Ship? (UK)	Yes
Delivers to:	Worldwide	Gift Wrap?	Yes
Based:	UK		

www.kiarie.co.uk

Kiarie has one of the best ranges of scented candles, by brands such as Geodosis, Kenneth Turner, Manuel Canovas, Creation Mathias, Rigaud and Millefiori – there are literally hundreds to choose from at all price levels and you can also choose your range by price, maker, fragrance, colour and season. Once you've made your selection you can ask them to gift wrap it for you and include a handwritten message.

Prices:	Medium	Express Ship? (UK)	Yes
Delivers to:	Worldwide	Gift Wrap?	Yes
Based:	UK		

www.mycandles.eu

Candle lover that I am, it's always a real joy to come across a new website offering an excellent choice at very reasonable prices. My Candles are based in Zurich, Switzerland and they've gone to a lot of trouble to produce an exceptionally attractive and tempting choice. The fragrances range from Orange and Cinnamon to Royal Rose and Red Grapefruit and there are unusual products (great for gifts) such as soap mobiles and wax medals.

Prices:	Medium/Very Good Value	Express Ship? (UK)	Call them
Delivers to:	EU	Gift Wrap?	No
Based:	Switzerland		

www.naturalmagicuk.com

Unlike almost all conventional candles (which contain paraffin wax and synthetic oils), Natural Magic candles are made from clean, pure vegetable wax, scented with the best quality organic aromatherapy oils. They're also twice the size of the average candle (1kg) with 3 wicks and up to 75 hours of burn time. Each candle has a specific therapeutic task, such as uplifting, inspiring, soothing and de-stressing.

Prices:	Medium	Express Ship? (UK)	Yes
Delivers to:	Worldwide	Gift Wrap?	No
Based:	UK		

www.simplyroses.com

This is a handpicked collection of luxurious rose-inspired products, which includes delicately scented pomanders, the Roses de Jardin vintage rose interior fragrance, beautiful pink Indian incense sticks and the signature pale, pink wax, early summer, rose-scented candle which comes in a black glass votive. Then you can choose from foaming bath oil, prettily packaged soaps, Savon de Marseilles and bath truffles.

Prices:	Medium	Express Ship? (UK)	No
Delivers to:	UK	Gift Wrap?	No
Based:	UK		

www.theluxurycandlecompany.com

Candles are always, to my mind, an excellent gift. They're pampering and lovely to receive and to use, particularly when they're as beautifully packaged as they are here. At The Luxury Candle Company there are fragrances such as geranium, orange, lavender and ylang ylang presented in four sizes of candles from the Piccolo to the Grande and all are reasonably priced.

Prices:	Medium	Express Ship? (UK)	Yes
Delivers to:	UK	Gift Wrap?	Yes
Based:	UK		

www.timothyhan.com

If you haven't already come across these luxurious candles then take a look now. Timothy Han has a small but gorgeous range, including aromatherapy candles with names such as Orange Grapefruit and Clove, Lavender, and Scent of Fig and his unscented candles, which are perfect for entertaining.

Prices:	Luxury/Medium	Express Ship? (UK)	Yes, but call them
Delivers to:	Worldwide	Gift Wrap?	Yes
Based:	UK		

www.truegrace.co.uk

If you want to pamper someone with something small and beautiful and you don't want to spend a fortune you should choose from the gorgeous candles here. All beautifully wrapped and in glass containers, you'll find the 'Never a Dull Day' range in pretty printed boxes with fragrances such as Vine Tomato, Stem Ginger and Hyacinth and 'As it Should Be' the slightly more simply boxed candle in 37 fragrances including Citrus, Cappuccino and Raspberry.

Prices:	Medium	Express Ship? (UK)	No
Delivers to:	Worldwide	Gift Wrap?	No
Based:	UK		

Interior Inspirations

Here you'll find different and specific accessories for your home, from fabric accessories such as rugs, wall hangings, cushions and throws to lighting and accent furniture. For some really beautiful ideas take a look round Black Orchid Interiors for exceptionally stylish, mainly neutral-based living, and Elanbach for wonderful country style. I would live happily ever after surrounded by either.

Fabrics and Accessories

www.atlanticblankets.com

At Atlantic Blankets they quite rightly say that one of the problems is which one to choose. There's everything from the fleece and picnic variety right up to patterned cashmere throws, then there are striped, checks, brights, pastels, boucle and alpaca blankets to choose from plus a pretty nursery selection. This is a great place too if you're looking for a gift as they offer gift vouchers plus cushions, hot water bottle covers and scented candles.

Prices:	Luxury/Medium	Express Ship? (UK)	Yes
Delivers to:	Worldwide	Gift Wrap?	No
Based:	UK		

www.blackorchidinteriors.co.uk

There are beautiful, sophisticated ideas for your home here concentrating on rich and tactile pieces of superb quality. Nearly everything, from the modern to the traditional, is in deep neutral colours with black being the dominant colour in every room whether it's the black lacquer dining furniture, the French black glass chandeliers, or the black upholstered 'Louis' chairs.

Prices:	Luxury	Express Ship? (UK)	No
Delivers to:	Worldwide	Gift Wrap?	No
Based:	UK		

www.elanbach.com

This is a pretty website run by a family business offering lovely traditional Welsh fabrics which they design and print using the latest digital technology. You can buy the fabrics themselves by the metre, have them make up curtains and blinds for you using their online measuring calculator or buy cushions, bags and boxfiles.

Prices:	Medium	Express Ship? (UK)	No
Delivers to:	Worldwide	Gift Wrap?	No
Based:	UK		

www.macculloch-wallis.co.uk

MacCulloch and Wallace have specialised in supplying the fashion trade with trimmings and fabrics since 1902. Now you can order directly from them on their colourful website and choose from a wonderful selection of ribbons, threads and fabrics both for furnishing and dressmaking plus beautiful extras such as silk and velvet roses, feather boas and star sequins. Buy your Christmas ribbons here as well.

Prices:	Luxury/Medium	Express Ship? (UK)	No
Delivers to:	Worldwide	Gift Wrap?	No
Based:	UK		

www.marston-and-langinger.com

With stores in London and New York, Marston and Langinger have the enviable reputation as the market leader in the manufacture of custom-made timber-and-glass conservatories, poolhouses and garden rooms. On their attractive website you can order from their range of furniture, lighting, garden tools, accessories, textiles, and Marston & Langinger's own-label domestic paint.

Prices:	Luxury/Medium	Express Ship? (UK)	No
Delivers to:	Worldwide	Gift Wrap?	No
Based:	UK		

www.pretavivre.com

This is an excellent interiors website offering a bespoke service for curtains where you can order fabric samples, then when you've made your choice use their guide to decide on the heading style and lining and input your measurements. They also offer high-quality tie-backs and posts, fabrics by the metre, blinds, poles, valances, headboards and quilts.

Prices:	Medium/Very Good Value	Express Ship? (UK)	No
Delivers to:	UK	Gift Wrap?	No
Based:	UK		

www.queenshill.com

Queenshill is a family-run business offering a lovely selection of fabrics, wallpapers, gifts and home accessories from brands such as Mulberry, GP and J Baker, Harlequin and Fired Earth. The selection of mouthwatering gift ideas includes Mulberry candles, pot pourri, cushions and throws – including James Brindley's range of faux-fur throws (think leopard, llama, bear and cheetah), cushions and hot-water-bottle covers.

Prices:	Luxury/Medium	Express Ship? (UK)	No
Delivers to:	Worldwide	Gift Wrap?	No
Based:	UK		

www.thelondoncushioncompany.com

Cushions must surely be one the easiest ways of updating the living areas of your home without having to spend a fortune. The London Cushion Company is a new online store with a gorgeous selection from richly coloured Kenzo florals to Union Jacks, children's prints and modern metallics. There's an excellent choice at a wide range of prices so have a browse now. Call for overseas delivery.

Prices:	Luxury/Medium	Express Ship? (UK)	Yes
Delivers to:	Worldwide	Gift Wrap?	No
Based:	UK		

www.vvrouleaux.com

This famous ribbon and trimmings emporium based in Marylebone Lane, London, is now online. Click through to the product section of their website to choose from grosgrain, organdie, wire edged, velvet and gingham ribbons plus beaded strands feathers and much more. There's so much here that you'd be well advised to have a good idea of what you're looking for before you start or you may well get lost.

Prices:	Luxury/Medium	Express Ship? (UK)	No
Delivers to:	Worldwide	Gift Wrap?	No
Based:	UK		

Lighting

www.ascolights.co.uk

So you're looking for a new lamp for your recently decorated living room? Or do you have a friend who's getting married and you want to give her something other than the tableware and household goods from her wedding list? If either is the case you could take a look at this lighting website where there are lots of mainly contemporary ideas at not unreasonable prices, from modern table and desk lighting to floor standing uplighters.

Prices:	Medium	Express Ship? (UK)	Yes
Delivers to:	UK	Gift Wrap?	No
Based:	UK		

www.besselink.com

For really beautiful lighting stop here. This may well not be the place from which you're going to replace all your lighting in your home but it's one where you'll find some really beautiful and unusual ideas. Click through to their ceramics, urns and balusters and in particular their lamps with decorated figures and I think you'll see exactly what I mean. They're not cheap but very, very special and would make excellent presents as well.

Prices:	Luxury/Medium	Express Ship? (UK)	No
Delivers to:	Worldwide	Gift Wrap?	No
Based:	UK		

www.italian-lighting-centre.co.uk

All the lights on this website are designed and manufactured by Italian companies and although you'll be buying from a British company they'll be shipped to you straight from the manufacturer; so if you order a craftsman made light you may well have to wait a few weeks, but it'll be well worth it. You'll find a wide range, from the gorgeous and breathtakingly priced Murano chandeliers to more reasonable and classic floor and table lights.

Prices:	Luxury/Medium	Express Ship? (UK)	No
Delivers to:	Worldwide	Gift Wrap?	No
Based:	UK		

www.jglighting.co.uk

If you're looking for lighting and want something a little unusual and modern then this is your place. The range, which includes everything from fabulous barleytwist arm chandeliers to modern picture lighting (plus fibre optics, downlighters, garden lighting, track lights, spot lights and kids' lighting from flying planes to bugs and dinosaurs) is huge so allow time to have a good look round.

Prices:	Luxury/Medium	Express Ship? (UK)	No
Delivers to:	Worldwide	Gift Wrap?	No
Based:	UK		

Wall Hangings, Rugs and Pictures

www.artrepublic.com

There's a huge range here of well-presented posters and prints by artists such as Matisse, Hockney, Chagalle, Warhol and many, many more. You can search by artist, title or style or just browse through the range until you find something to suit. Delivery is free and they give you the choice, if you want framing, of aluminium or wood frames. There's also comprehensive information on exhibitions all over the world.

Prices:	Medium	Express Ship? (UK)	No
Delivers to:	Worldwide	Gift Wrap?	No
Based:	UK		

www.haywoods-tapestries.com

There's a lovely selection here of not overpriced tapestries and wall hangings which you can order mainly from stock and which are available in a choice of sizes. This collection of tapestries is reproduced from originals dating back to medieval times, many of which are now on display in famous museums throughout the world. You can expect to receive your delivery within 14 days and they welcome overseas enquiries.

Prices:	Luxury/Medium	Express Ship? (UK)	No
Delivers to:	Worldwide	Gift Wrap?	No
Based:	UK		

www.postershop.co.uk

Choose from their selection of lithographics by artists such as Bacon, Bracque and Miro, Art prints and posters by Kandinsky, Delaunay or Cocteau, plus a huge range of etchings and screen prints. There are also some particularly good sport prints including sailing ships, surfing and fishing. Once you've chosen your poster or print you have the option of taking it to the virtual framing studio or just sending it straight to your shopping cart.

Prices:	Medium	Express Ship? (UK)	No
Delivers to:	Worldwide	Gift Wrap?	No
Based:	UK		

www.rugsdirect.co.uk

A rug can add so much atmosphere to a room, so if you haven't inherited a few from your great grandmother you can choose from the very good selection on this website, from traditional patterned rugs (think Chinese or Turkish in deep dark rich colours) to extremely modern designs, such as animal prints and abstracts.

Prices:	Luxury/Medium	Express Ship? (UK)	Yes
Delivers to:	Worldwide	Gift Wrap?	No
Based:	UK		

www.worldgallery.co.uk

World Gallery have a huge, easily searchable, interactive database and deliver prints, posters and frames worldwide. Choose from the selection by artist, subject and style; such as classic, contemporary, modern or impressionist. Once you've decided on your picture you can select your mount and frame online and see exactly what the finished product will look like. This is a really excellent website – try it and you'll see.

Prices:	Medium/Very Good Value	Express Ship? (UK)	No
Delivers to:	Worldwide	Gift Wrap?	No
Based:	UK		

Storage Solutions

Here are a few suggestions where you'll find something in which to keep tidy everything in your house, from CDs to magazines to clothes. The fact that this may be totally aspirational on your part and no one else will indulge your tidy fantasies is a problem that you, like me, will have to put up with. There's always hope, of course.

www.aplaceforeverything.co.uk

I'm one of those people who always feels more relaxed when everything's tidy and in its proper place (not that my family help me in this) and if you're anything like me you'll enjoy having a browse round here where you can find innovative ideas to keep everything tidy (hah!). Anyway, no more of that, there are attractive, useful and helpful items here from wicker baskets and magazine racks to cuboid CD racks, shelves and side tables.

Prices:	Medium	Express Ship? (UK)	No
Delivers to:	UK	Gift Wrap?	No
Based:	UK		

www.originalbooks.net

So you're one of those people who like to keep their papers, CDs and even the TV remote control tidied up and elegantly stored – this is the place for you. You'll find every kind of storage covered in what looks like antique embossed leather but which is actually a special resin. They offer booksafes, box files and journals, drinks accessories, photo frames and much more and they'll deliver worldwide.

Prices:	Medium	Express Ship? (UK)	No
Delivers to:	Worldwide	Gift Wrap?	No
Based:	UK		

www.theholdingcompany.co.uk

If you've suddenly decided that it's time you went for the tidy, well-organised look you'll need this website, where you'll find every type of storage for the home, including, for the bathroom, laundry baskets, hooks, trolleys, corner shelves and shaving mirrors (not storage but hey). Chic and clever storage for everywhere you can think of, in fact.

Prices:	Medium	Express Ship? (UK)	No
Delivers to:	UK	Gift Wrap?	No
Based:	UK		

Gardeners' Paradise

Here you can find just about everything for your garden from an exceptional selection of barbeques to perfect garden furniture, tools and equipment, and on to trees, plants and seeds. On a fine day, wandering round your nearest really good garden centre can be a very pleasant past-time; however, if it just happens to rain on the day you've chosen or you really can't spare the time, then pour yourself a cuppa, relax and have a good look round online.

Equipment, Furniture and Barbeques

www.alfrescolivingonline.co.uk

Alfresco Living offers an extensive range of garden furniture to suit most styles and budgets, which includes bistro, aluminium, contemporary and hardwood furniture and Australian barbeques by Outback, Leisuregrow, Beefeater and Lifestyle. There are garden benches, parasols and patio heaters here as well plus some very good discounts.

Prices:	Luxury/Medium/Very Good Value	Express Ship? (UK)	Some items
Delivers to:	UK, mostly included in price	Gift Wrap?	No
Based:	UK		

www.birstall.co.uk

Here you can buy just about everything for the garden and gardening enthusiast, from seeds to recliners, barbeques to poultry houses and swimming pool lighting, high-quality secateurs, brass watering cans and Leatherman knives. There are so many products bursting out from the site that it looks a bit confusing but it's well worth the effort.

Prices:	Medium	Express Ship? (UK)	No
Delivers to:	Worldwide	Gift Wrap?	No
Based:	UK		

www.dobbies.co.uk

At Dobbies you'll find everything you need for your garden, from Weber and The Australian Barbeque Company barbeques, garden furniture from the highest quality teak to well-priced garden sets and equipment from pond pumps to propagators. There's also an excellent range of gifts plus Christmas trees, lights and ornaments. Whatever you're looking for for your garden you're almost bound to find it here.

Prices:	Medium	Express Ship? (UK)	Yes
Delivers to:	Worldwide	Gift Wrap?	No
Based:	UK		

www.flamingbarbeques.co.uk

Flaming Barbeques offer everything from a wide range of gas, charcoal and portable barbeques by Outback, BillyOh, Big K, Landman, Weber, Beefeater and Sunshine to outdoor heating, smokers and all you could need in the way of accessories. You can buy barbeques at all price levels here, read their recommendations and find some very good discounts and ends of lines as well.

Prices:	Luxury/Medium/Very Good Value	Express Ship? (UK)	No
Delivers to:	UK	Gift Wrap?	No
Based:	UK		

www.gardencentredirect.co.uk

This is another of those extremely comprehensive garden websites where there's a wide choice from garden sheds, summer houses and log cabins to wheelbarrows, ladders and pruners, trimmers, shredders and brushcutters. You can enlarge everything to see it really clearly and they have a lot of special deals.

Prices:	Medium	Express Ship? (UK)	No
Delivers to:	UK	Gift Wrap?	No
Based:	UK		

www.greenfingers.com

Calling themselves the Garden Superstore and with good reason, Greenfingers has a well laid-out website that's easy to use as all the departments are very clearly listed on the Home Page. So you can choose from Garden Furniture, Water Butts, Plant Care, Barbeques, Garden Lighting, Pots and Planters (and much more) and be taken to exactly what you're looking for.

Prices:	Medium	Express Ship? (UK)	No
Delivers to:	UK	Gift Wrap?	No
Based:	UK		

www.kitstone.co.uk

Kit Stone offers a small but beautiful range of furniture for your home and garden, including hand-painted chests of drawers, dining sets and workstations. The garden collection includes teak, wrought iron and granite plus café folding tables and chairs and loom chairs. Buy cushions and parasols here as well.

Prices:	Luxury/Medium	Express Ship? (UK)	No
Delivers to:	UK	Gift Wrap?	No
Based:	UK		

www.thecountrygardener.co.uk

Calling themselves 'the online emporium for country gardeners', here you can find an exceptional selection of tools, planters and accessories, from plant ties and net tunnels to potting benches and planters. Then you can take a look at the furniture which includes Lloyd Loom loungers and tree seats and there's a small selection of plants and seeds. Everything is extremely well described and easy to see.

Prices:	Luxury/Medium	Express Ship? (UK)	No
Delivers to:	UK	Gift Wrap?	No
Based:	UK		

Plants and Seeds

www.chilternseeds.co.uk

At Chiltern Seeds you'll find over 4500 species and varieties including a rare and unusual selection, with the majority being available for immediate despatch worldwide. There are old and new annual and perennial flower seeds for beds, borders and rockeries plus exotic and tropical seeds for greenhouse and conservatory, ornamental grasses, giant bamboos and bonsai.

Prices:	Medium	Express Ship? (UK)	No
Delivers to:	Worldwide	Gift Wrap?	No
Based:	UK		

www.crocus.co.uk

Crocus is one of the best gardeners' websites. It offers you not only attractive flowers and plants, giving you more information than most about them but just about everything else you might need for the garden, all presented in a really attractive and informative way. If you want some advice they're just waiting to give it and they'll always have clever ideas for gifts for occasions such as Mother's Day and Easter.

Prices:	Medium	Express Ship? (UK)	Yes
Delivers to:	UK	Gift Wrap?	No
Based:	UK		

www.davidaustin.com

David Austin is famous for developing new types of English Roses, with his first, 'Constance Spry', launched in 1963. On his website you can find many varieties, including Modern Hybrid Tea Roses and Floribundas, Climbing Roses, Ramblers, Modern Shrub Roses and Wild Species Roses. You'll also find his new fragrant English Roses created specially for the home. You can order his gift boxed container roses and exquisite rose bouquets here as well for UK delivery.

Prices:	Luxury/Medium	Based:	UK
Delivers to:	Worldwide except for container roses	Express Ship? (UK)	Yes
	and bouquets	Gift Wrap?	Yes, for container roses

www.duchyofcornwallnursery.co.uk

This is a unique nursery, offering for sale some 4000 varieties of plants, including many rarely available elsewhere, with the majority grown on site. On this extremely attractive website you can download the full product and price list or visit the plant shop, offering a wide range, beautifully photographed and with detailed descriptions.

Prices:	Medium		Express Ship? (UK)	No
Delivers to:	UK		Gift Wrap?	No
Based:	UK			

www.plantconnection.com

Plant Connection offer a very good selection of bedding and young plants together with a specialist range of organic vegetables and herbs. The different plant categories are very clearly displayed and once you click on the area you're interested in you'll fine even more choice. With the excellent range available together with lots of advice you may well find what you're looking for here.

Prices:	Medium		Express Ship? (UK)	No
Delivers to:	UK		Gift Wrap?	No
Based:	UK			

www.suttons.co.uk

Founded in 1806, Suttons is one of the most famous flower and vegetable seed retailers with the exceptional range as you might expect. If you don't have the time to plant from seed you can also order plants here, plus organic vegetable seed, Groweasy mats, seed potatoes, lawn seed and gardening equipment. Allow 7–10 days for delivery.

Prices:	Medium		Express Ship? (UK)	No
Delivers to:	UK		Gift Wrap?	No
Based:	UK			

Gardening Tools and Accessories

www.baileys-home-garden.co.uk

Baileys offer a wonderfully eclectic mix of home and garden accessories, from pretty Welsh blankets and paint buckets to big sinks, garden lighting, Bailey's Bath Soak and Carrot Hand Cream. There are ideas for junior gardeners' gifts from tools, watering cans and buckets (all in a gorgeous cherry red) and vintage style garden forks, pots and twine reels. To order anything on their website you need to phone them – hopefully that will change soon.

Prices:	Medium		Express Ship? (UK)	No
Delivers to:	UK		Gift Wrap?	No
Based:	UK			

www.franceshilary.com

Here the products combine practicality with style and there's quite a selection including well-priced essentials such as dibbers and tags, beautifully made classic tools, gloves, aprons and Le Chameau boots. As well as the adults' range there are some good ideas for encouraging kids to take an interest in the garden, such as ladybird towers and bird tables, growing buckets and colourful tools.

Prices:	Medium	Express Ship? (UK)	No
Delivers to:	Worldwide	Gift Wrap?	Yes
Based:	UK		

www.qualitygardentools.com

So no guessing what this website is about then? Here you'll find exactly what the name suggests. You can order your next Hammerlin wheelbarrow, garden scythe and leafblower online plus hoses and sprinklers, secateurs, pruners, twine and gloves. You're able to view everything within each section together which makes life very easy and although you should always compare prices there are some very good discounts here as well.

Prices:	Medium	Express Ship? (UK)	No
Delivers to:	UK	Gift Wrap?	No
Based:	UK		

www.rkalliston.com

RK Alliston is a garden design business based in London, which has branched out (no pun intended) into a well put-together range of products for both home and garden. The site is well worth having a good look round and includes planters and storage, potting shed essentials, wasp catchers and bird feeders plus natural toiletries.

Prices:	Medium	Express Ship? (UK)	Yes
Delivers to:	Worldwide	Gift Wrap?	No
Based:	UK		

www.treesdirect.co.uk

Fruit and nut trees, ornamentals and aromatic, evergreen bays are just some of the unusual gift ideas you can find here. The trees are chosen for their colour, blossom, shape and size to suit all types of gardens and patios and they arrive dressed in a hessian sack tied with green garden string, planting instructions and handwritten message card. You can request that your tree arrives on a specific date and if you want advice just give them a call.

Prices:	Medium	Express Ship? (UK)	Yes
Delivers to:	Europe	Gift Wrap?	No
Based:	UK		

www.wyevale.co.uk

Wyevale is a leading specialist garden retailer and here you can find everything for enthusiastic gardeners to those who just want to lounge outside and enjoy the sunshine. You'll find plants, flowers, tools and equipment, power tools, furniture and barbeques, making this a superb one-stop shop for your garden. Visit their hire station online as well if you need to hire a major piece of equipment.

Prices:	Medium	Express Ship? (UK)	Yes
Delivers to:	Europe	Gift Wrap?	No
Based:	UK		

Flower Shop

It's now so easy to order flowers online from a vast selection of websites including department stores such as Marks and Spencer and John Lewis, select the type of flowers you want to send and then include chocolates and champagne, that there's never been an easier way to say 'happy Mother's Day', 'thank you', 'congratulations' and 'happy anniversary'.

Here are some of my favourite florists with attractive websites to browse round and a beautiful selection to choose from. You can call any of them if you want something different.

www.bloom.uk.com

If you're fed up of throwing out dead flowers and having to spend real money to replace them then take a look at this website, offering the new generation of silk flowers online. They are incredibly real looking in most cases (you may well have admired some in a friend's house without realising they were silk, I certainly have) and they offer all types of arrangements from Dorset cream roses and cabbages to orchids and seasonal arrangements.

Prices:	Medium	Express Ship? (UK)	Yes
Delivers to:	UK		
Based:	UK		

www.designerflowers.org.uk

At Designer Flowers all the arrangements are created by their own florists and delivered direct by courier in secure boxes to London and the UK. You can also include champagne, Belgian chocolates and soft toys and choose from their selection of special occasion bouquets. Prices are not inexpensive and delivery is extra at £4.50.

Prices:	Luxury/Medium	Express Ship? (UK)	Yes
Delivers to:	UK		
Based:	UK		

www.imogenstone.co.uk

Imogen Stone is an exclusive online florist and luxury gift store, and their flower and plant collection includes hand-tied bouquets, Fairtrade flowers, scented flowers and seasonal plants plus special designs for Valentine's Day, Mother's Day, Easter and Christmas. You can include Rococo Chocolate Truffles, Abahna Toiletries, Nougat and LSA vases with your order.

Prices:	Luxury/Medium	Express Ship? (UK)	Yes
Delivers to:	Worldwide		
Based:	UK		

www.janepackerdelivered.com

Here are the most beautifully presented, reasonably priced modern flowers to send as a gift or if you want to give yourself a treat, to yourself. The range in her stores is much larger than what's offered online, but here you'll find roses, hyacinths, pink parrot tulips, orchids and mixed bouquets all presented in her unique, chic style. You can buy Jane Packer's books, fragranced bath and body gifts, champagne and chocolates and gift vouchers here as well.

Prices:	Luxury/Medium	Express Ship? (UK)	Yes
Delivers to:	UK		
Based:	UK		

www.jwflowers.com

The flowers here are really exquisite, with unusual combinations (such as pale pink hyacinths, white ranunculas and Candy Bianca roses, or burnt orange Adrema tulips with china grass loops and Guelda roses) used to create designs you won't find anywhere else. Their Christmas selection is beautiful as well.

Prices:	Luxury	Express Ship? (UK)	Yes
Delivers to:	UK		
Based:	UK		

www.lambertsflowercompany.co.uk

On this stylishly designed website Lamberts offer a small but cleverly thought out collection of bouquets and arrangements. There are gorgeous new baby gifts, special flowers for Valentine's Day and other occasions plus teddies, chocolates and vases. Lamberts also specialise in wedding flowers, including bouquets, church and reception arrangements and buttonholes plus stylish arrangements for the home.

Prices:	Luxury/Medium	Express Ship? (UK)	No
Delivers to:	UK		
Based:	UK		

www.moysesflowers.co.uk

Since 1876, when Miss Moyses and Mr Stevens started their business, Moyses have been known for the artistry and quality of their floristry. They choose their in-house florists specifically for their originality and capacity to inspire, and create designs that are innovative, stylish and fun. You can order orchids and small plants here too plus elegant handmade glass vases and unusual floral themed gifts.

Prices:	Luxury/Medium	Express Ship? (UK)	Yes, for some bouquets, provided you order early enough
Delivers to:	UK		
Based:	UK		

Also look at the following who you'll find in the wedding flowers section: www.realflowers.co.uk

Pet Store

As the owner of a couple of large dogs I know only too well how marvellous the web can be for everything from delivering huge quantities of dog food to name tags and dog beds. I have to say right now that I'm not a tiny fluffy dog person so you won't find a huge range of diamante collars or tartan jackets here, but a very good choice of all the essentials for just about any normal pet.

www.barkerandball.com

With all the incredibly busy pet supermarkets which you can find online it's a real pleasure to come across one which is slightly different – in this case just for dogs. If you like to spend just that little bit extra and enjoy something a bit different just take a look at their selection of 'nest' beds, colourful dog bowls and toys and doggy gift ideas including fun ID tags. UK delivery is free on orders over £70.

Prices:	Medium	Express Ship? (UK)	Yes, worldwide express delivery
Delivers to:	Worldwide	Gift Wrap?	No
Based:	UK		

www.petplanet.co.uk

This is another excellent pet supermarket and one which I have to admit I've used many times with excellent results. It's a busier website than some, but as long as you immediately click through to the type of animal you're buying for you should be fine. Register with them and they'll store the details of your previous purchases to make it really easy for repeat orders.

Prices:	Medium	Express Ship? (UK)	Yes
Delivers to:	Europe	Gift Wrap?	No
Based:	UK		

www.petspantry.tv

Here you can find one of the best online ranges for dogs, cats, fish and small animals plus wild bird and reptile (!) food and equipment, horse food, supplements and grooming products and lovely animal themed birthday and greeting cards. Also flea sprays and powders, grass seed, rose food, stain and odor removers and everything to get rid of vermin, although I have to say I prefer to leave that to the experts, coward that I am.

Prices:	Medium	Express Ship? (UK)	No
Delivers to:	Worldwide	Gift Wrap?	No
Based:	UK		

Section 8
Eat and Drink

Now that we're all being pushed more and more towards supermarkets for our food and there's a dearth of fresh food merchants on the high street (or at least most of them) the web has truly come into its own. The days when you could wander down the road and come back with produce from your local greengrocer and fishmonger have totally disappeared for most people and it was only a very few years ago that you were forced to buy frozen shellfish at the fishcounter and overpriced organic veg at which ever your 'best' stocked food store was.

Now you can have your freshly caught lobster, cod and skate by next-day delivery, every cut of meat that you could possibly want, totally organically farmed fruit and veg and even fresh, wholesome bread and if you take a look at what's on offer below you'll see that you don't even have to look very far to find it all.

Just one word of advice, check out the delivery costs before you order from too many different retailers. It's best to find a few favourites and order as much as you can at a time, otherwise delivery can stack up and become extremely expensive, outweighing the benefits of ordering from Devon, Cornwall and the Scottish Isles.

Bakery

If you bake your own bread of course you can skip right on past this section but if, like me, you don't, then close your eyes, imagine that smell of freshly baked bread for a second and read on. Just a couple of years ago, pretty much the only bread you could buy online was the sliced variety which you included with your supermarket order. Now that's changed completely and not only is there so much more choice from the major foodstores, but you can order freshly baked bread for special diets, organic bread, Poilane from France, croissants and everything else you might wish for. Keep your eyes open this time, click away and it can all be yours tomorrow plus pretty cupcakes, chocolate brownies, superb fruitcakes and more.

www.artisanbread.co.uk

Artisan Bread mill their own grain, add less salt, no yeast and use only spring water in their biodynamic/organic bread. They offer breads for wheat free, gluten free, dairy free, salt free and many other diets and several unusual types of bread such as deli pumpkin seed, spelt 7 grain and seed, and quinoa bread. If you're looking for bread for any special diet you're more than likely to find it here.

Prices:	Medium	Express Ship? (UK)	No
Delivers to:	UK	Gift Wrap?	No
Based:	UK		

www.bettysbypost.com

Since 1919, Bettys famous Cafe Tea Rooms have been tempting customers with a delicious array of Yorkshire and Continental cakes, biscuits and chocolates, afternoon teas and freshly prepared meals. Choose from celebration cakes, luxury fruit cakes, teatime treats, gift boxes and hampers and teas and coffees selected by sister company Taylors of Harrogate.

Prices:	Medium	Express Ship? (UK)	No
Delivers to:	Worldwide	Gift Wrap?	No
Based:	UK		

www.beverlyhillsbakery.com

If you live outside London don't even think of looking at the full range here, as you'll probably be really disappointed when you realise that they can't deliver to you. Do, however, click through to the selection that they will send to you anywhere in the UK (and overseas, in some cases), which includes their carrot cake, apple and cinnamon cake and pear and ginger cake or one of their attractive gift tins containing delicious mini muffins, cookies and brownies.

Prices:	Medium	Express Ship? (UK)	No
Delivers to:	Worldwide for some items	Gift Wrap?	No
Based:	UK		

www.biscuiteers.com

Give something fun and different the next time you want to say thank you, happy birthday or congratulations and send a gorgeous tin of wonderfully iced biscuits from Biscuiteers. There's the Bootilicious Shoes tin, the Oodles of Poodles tin and the Creepy Crawlies tin, and the biscuits are all as you might imagine. Also buy biscuit cards from them as an alternative to paper ones and choose from Christmas trees, 'Hot Pants,' Flowers, 'Home Sweet Home' and more.

Prices:	Medium	Express Ship? (UK)	No, but call for rush delivery
Delivers to:	UK	Gift Wrap?	Gift tins
Based:	UK		

www.cheesecake.co.uk

There's everything here for cheesecake addicts (and I have one in my house) from Chocolate Toffee Walnut Smash and Raspberry Split to Charlie's Original New York New York double baked and far too many more to list. You can order yours personalised for birthdays and other celebrations, there are special cakes for Valentine's Day and weddings and you can have them pre-sliced too.

Prices:	Medium	Express Ship? (UK)	Yes
Delivers to:	UK	Gift Wrap?	No
Based:	UK		

www.forgoodnesscake.co.uk

The next time you're considering sending flowers to someone as a thank-you gift have a look at this website and you may well be persuaded to send something entirely different. The Classic Box from For Goodness Cake arrives brimming with dainty fairy cakes, prettily packaged in a high-quality, pale blue box and tied with fuchsia ribbon. They make a perfect gift.

Prices:	Medium	Express Ship? (UK)	48 hours if you order by midday
Delivers to:	UK	Gift Wrap?	Packaging is lovely
Based:	UK		

www.jane-asher.co.uk

Click through to Jane Asher's website and her Mail Order cake section and you'll find a choice of about 40 different designs for all sorts of different occasions. You can choose from three sizes of cake and sponge or fruit filling. UK delivery only and you need to allow up to ten days for your cake to arrive.

Prices:	Medium	Express Ship? (UK)	No
Delivers to:	UK	Gift Wrap?	No
Based:	UK		

www.megrivers.com

Meg Rivers has an extremely tempting website offering 'homemade' beautifully decorated cakes, biscuits and traybakes (flapjacks, chocolate brownies and the like). Their traditional fruit cake is extremely good and made well in advance so if you can't be bothered to bake yourself you can shop here. Overseas delivery by request.

Prices:	Medium	Express Ship? (UK)	No
Delivers to:	UK and overseas by request	Gift Wrap?	Yes
Based:	UK		

www.need-a-cake.co.uk

There's a quite amazing selection of cake designs here, from Whinny the Pooh and Tigger to guitar and rugby ball shaped cakes. This is a family run cake company who will send out most of their cakes to you anywhere in the UK. You can order a small selection directly online and if you want something else from their range you need to give them a call.

Prices:	Medium/Very Good Value	Express Ship? (UK)	No, but call for rush orders
Delivers to:	UK	Gift Wrap?	No
Based:	UK		

www.poilane.fr

This is an exceptionally attractivek, famous French bakery which ships to many countries throughout the world. Click on the products on the shelves and drag them to your basket and buy Poilane breads, boxed cookies, bowls, bread knives and more. They'll tell you when they're baking for you and when you should receive delivery, how to store your bread and there are recipes as well. Take a look.

Prices:	Medium	Express Ship? (UK)	No
Delivers to:	Most worldwide	Gift Wrap?	No
Based:	France with UK store		

Also find breads and cakes at:
www.formanandfield.com
www.valvonacrolla.co.uk
www.graigfarm.co.uk

Meat Store

It has to be said that if you want really good meat you are now bound to find more choice, better pricing and higher quality online. Apologies to your favourite neighbourly butcher, but as one who lives out in the country and can find very good, non-supermarket meat at several destinations practically on their doorstep I can tell you unfortunately that it's true, particularly where pricing is concerned. If you browse the websites here for that perfect 10oz sirloin steak you'll see what I'm talking about. The real difference now is the number of butchers you have to choose from, rather than the two or three round the corner – it doesn't matter if your meat is coming to you from deepest Devon or the highlands of Scotland, you can still have it by next-day delivery. Try it and see.

www.aubreyallen.co.uk

This is not the least expensive meat that you can find online but it will almost certainly be some of the highest quality. Aubrey Allen is an award-winning catering butcher offering Aberdeenshire beef, free range poultry and Cornish lamb alongside their venison, game and sausages. You can also order barbecue packs plus chef prepared meals and sauces.

Prices:	Luxury/Medium	Express Ship? (UK)	No
Delivers to:	UK	Gift Wrap?	No
Based:	UK		

www.blackface.co.uk

Heather-bred Blackface lamb, organic lamb, haggis, iron-age pork, oven-ready grouse, partridge and bronze turkeys are all available to order online on this site based in Scotland. Note that deliveries and availability depend on seasonality and you may have to wait for some products. Delivery is free and if you want to order your Christmas turkey from them this year they'll send them out by carrier to you a few days before Christmas.

Prices:	Medium	Express Ship? (UK)	No
Delivers to:	UK	Gift Wrap?	No
Based:	UK		

www.donaldrussell.com

This is a superb website from an excellent butcher, beautifully photographed and laid out and extremely tempting. You can buy just about every type of meat here, from goose and game (in season) to pork, beef and lamb plus natural fish and seafood. Most of the pictures show the products as you'd like them to arrive on your plate and you can either buy from their ready prepared dishes such as Salmon en Croute or Bolognese sauce or you can follow their excellent recipes.

Prices:	Luxury	Express Ship? (UK)	No
Delivers to:	UK	Gift Wrap?	No
Based:	UK		

www.macbeths.com

For a high-quality product, well-designed site and enthusiastic service this online butcher takes a lot of beating. Based in the north of Scotland near Inverness (and yes near to Cawdor Castle in case any of you are up on your Shakespeare) this is a traditional Scottish butcher and game dealer. Order your haggis here for Burn's night and if you're giving a big party call them and ask to speak to Jock who will almost certainly be as helpful to you as he is to us on our visits to the north.

Prices:	Medium	Express Ship? (UK)	Call them
Delivers to:	UK	Gift Wrap?	No
Based:	UK		

www.pampasplains.com

Pampas Plains offers British beef from Aberdeen Angus and Hereford cattle reared in Argentina. Shop for the highest-quality sirloin, ribeye and whole fillet here plus different types and sizes of steaks, ribs, burgers and mince. Then take a look at their Patagonian lamb racks, chorizo sausage and empanadas. They also offer a selection of Argentinian wines. This is a beautifully designed website and a pleasure to browse.

Prices:	Medium	Express Ship? (UK)	Order before mid-day
Delivers to:	UK	Gift Wrap?	No
Based:	UK		

Cheese Larder

Here's a real cheese lover's paradise and although I really couldn't go as far as a cheese wedding cake (which frankly I think is an exceptionally strange idea), the thought of having a selection of mouthwatering cheeses delivered to me on a regular basis is something I can readily identify with. Here we're talking about real cheese from all over the world, nothing like the basic Brie, Camembert, Stilton and Cheddar you can find at your local store (although they are getting much, much better) but a serious range of serious cheeses from the runny, smelly and eat-me-immediately varieties to wonderful, hard-to-find cheeses. Be warned. It's all too easy to spend a fortune.

www.fromages.com

Fromages.com is based as you might expect in France, and delivers its French cheeses to most countries in the world in 24 hours. For a really grown up selection you can choose their Party Cheese Board containing their selection of ten cheeses including some well known and some you'll probably never have heard of. Alternatively you can choose your own.

Prices:	Medium	Express Ship? (UK)	Yes
Delivers to:	Worldwide	Gift Wrap?	No
Based:	France		

www.houseofcheese.co.uk

This is one of those websites you know you're going to enjoy looking round as soon as you arrive at the home page. Not only is it clearly designed and well photographed but the choice on offer, from Farm Red Leicester to Parmegiano Reggiano, Chatel and Pont l'Eveque is very good indeed. There are lots of varieties you'll have heard of here and many that you may well not have so, cheese lovers, prepare to be inspired.

Prices:	Luxury/Medium	Express Ship? (UK)	No
Delivers to:	UK	Gift Wrap?	No
Based:	UK		

www.nealsyarddairy.co.uk

Originally the Neal's Yard Dairy only sold cheeses that it made on the premises. Today the Dairy has two retail shops, supplies other shops and restaurants across the UK and exports to businesses across the world. You can order selections of cheeses under names such as 'Strictly Traditional,' 'Box of Cheddars,' or 'West Country Selection,' whole cheeses, and large pieces of Colston Basset Stilton, Montgomery's Cheddar and Lincolnshire Poacher, among others.

Prices:	Luxury/Medium	Express Ship? (UK)	No
Delivers to:	UK	Gift Wrap?	No
Based:	UK		

www.norbitoncheese.co.uk

Sometimes a website is designed in such a way that you just have to go in and have a browse and I warn you, this is one of those. Whether you're specifically looking for Explorateur from France, Keen's Farmhouse Cheddar, or Irish Cashel Blue, or if you just want to have a look round, you're bound to find a) what you're searching for and b) something else as well. All the cheeses are beautifully photographed and there's a great deal of information: where they're from, how to store them and which wines will go with them.

Prices:	Medium	Express Ship? (UK)	No
Delivers to:	Worldwide	Gift Wrap?	No
Based:	UK		

www.paxtonandwhitfield.co.uk

This famous cheese company has a mouthwatering online shop and offers overnight delivery. You can buy specialty British, French and Italian cheeses here and join the Cheese Society to receive their special selection each month. They also sell biscuits, chutneys and pickles, York ham and patés, beautifully boxed cheese knives and stores, fondue sets and raclette machines.

Prices:	Medium	Express Ship? (UK)	Yes
Delivers to:	Worldwide	Gift Wrap?	No
Based:	UK		

www.thecheesesociety.co.uk

Although you can find other European cheeses here, the vast majority of those on offer are of the specialist, unpasteurised variety, which they source throughout England and France. There are some excellent gift selections, with which they can include a handwritten card with your personal message. If you want to just give them a call, and they'll be delighted to give you advice on choosing old favourites and making new discoveries.

Prices:	Luxury/Medium	Express Ship? (UK)	Yes
Delivers to:	Worldwide	Gift Wrap?	No
Based:	UK		

www.thecheeseworks.co.uk

Cheese shop owner and Masterchef finalist Ben Axford offers some of the UK's finest artisanal cheese, gift boxes, hampers and more from his shop in Cheltenham and online. Expect to find a perfectly chosen range which includes Camembert with Calvados, Langres, Munster and Selles sur Cher alongside Godminster Cheddar and Celtic Promise. You can have your selection gift boxed and sent out on your behalf, and there are chutneys, biscuits and other goodies here as well.

Prices:	Luxury/Medium	Express Ship? (UK)	Yes
Delivers to:	UK	Gift Wrap?	Yes
Based:	UK		

Seafood Special

There's a superb range of fish available online here from cod and halibut to lobster and scallops. Don't expect all the websites themselves to be beautiful; some of them are and others are not – they're fishmongers, after all. Do, however, expect wonderful quality, and now that your local high street fishmonger is a thing of the past they are the best places to buy fish. Yes of course you can go to your local supermarket counter (and some of what they offer is good) but most of what you buy will have been frozen first. For fish virtually straight out of the sea buy here.

www.andyrace.co.uk

Rick Stein accredited Andy Race offers undyed, organic, peat smoked salmon, kippers and smokies to hake, mackerel, sole and more. He also has hot smoked langoustines, mussels and oysters and taster packs of the most popular products so although you can't exactly 'try before you buy' you don't have to invest too heavily to start with.

Prices:	Medium	Express Ship? (UK)	No
Delivers to:	UK	Gift Wrap?	No
Based:	UK		

www.deadfreshfish.co.uk

Choose how you like to have your fish prepared, by this family fishmonger who buys most of their fish from Brixham in Devon, whether you prefer it scaled, trimmed and/or filleted. Fish on offer depends on the season but includes cod, brill, monkfish and John Dory and shellfish such as Canadian lobster, crab and mussels. This is not the prettiest of websites but after all it's the fish that counts, isn't it?

Prices:	Medium	Express Ship? (UK)	No
Delivers to:	UK	Gift Wrap?	No
Based:	UK		

www.fishworks.co.uk

From their premises in Brixham, Fishworks buy from fishermen in Dartmouth, Scotland, the East Coast, France, Italy (and as far away as the Maldives for fresh tuna), which means that you have access to one of the widest ranges of fish and shellfish available in the UK. You can choose from shellfish such as wild caught white prawns and Pallourde Clams, fresh fish from Brixham, Lemon Sole to Gilthead Bream and loads in between.

Prices:	Medium	Express Ship? (UK)	Yes
Delivers to:	UK	Gift Wrap?	No
Based:	UK		

www.foweyfish.com

Fowey fish are retail and wholesale fishmongers. Fresh supplies come into their shop every day and they operate a nationwide mail order service for fresh fish, shellfish and some specialist fine wines including the much sought after and hard to find Cloudy Bay. They despatch four days a week, Monday to Thursdays, for next-day delivery all over the UK. This is a simply designed website but you know that the fish will be fresh and there's an excellent choice.

Prices:	Medium	Express Ship? (UK)	No
Delivers to:	UK	Gift Wrap?	No
Based:	UK		

www.gallowaysmokehouse.co.uk

Nestling on the banks of Wigtown Bay is the Galloway Smokehouse, home of prize-winning smoked salmon, trout, seafood and game all waiting for you to order online. From the simple kipper to the grand salmon a huge variety of smoked food is on offer and both hot and cold smoked foods are available as well such as kippers, smoked mackerel and even smoked cheese.

Prices:	Medium	Express Ship? (UK)	Yes
Delivers to:	Worldwide	Gift Wrap?	No
Based:	UK		

www.lochfyne.com

You may well have eaten in one of their chain of seafood restaurants which are excellent and not overpriced but you may not know that you can buy a selection of their goods online from their beautifully laid out and photographed website. They offer fresh and smoked trout and salmon, oysters, mussels and langoustine plus Glen Fyne beef, pork, lamb and venison and lots of other goodies such as patés and gift boxes.

Prices:	Luxury/Medium	Express Ship? (UK)	No
Delivers to:	EU	Gift Wrap?	No
Based:	UK		

www.skye-seafood.co.uk

Isle of Skye Smokehouse is a small, dedicated producer, supplying traditionally smoked fish to some of the finest hotels in Scotland and now they're happy to sell to you directly online. If you didn't know it already, smoked Scottish wild salmon is completely different to the farmed variety. Once you've tried wild salmon you'll probably never look back, although it frequently costs at least twice as much.

Prices:	Luxury/Medium	Express Ship? (UK)	Yes
Delivers to:	Worldwide	Gift Wrap?	No
Based:	UK		

www.smokedsalmon.co.uk

At the Inverawe Smokehouse you'll find classic smoked salmon and trout, smoked Wild Atlantic salmon, gifts, hampers and gourmet boxes. In their deli section they offer smoked patés, cod's roe and salmon and lumpfish caviar. As well as the above, hiding in the 'Larder' section, you'll find beef and pies, shortbread and fruit cakes, pickles, chutneys and jellies and cheeses.

Prices:	Luxury/Medium	Express Ship? (UK)	Yes
Delivers to:	EU	Gift Wrap?	No
Based:	UK		

www.summerislesfoods.com

Established in 1977 and based in Achiltibuie near Ullapool, this is a small family smokehouse producing an extensive range of smoked salmon and smoked fish products as well as smoked meats, herring marinades and Scottish cheeses. You can order whisky, peat, sweet cured and hot roast smoked salmon here plus select from their extensive organic range and buy your organic Crowdie and Isle of Mull cheddar here too.

Prices:	Luxury/Medium	Express Ship? (UK)	No
Delivers to:	EU	Gift Wrap?	No
Based:	UK		

www.thefishsociety.co.uk

Here you can choose from over 200 kinds of fish and seafood, all of which will be delivered frozen. There's everything from organic salmon to Dover sole, turbot and tuna plus wild smoked salmon, gigantic prawns and dived scallops. They also have a range of fish recipe books and accessories such as fish kettles and claw crackers. Deliveries are twice a week on Wednesday and Friday, delivery is £5 on orders from £65–£100 and free after that.

Prices:	Medium	Express Ship? (UK)	No
Delivers to:	UK	Gift Wrap?	No
Based:	UK		

Gorgeous Gourmets

This is the place to find those gourmet treats that can make such a difference to a special occasion, from caviar and cured hams to salamis, terrines and other delicacies. You can find excellent cheeses here as well as in the cheese section, truffles, truffle oils and more. Choose your favourite foodie retailer and order as much as possible from the same place to avoid paying too much postage.

www.caspiancaviar.co.uk

If caviar is something that you really enjoy but you can't buy the real thing where you live then take a look at this website which offers Beluga, Oscietre and Sevruga caviar right up to 500g tins although thankfully, bearing in mind the price, you can also order their 50g tins. To go with your caviar celebration you can buy crystal caviar bowls, vodka shot glasses, horn spoons, vodka and blinis.

Prices:	Luxury	Express Ship? (UK)	Yes
Delivers to:	EU	Gift Wrap?	No
Based:	UK		

www.dukeshillham.co.uk

Dukeshill was founded over 20 years ago with the aim of producing the very best hams, cured the 'old fashioned' way (where flavour and texture are more important than speed or yield). Today you can also buy bacon and other cured meats, fish terrines and smoked salmon, regional cheeses, condiments, preserves and mouthwatering looking cakes. Once you've ordered your ham you'll no doubt be tempted by the rest – I certainly was.

Prices:	Medium	Express Ship? (UK)	Yes
Delivers to:	UK	Gift Wrap?	No
Based:	UK		

www.efoodies.co.uk

This is an extremely tempting website where you can order the highest quality olive oil and balsamic vinegar, British and French cheese, caviar, foie gras, black and white truffles and truffle oil, spices, mushrooms and champagne. Everything is beautifully photographed with lots of information about every product – where it comes from and what makes it special. The prices here are good, particularly when you consider the quality of what you're buying.

Prices:	Luxury/Medium	Express Ship? (UK)	Yes
Delivers to:	UK	Gift Wrap?	No
Based:	UK		

www.formanandfield.com

Forman & Field is a luxury delicatessen specialising in traditional British produce from small independent producers. There's a delicious selection of luxury cakes and puddings, smoked salmon, ham and cheeses all beautifully photographed and extremely hard to resist. Don't miss their homemade, award-winning fish patés and pies, perfect for the next time you're entertaining. They offer speedy delivery to UK, Ireland and the Channel Isles

Prices:	Luxury/Medium	Express Ship? (UK)	Yes
Delivers to:	UK	Gift Wrap?	No
Based:	UK		

www.mortimerandbennett.co.uk

This online deli is crammed full of speciality foods from around the world, many of which are exclusive to them. You'll find an extensive range of cheeses, breads, oil and charcuterie, as well as a selection of fun foodie gifts such as the La Maison du Miel honey, Italian flower jellies and gold and silver buttons. There's also panettone from Turin, extra virgin olive oil from New Zealand and biscuits from Sardinia – lots to choose from and all easy to see.

Prices:	Luxury/Medium	Express Ship? (UK)	Yes
Delivers to:	UK	Gift Wrap?	No
Based:	UK		

www.valvonacrolla-online.co.uk

Valvona & Crolla is an independent family business based in Edinburgh, specialising in gourmet Italian products plus their excellent range of good value, quality Italian wines from artisan producers and progressive co-operatives. In their wonderful deli you'll find a wide choice, including well-priced and high-quality prosciutto and pancetta, cheeses, smoked salmon and all your larder essentials.

Prices:	Luxury/Medium	Express Ship? (UK)	Yes
Delivers to:	UK	Gift Wrap?	No
Based:	UK		

The World of Food

Here's a selection of foods and ingredients from around the world, from countries such as Italy, Spain, France, Japan and India. Some are based here in the UK and others offer you speedy delivery from abroad and whether you're preparing for your next pasta or paella party, sushi dinner or Indian feast, you should find everything you need here.

www.carluccios.com

You may have been lucky enough to eat in one of his restaurants or to receive some of wonderful regional Italian delicacies as a gift. Even if you haven't done either of the above you can now buy from Antonio Carluccio's attractively presented range online which includes pasta, olive oil, antipasti and confectionery. Everything is packaged beautifully with lots of information about where the product originated and what you can use it for.

Prices:	Luxury/Medium	Express Ship? (UK)	No
Delivers to:	UK	Gift Wrap?	No
Based:	UK		

www.delinostrum.com

This is an extremely attractive website vased in Barcelona, offering Spanish foods online, 24-hour delivery within Spain and 3-day delivery elsewhere in Europe. You can buy everything you would expect here, from olive oils and vinegars, Iberico and Serrano ham to specialist cheeses and Catalan sparkling wine.

Prices:	Medium	Express Ship? (UK)	No
Delivers to:	EU	Gift Wrap?	No
Based:	Spain		

www.frenchgourmetstore.com

Here you'll discover a marvellous choice of regional gourmet products from France all prepared according to traditional recipes and including mushrooms and truffles, mustards, oils and vinegars and gorgeous chocolates. They also have a small but excellent range of hampers and gift baskets. They're actually based in the UK, will ship to you anywhere in the world and offer an express service.

Prices:	Luxury/Medium	Express Ship? (UK)	Yes
Delivers to:	Worldwide	Gift Wrap?	No
Based:	France		

www.gusti.co.uk

Calling themselves 'Your Online Mediterranean Delicatessen Store' should give you some idea of what you'll discover here. The products on offer all look wonderful, from the stuffed chillies in olive oil and Bresaola to the black truffle oil and jars of Bagna Cauda. This is a great place to shop if you enjoy Mediterranean cooking and there are enough ideas to create an excellent choice of antipasti for your next dinner party with no effort at all.

Prices:	Medium	Express Ship? (UK)	Yes
Delivers to:	UK	Gift Wrap?	No
Based:	UK		

www.iberianfoods.co.uk

If you like Spanish cuisine this is a great website to have a look around, offering a good choice of products from Spain such as Serrano Ham, Chorizo and other cured meats and fish, herbs and spices and Spanish cheese. You can also shop from their range of Tapas, and paella dishes, cookers and ingredients, there's a lot of information on where to find good Spanish restaurants in the UK and a Spanish food glossary.

Prices:	Medium	Express Ship? (UK)	No
Delivers to:	UK	Gift Wrap?	No
Based:	Spain		

www.okinami.com

Okinami is based in Brighton and stocks an extensive range of Japanese products, from cooking ingredients to kitchen utensils. Online you can buy a wide range of Japanese ceramics, sushi ingredients and cookery books. They also stock martial arts books although I suspect that *Advanced Shokotan Karate* will not be my next bedtime reading.

Prices:	Medium	Express Ship? (UK)	Depends on the day you order
Delivers to:	UK and USA	Gift Wrap?	No
Based:	UK		

www.savoria.com

Savoria is an online retailer run by obviously passionate 'foodies' offering you the very best from all over Italy, including cheese, meat, pasta, olive oil and antipasti. There's lots of friendly information about each product and which part of the country it comes from plus suggestions for use. Delivery comes to you direct from Italy – orders placed by Sunday night are delivered by the end of the following week. They'll deliver to most EU countries.

Prices:	Luxury/Medium	Express Ship? (UK)	No
Delivers to:	EU	Gift Wrap?	No
Based:	UK		

www.spicesofindia.co.uk

Everything you'd expect is here for great Indian cooking including an excellent choice of (well-photographed) pulses and lentils, pickles and chutneys, appetisers, drinks and beverages. They also offer kitchen and tableware such as balti dishes and pickle servers plus gift baskets such as The Pickle Basket and the Deluxe Indian Spice Basket. One of the great things about this website is the amount of information, plus their constantly updated recipe section.

Prices:	Medium	Express Ship? (UK)	No
Delivers to:	Worldwide	Gift Wrap?	No
Based:	UK		

www.steenbergs.co.uk

This is an attractive website offering a wide choice of organic salts and peppers, herbs and spices sourced directly from the producers, from succulent vanilla to the heady Herbs de Provence. Steenbergs were the first company offering Fairtrade spices in the UK and you can find their new organic Fairtrade vanilla extract and home baking range here as well as Peace (black) and green tea.

Prices:	Medium	Express Ship? (UK)	Yes
Delivers to:	Worldwide	Gift Wrap?	No
Based:	UK		

www.vallebona.co.uk

At Sardinian gourmet store Vallebona you'll find unusual cheeses such as saffron and peppercorn Pecorino and Robiola, wild boar prosciutto and pancetta, antipasti, confectionary, oils and vinegars and much more. There's a selection of Italian wines on offer and hampers with names such as The Italian Job and Tuscan Treat (or you can create your own). This is a great place for anyone who appreciates real Italian food.

Prices:	Luxury/Medium	Express Ship? (UK)	No
Delivers to:	UK	Gift Wrap?	No
Based:	UK		

Organic Everything

If you had any doubts before from looking over the less than wonderful quality, overpriced organic fruit and veg at your local supermarket then what you'll find here will surely change your mind. How 'organic' you go is of course totally up to you, particularly with the choice available online which includes everything from vegetables, meat, seafood, cheese and bakery goods. Some of these look so good that you'll be ordering without thinking that you're eating more naturally. With the organic age now definitely upon us, ordering like this must be the way forward.

www.abel-cole.co.uk

Abel & Cole deliver delicious boxes of fresh organic fruit and veg, organic meat, sustainably sourced fish and loads of other ethically produced foods, buying as much as possible from UK farms. They offer regular selection boxes of fresh produce, and providing you live in the

South of England then you can order all of their other food and drink too, including locally baked bread.

Prices:	Medium	Express Ship? (UK)	No
Delivers to:	UK	Gift Wrap?	No
Based:	UK		

www.rodandbens.com

Rod and Ben's, just in case you're wondering, is run by the team of Rodney Hall and Ben Moseley and offers you the opportunity of buying into their box schemes of organic fruit and veg from their Soil Association certified farm. There are several sizes of box available for delivery each week and they also produce a range of seasonal organic soups.

Prices:	Medium	Express Ship? (UK)	No
Delivers to:	UK	Gift Wrap?	No
Based:	UK		

www.daylesfordorganic.com

As one of the best known of the organic food suppliers you may well already have heard of Daylesford and they certainly have one of the most attractive websites, organic or otherwise. There's an excellent range of fresh, seasonal organic foods here, including vegetables from their kitchen gardens, award-winning handmade cheeses, breads and cakes from their bakery and fresh meat from their organic estate in Staffordshire.

Prices:	Medium	Express Ship? (UK)	Yes
Delivers to:	UK	Gift Wrap?	No
Based:	UK		

www.eversfieldorganic.co.uk

Eversfield Organic is an 850-acre organic farm nestling deep in the heart of the West Devon countryside and farmed to the highest Soil Association standards. Aberdeen Angus Beef, Romney Marsh sheep and Large Black pigs are prepared in the traditional manner by their professional butchers, guaranteeing extremely tasty and tender cuts of meat.

Prices:	Medium	Express Ship? (UK)	No
Delivers to:	UK	Gift Wrap?	No
Based:	UK		

www.goodnessdirect.co.uk

There's really a vast range here with 3000+ health foods, vitamins and items selected for those with special dietary needs. You can search for foods that are dairy free, gluten free, wheat free, yeast free and low fat, plus organic fruit, vegetables (in a selection of boxed choices), fish and meat. You'll also find frozen and chilled foods so you can do your complete shopping here.

Prices:	Medium	Express Ship? (UK)	No
Delivers to:	UK	Gift Wrap?	No
Based:	UK		

www.graigfarm.co.uk

Graig Farm Organics is an award-winning pioneer of organic meats and other organic foods in the UK. The range is very extensive and includes meat (organic beef, lamb, mutton, pork, chicken and turkey, as well as local game and goat meat) ready meals, fish, baby food, dairy, bread, groceries, vegetables and fruit, soups and salads, alcoholic drinks, a gluten-free range, and even pet food, plus herbal remedies and essential oils.

Prices:	Medium	Express Ship? (UK)	No
Delivers to:	UK	Gift Wrap?	No
Based:	UK		

www.organicsmokehouse.com

The award-winning organic smokehouse uses centuries-old traditions to give greater depth of flavour to their products, and all the smoking is carried out without any mechanical intervention. As one of Rick Stein's 'Food Heroes' and a Gold winner in several of the Great Taste Awards you should try out their smoked salmon and chicken and specialities such as smoked butter, brie, olive oil, sea salt and parmesan.

Prices:	Medium	Express Ship? (UK)	Call them
Delivers to:	Worldwide	Gift Wrap?	No
Based:	UK		

www.organics-4u.co.uk

Organics4u supply top quality organic vegetables, fruit and dry goods direct to your home or place of work anywhere in the UK. Their fruit and vegetables are delivered in boxes of different sizes, and you can choose to have them delivered weekly, fortnightly or monthly. They also offer dry goods boxes, containing items such as pasta, spices, pulses and oil although you can buy these products separately if you want to.

Prices:	Medium	Express Ship? (UK)	No
Delivers to:	UK	Gift Wrap?	No
Based:	UK		

www.riverford.co.uk

Riverford Organic Vegetables is situated along the Dart Valley in Devon and delivers fresh organic vegetable boxes direct from the farm to homes across the South of the UK. They started organic vegetable production in 1987 and have become one of the country's largest independent growers, certified by the Soil Association. Simply enter your postcode to check that they deliver to your area then select which of their fruit and vegetable boxes is most suitable for you.

Prices:	Medium	Express Ship? (UK)	No
Delivers to:	UK (South)	Gift Wrap?	No
Based:	UK		

www.somersetorganics.co.uk

Depending on the season, Somerset Organics provide their own organic Angus beef, Rare Breed Berkshire Pork and Organic Lamb, all of which they farm at Gilcombe Farm. They also stock a full range of meat and poultry reared on local organic farms plus non-organic freerange meats. The dairy range includes Stilton, Brie and vintage Cheddar, plus milk and cream, and you can order your fruit and veg boxes here as well.

Prices:	Medium	Express Ship? (UK)	No
Delivers to:	UK	Gift Wrap?	No
Based:	UK		

Chocolate Heaven

Are you a chocoholic? If so, beware stopping too long here, particularly if a bar of best fruit and nut simply won't do. Most of these online retailers have created their stores specifically to lure you in with outrageously tempting photographs of chocolates of all shapes and sizes, sometimes covering luscious fruits such as cherries and oranges and sometimes filled with liqueurs, nuts and amazing truffles. Why do I sense that no one is reading this any more?

www.chococo.co.uk

This is a small husband and wife-led team based in Purbeck in Dorset. Passionate about proper chocolate, they have developed their own, totally unique, award-winning range of fresh chocolates in vibrant, stylish packaging and use only the finest origin chocolate from Venezuela, Tanzania and Ghana, fresh Dorset cream and fairly traded ingredients wherever possible.

Prices:	Medium	Express Ship? (UK)	Yes
Delivers to:	Europe	Gift Wrap?	No
Based:	UK		

www.chocolatetradingco.com

Here's a mouthwatering selection of chocolates, from Charbonel et Walker serious chocolate indulgences and chocoholics' hampers to funky and fun chocolates such as chocolate sardines and Jungle Crunch. They'll send your chocolates out for you with a personalised gift card and also offer you lots of information on how to tell when you're tasting the highest-quality chocolate.

Prices:	Medium	Express Ship? (UK)	Yes
Delivers to:	UK	Gift Wrap?	Yes
Based:	UK		

www.greenandblacksdirect.com

For beautifully packaged, high-quality organic chocolate at a reasonable price this company is a must. You can order ribbon tied selections of their bars, gift boxes such as The Chocolate Gardener and Coffee Indulgence or use their bespoke service where you choose which of their products should go into one of their stylish gift boxes. They also offer ribbon-decorated wedding favours and again you can choose what you want to include.

Prices:	Medium	Express Ship? (UK)	Yes
Delivers to:	UK	Gift Wrap?	Yes
Based:	UK		

www.hotelchocolat.co.uk

This is a lovely and well-designed website with a large selection of beautifully packaged chocolates. Send someone a Chocogram Delux, Champagne Truffles, their Seasonal Selection or let them choose for themselves. They also have some unusual goodies such as Happy Eggs (for Easter) Strawberries in White Chocolate, Christmas Crates, Chocolate Logs, Goody Bags and Rocky Road Slabs. Resist if you can.

Prices:	Luxury/Medium	Express Ship? (UK)	Yes
Delivers to:	Worldwide	Gift Wrap?	No
Based:	UK		

www.leonidasbelgianchocolates.co.uk

For the ultimate in Belgian chocolates click through to this dedicated website and make your choice. First you select the size of box you want to order and then choose from the chocolate menu with possibilities such as Butter Creams, General Assortment, milk or dark chocolates, Neapolitans and Liqueurs, all of which will be boxed up and despatched to wherever you want.

Prices:	Luxury	Express Ship? (UK)	Yes
Delivers to:	UK	Gift Wrap?	No
Based:	UK		

www.meltchocolates.com

Here you'll find such wonders as raspberry and white chocolate bonbons, sea salted caramels, champagne truffles and Choconola jars, and doesn't just the sound of all of that make you want to try? Visit their website and it gets even worse, as you can ask their master chocolatier to handpick a selection of their amazing truffles straight from the kitchen to fill your chosen box size. Oh dear.

Prices:	Luxury/Medium	Express Ship? (UK)	Call them
Delivers to:	UK	Gift Wrap?	No
Based:	UK		

www.montezumas.co.uk

Montezumas produce a range of around 40 different handmade truffles, with names such as Caribbean Rhythm, Irish Tipple and Lost in Space. You can order by selecting one of their ready made collections or choose your own from the complete list. Buy organic cocoa drinking chocolate, fantastic fudge and chocolate hampers here too.

Prices:	Luxury	Express Ship? (UK)	Yes
Delivers to:	Worldwide	Gift Wrap?	No
Based:	UK		

www.thorntons.co.uk

Thorntons are ideal for Easter, birthdays, anniversaries and weddings or simply when you want to treat yourself. You can buy their delicious chocolate hampers, choose 800g of continental chocolates or one of Thorntons' classic boxes and you'll also find gifts to add such as wine, flowers and Steiff bears. As well as all of this they have a small collection of cards which they'll personalise for you and send out with your gift.

Prices:	Medium/Very Good Value	Express Ship? (UK)	Yes
Delivers to:	Worldwide for most products	Gift Wrap?	No
Based:	UK		

The Superstores

The web has moved on a huge amount, food-wise, over the past year or so, with the launch or several extremely good 'super stores' where you can order your meat, fish, fruit and veg, breads, cheeses and other foods all together in one place, sometimes through lots of individual suppliers but one shopping cart and sometimes from just one provider.

You're almost certainly by now ordering your basics from Ocado, Tesco or Sainsbury's but now you have far more choice online and you don't need to shop around so much for specialities. Yes if you have a great supplier for meat or cheese you'll probably want to go on buying from them, but if you haven't bought fresh food online before and you can't be bothered to go to lots of different stores, you'll be delighted with what you find here.

Just a few words about my favourite three online supermarkets:

www.ocado.com
www.sainsburys.co.uk
www.tesco.com

Check they deliver to your area (this has hugely expanded), set up your favourites list and if you want to order for Christmas delivery place your order well in advance. Now that they're all price matching like mad there isn't a huge amount to choose between them although I personally think that Ocado is the best for 'proper' food such as meat and fruit and veg, and offers one hour time slots which can be much more convenient. If you have a favourite off-line no doubt you'll be shopping online from them too.

Take a look at these as well:

www.foodfullstop.com

If you'd like to have the time to do all your shopping from farmer's markets but you just can't get there then this would be a great place for you to shop, where they've done it for you. Here you can find rare breed meats, organic fruit and veg, artisan cheeses and much more, and you can see immediately which supplier your produce is coming from, whether it's Isle of Lewis smoked salmon or Pied Blue mushrooms.

Prices:	Medium	Express Ship? (UK)	No
Delivers to:	UK	Gift Wrap?	No
Based:	UK		

www.natoora.co.uk

Natoora offers British, French and Italian food sourced directly from individual producers and sent to you by speedy delivery. You can order cheeses from across France and Italy, organic vegetables from Devon, fish from Cornwall, veal from Auvergne or wild goose salami from Italy and everything you order will arrive in one delivery when you choose.

Prices:	Medium	Express Ship? (UK)	Some items
Delivers to:	UK	Gift Wrap?	No
Based:	UK		

www.partridges.co.uk

Famous London-based grocers and Royal Warrant holders Partridges make it easy for you to buy from their excellent selection online, including their own-brand preserves and chocolates, olives oils and vinegars, deli products, wines and spirits. If you know them you'll probably be delighted to be able to buy from them here throughout the year without having to step out of your door.

Prices:	Luxury/Medium	Express Ship? (UK)	No
Delivers to:	UK	Gift Wrap?	No
Based:	UK		

www.solstice.co.uk

When I discovered this website I have to confess to feeling a bit confused: was this a butcher, greengrocer, delicatessen, dairy or what, exactly? Having had a good look round I've simply given up the questions and decided that I'll just carry on and buy my walnut bread (sliced or unsliced), Shitake mushrooms, orange blossom honey, fresh coriander, Lincolnshire Poacher (cheese), Scotch sirloin steak and brown trout without a thought.

Prices:	Luxury/Medium	Express Ship? (UK)	Yes, in London, one extra day elsewhere
Delivers to:	UK	Gift Wrap?	No
Based:	UK		

Caffeine Zone

I really am not a strong coffee person and I'm not going to tell you what happens to me when I try to be – as I have many times – because I love that image of a mug brimming with dark, aromatic, caffeine-filled coffee. So, moving on swiftly, I can say that I know a lot of people who are and I keep a cafetiere and high-quality grounds close at hand for when they visit and really need a coffee fix.

There are many beautiful coffee and tea websites with an amazing selection, perfect if you know exactly what you like and extremely helpful if you don't, so for your next cup of Lapsang Souchong, mint tea or after dinner Java roast you can browse to your heart's content.

www.coffeebypost.co.uk

This is a website for the real coffee connoisseur, as Coffee by Post only offer slow roasted beans from 100% Arabica coffee. So if you think you're being asked to pay a little more, remember that you're buying the best. You can order everything from Columbia Supremo to Italian Dark Espresso Roast, flavoured coffees such as Amaretto and Havana Rum plus accessories such as cafetières and grinders.

Prices:	Medium	Express Ship? (UK)	Yes
Delivers to:	UK	Gift Wrap?	No
Based:	UK		

www.drury.uk.com

Established in central London in 1936 Drury supply a huge variety of coffee, both beans and ground. They also offer espresso machines, coffee makers and accessories and are waiting to offer you advice. You can choose from an extensive range of leaf teas and tea bags too including black, green, herbal or flavoured and from the finest English Breakfast to aromatic Earl Grey and Lapsang.

Prices:	Medium	Express Ship? (UK)	No
Delivers to:	UK	Gift Wrap?	No
Based:	UK		

www.realcoffee.co.uk

The original founders of the Roast & Post Coffee Company were in the coffee business for over 150 years and owned coffee trading companies and estates in Kenya, Tanzania and

Uganda, so now they're using the knowledge and expertise perfected over three generations in roasting and blending the finest coffees in the world. You can buy organic and fairtrade coffees as well as their blended and premium collections and read lots of information about each one.

Prices:	Medium	Express Ship? (UK)	Yes
Delivers to:	Worldwide	Gift Wrap?	No
Based:	UK		

www.taylorsofharrogate.co.uk

This is not only a wonderful place to shop for tea and coffee but also a really attractive website to browse. Choose your coffees from Java, Jamaica Blue Mountain or Mysore plus lots more, and your teas from China Rose Petal, Afternoon Darjeeling or Scottish Breakfast. Then buy your Chamomile, Rosehip and Hibiscus and Organic Peppermint teas here as well.

Prices:	Medium	Express Ship? (UK)	Yes
Delivers to:	Worldwide	Gift Wrap?	No
Based:	UK		

www.thebeanshop.com

With its clear, well-photographed website and excellent selection of coffee, tea and hardware this is a very good place to come to order your next cup. There's a lot of information about all the different ranges plus clear roast/body/acidity/strength ratings so you can see straight away what you're buying. You can also buy espresso machines, coffee grinders, teapots, milk frothers and unusual (and humorous) mugs and cups.

Prices:	Luxury/Medium	Express Ship? (UK)	Yes
Delivers to:	Worldwide	Gift Wrap?	No
Based:	UK		

www.whittard.co.uk

Whittard of Chelsea offers a wide range of teas and coffees (choose from Monsoon Malabar, Old Brown Java and Very Very Berry Fruit Infusion) and also offers instant flavoured cappuccinos plus coffee and tea gifts. They have a very high-quality hot chocolate to order here and you'll also find machines, grinders, roasters and cafetières, accessories and equipment spares as well as very attractive ceramics, fine bone chine and seasonal hampers.

Prices:	Medium	Express Ship? (UK)	No
Delivers to:	Worldwide	Gift Wrap?	No
Based:	UK		

Drink and be Merry

Online shopping and choosing wines and champagne seem to me to go perfectly hand in hand, you can take your time deciding what to order, find some great discounts and have everything delivered to your door. Alternatively you can pick one of your favourite wines and instead of having to trawl round various supermarkets and wine merchants you can find it speedily online using www.wine-searcher.com (did you know about that one?) choose your vintage, discover who's selling it at the best price and again, have it delivered to your door.

Of course if you really want to you can go down the crawl and trawl route and you can also carry boxes of wine out to your car and unload them at the other end. If that's your thing I won't try and discourage you and you'll take no pleasure from looking through the wonderful spirits, wines and champagnes to be found online. Save a glass of the latter for me – I'll take bubbles over coffee any day.

www.ballsbrothers.co.uk

Balls Brothers is a long-established business having shipped and traded wines for over 150 years. You'll discover a handpicked selection of over 400 wines and you can be sure that everything has been carefully chosen from the least expensive (reds starting at around £4.50 a bottle) right up to Chateaux Palmer Margaux at over £100.

Prices:	Luxury/Medium	Express Ship? (UK)	No
Delivers to:	Worldwide	Gift Wrap?	No
Based:	UK		

www.bbr.com

Berry Bros. & Rudd is Britain's oldest wine and spirit merchant having traded from the same shop for over 300 years. Today members of the Berry and Rudd families continue to own and manage the business and their website is a surprisingly busy one. You can not only find out about the wines you should be drinking now but you can also start a BBR Cellar Plan, use their Wedding List services and join their Wine Club.

Prices:	Luxury/Medium	Express Ship? (UK)	Yes
Delivers to:	Worldwide	Gift Wrap?	No
Based:	UK		

www.bibendum-wine.co.uk

Bibendum has been involved in the fine wine market in the UK for over 25 years and on their interesting and friendly website you can buy their wines online, from fine Bordeaux and Burgundies to the best from the New World. You can search their fine wine list which is updated daily and discover wines from all over the world, from the reasonably priced to the extremely expensive.

Prices:	Luxury/Medium	Express Ship? (UK)	Yes
Delivers to:	Worldwide	Gift Wrap?	No
Based:	UK		

www.cambridgewine.com

This is a really beautifully designed website from a Cambridge-based independent wine merchant and a site that's a pleasure to browse through. You can choose by category and by country, select from their mixed cases and promotional offers and take advantages of their gift and En Primeur services. It's the perfect website if you want one that isn't too busy and where it's very easy to place your order.

Prices:	Luxury/Medium	Express Ship? (UK)	No
Delivers to:	UK	Gift Wrap?	Yes
Based:	UK		

www.corneyandbarrow.com

Independent wine merchant Corney and Barrow was established in 1780 and offers you exclusive wines from around the world. On the beautiful deep fuchsia website you can choose your wine by country, type, price or vintage or just put one word from the label of a wine you like into the keyword box to see if they stock it here. Expect to find some marvellous wines here and a great deal of information as well from this expert merchant and broker.

Prices:	Luxury	Express Ship? (UK)	No
Delivers to:	UK and most worldwide	Gift Wrap?	No
Based:	UK		

www.jeroboams.co.uk

This is a beautifully photographed website, from a fine wine (and cheese) importer based in South Kensington. On this site you can order from their extensive list of wines, champagnes and spirits, choose from gifts of food and wine which include port with Stilton, vodka and caviar or whisky and Cheddar, and visit their online cheese store. You can also order Riedel glasses and your next box of Cohiba Siglo IV.

Prices:	Luxury	Express Ship? (UK)	No
Delivers to:	Wine and spirits worldwide	Gift Wrap?	No
Based:	UK		

www.justerinis.com

It's quite a surprise when you first visit this long established wine merchant to be asked where you are and how old you are: very much a first for me online. Anyway, once you're past that you can pay a proper visit to this gorgeous website where the wines are certainly expensive but you'll only find the best, plus lots of advice on what you're buying and how to look after it.

Prices:	Luxury/Medium	Express Ship? (UK)	No
Delivers to:	Worldwide on application	Gift Wrap?	No
Based:	UK		

www.laithwaites.co.uk

Laithwaites are an excellent, family-run online (and offline) wine merchant with a really personal and efficient service and a very good choice at all price ranges. They offer wines and champagnes, mixed cases, a wide range of fortified wines and spirits and there's also a clever food-matching service plus all the other options you would expect including bin ends, mixed case offers and wine plans.

Prices:	Luxury/Medium/Very Good Value	Express Ship? (UK)	No
Delivers to:	UK	Gift Wrap?	No
Based:	UK		

www.laywheeler.co.uk

Based in Colchester and specialising in Bordeaux and Burgundy, Lay and Wheeler are also agents for wine producers in Australia, California, South Africa and other areas. There's a wide range of wine on offer on this busy website plus assistance if you need it. You can choose from their current offers or the full wine list, use their gift service, view the tastings programme and find out about their Bin Club and Wine Discovery Club as well.

Prices:	Luxury/Medium	Express Ship? (UK)	No
Delivers to:	UK	Gift Wrap?	No
Based:	UK		

www.majestic.co.uk

You've almost certainly heard of Majestic, but have you tried their online ordering service, which takes away all the hassle of having to go there, load up and then carry everything from your car when you get home? Not only do they make ordering really easy and offer the best prices on bulk orders but your nearest branch will give you a call once you've placed your order and bring it to you exactly when you want it. You can order right up to Christmas too.

Prices:	Luxury/Medium/Very Good Value	Express Ship? (UK)	Yes, if you request it by phone
Delivers to:	UK	Gift Wrap?	No
Based:	UK		

www.tanners-wines.co.uk

You'll find a comprehensive range of wine, champagne, liqueurs and spirits on this clear and well laid out site. Tanners are a traditional style wine merchant with a calm style (very different from the 'full on' style of Majestic and Oddbins') offering an excellent service and reasonable prices plus lots of advice and information about everything on offer. So you may not always find the cheapest deals here, but you'll certainly enjoy buying from them.

Prices:	Luxury/Medium	Express Ship? (UK)	No
Delivers to:	UK	Gift Wrap?	No
Based:	UK		

www.thesecretcellar.co.uk

This is an independant wine merchant offering a handpicked selection of wines, some of which are easy to find elsewhere and some which are not. It's well worth having a look round as not only are there some interesting wines on offer, but the website is very clear and uncluttered and offers lots of useful information which I not only found helpful (and I'm no expert here) but also made me want to buy.

Prices:	Medium	Express Ship? (UK)	Yes
Delivers to:	UK	Gift Wrap?	No
Based:	UK		

www.thewhiskyexchange.com

Although you can buy blended and some single malt whiskies from just about every supermarket and wine merchant, if you want a really good selection of specialist whisky you need to have a look here. They offer a very good range from the reasonably priced to the not so reasonably priced and include help and advice for the drinker, collector and the investor.

Prices:	Luxury/Medium	Express Ship? (UK)	No
Delivers to:	Worldwide	Gift Wrap?	No
Based:	UK		

www.wine-searcher.com

Looking for a particular vintage of Pomerol, or just Oyster Bay Chardonnay? With prices differing by as much as 40% you need this fantastic worldwide wine comparison website if you're considering buying more than a single bottle of wine. Do register for the pro-version to get all the benefits. There are literally hundreds of wine merchants online all over the world and it's simply not possible to list all the good ones. Wine-searcher will take you to many you've never heard of so take a good look at the sites you visit, make sure they're secure, compare the prices and enjoy.

www.yapp.co.uk

Specialising as importers of high-quality wines from small domains, Yapp is widely recognised as a leading specialist in wines from the Rhône, Loire and Provence, although they also now include Alsace, Champagne, the Savoie and Australia. Try them, you'll find an excellent, knowledgeable selection.

Prices:	Luxury	Express Ship? (UK)	Yes
Delivers to:	UK	Gift Wrap?	No
Based:	UK		

Section 9
Play Time

Whether you're a couch potato or sports and fitness enthusiast there may well be inspiration for you here, from websites that will make you think that you really could get up and have a go this year to others just begging to kit you out for Pilates, rock climbing, your next skiing holiday or a round of golf at La Manga.

The most popular sports in the UK include golf, fishing, running, fitness training and swimming and although as we all know it's too easy to sit for hours in front of the box and watch cricket, football, rugby and tennis it does makes you feel so much better to get up and do something. So create a bit of balance in your life by setting a new, new you (rather than New Year's) resolution and just get on with it.

Speaking as someone who has absolutely no hand/eye co-ordination (which my kids will be all too happy to tell you) and can't run because they've done something stupid to their foot I have, however, managed to make myself go swimming at least twice a week for the past three months (at time of writing). Do I feel better for it? Definitely, and not a little smug as well. Can I swim well? I'm not going to answer that one, either.

RELAX AND GET FIT

Yoga and Pilates

Whether you're looking for a new treadmill for your home gym, want to investigate the Power Plate craze – which is well worth looking at – or just the best ranges of kit and clothing for yoga and Pilates, take a look here and be inspired. It's sometimes extremely hard to get going on the path to fitness (sounds good, doesn't it) as I know only too well. I also know that signing up at an expensive gym more often than not isn't the answer. At least if you have just one really good piece of kit at home you can use it when the urge takes you and even if it's expensive to start with it'll be far cheaper in the long run than that gym membership you give up after a few weeks.

www.fitness-superstore.co.uk
You can see exactly why this fitness equipment calls itself the largest supplier of specialist fitness equipment in the UK – you'd be hard put to find a better range of top-brand equipment. Kit out your home gym from their selection of treadmills, elliptical trainers, rowing machines, bikes, multi-gyms, toners, dumbells, ab trainers and gym balls.

Prices:	Medium	Express Ship? (UK)	No
Delivers to:	UK	Gift Wrap?	No
Based:	UK		

www.gymworld.co.uk
This is another fitness store where you can buy just about everything from treadmills to elliptical cross trainers and rowers to multi-gyms. Then there are the weights, mats, benches and stability balls. Alongside all of this, Gym World offer Jacques croquet sets, multi-games tables, go-karts and sledges, rehabilitation and mobility aids, yoga and Pilates gear, pool tables and massage couches.

Prices:	Medium	Express Ship? (UK)	No
Delivers to:	Most items throughout EU	Gift Wrap?	No
Based:	UK		

www.powerplate.com
By now you may well have heard of these vibrating machines, seen them in John Lewis, on TV or read about them somewhere. As someone who was given a Power Plate last Christmas I can only say 'if you can, buy one now.' Forget all the jokes, they really work and they save so much time that you (might) otherwise spend in the gym.

Prices:	Medium	Express Ship? (UK)	No
Delivers to:	UK this site	Gift Wrap?	No
Based:	UK		

www.wellicious.com

Wellbeing lifestyle brand offers chic and feminine clothes for yoga and Pilates on one of the most attractive websites around, with a range which includes t-shirts, tops, pants, jackets and catsuits – wear them to class or out on the town, it's totally up to you. As well as the boutique you can browse their favourite spa retreats, learn how to make your own body scrubs and find other wellbeing accessories. For yoga or Pilates addicts this website is a must.

Prices:	Medium	Express Ship? (UK)	Yes
Delivers to:	Worldwide	Gift Wrap?	Yes
Based:	UK		

www.yogamatters.com

Yoga Matters is run by a group of enthusiastic yoga practitioners based in North London, and while you won't find an enormous range you can be sure that what's there has been extremely well thought out. They offer a selection of mats and bags, latex resistance bands and Pezzi gym balls plus clothing by Asquith London, prAna and more, plus a good selection of books and DVDs.

Prices:	Medium	Express Ship? (UK)	Yes
Delivers to:	Worldwide	Gift Wrap?	No
Based:	UK		

SERIOUSLY SPORTY

If you are seriously sporty you almost certainly won't have much time to go shopping for all the equipment you need, you'll be far to busy scaling the nearest peak. Finding good sports equipment and clothing without wasting time can sometimes be extremely difficult so this is where the online sports emporiums can made a big difference, so that you can make your list, order online where you find the best deals and quickest delivery and then load up your rucksack and be off.

Walking, Climbing and Camping

www.allweathers.co.uk

Their name really defines the products on this easy-to-use website which is perfect for the hiker and camper or really anyone who spends a lot of time braving the elements. With brands such as Hi-Tec and Berghaus you know you're in safe hands purchasing your rucksacks, tents, hiking boots, travel equipment and clothing. They also stock a very comprehensive range of Barbour jackets.

Prices:	Medium	Express Ship? (UK)	Yes
Delivers to:	UK	Gift Wrap?	No
Based:	UK		

www.blacks.co.uk

If you or any member of your family has ever taken part in any major outdoor excursions you'll probably already have visited Blacks, where they offer a well-priced range of clothing and accessories and good value skiwear in season. You'll find waterproof jackets and trousers, lots of fleece, tents, poles, footwear and socks and great gift ideas.

Prices:	Medium/Very Good Value	Express Ship? (UK)	No
Delivers to:	UK	Gift Wrap?	No
Based:	UK		

www.completeoutdoors.co.uk

Everything for walking, trekking, rambling, camping, climbing, and many other activities is available here with tents, rucksacks, sleeping bags, navigation equipment, boots, walking poles, and general camping accessories from brands such as Paramo, Berghaus, Brasher, Meindl, Bushbaby, Victorinox, Leki, Karrimor, Leatherman, Rohan, Nomad Medical and Regatta.

Prices:	Medium	Express Ship? (UK)	No
Delivers to:	UK	Gift Wrap?	No
Based:	UK		

www.cotswoldoutdoor.com

This is one of the very best websites for camping, hiking and adventure holiday equipment including tents, sleeping bags, clothing, hiking boots, rucksacks, travel equipment and gadgets and tools from brands such as The North Face, Osprey and Gerber. Service is friendly and speedy and they support youth adventure holidays and treks such as World Team Challenge.

Prices:	Medium	Express Ship? (UK)	Yes, if you call them
Delivers to:	Worldwide	Gift Wrap?	No
Based:	UK		

Snowsports

www.edge2edge.co.uk

The next time you're planning a skiing or snowboarding trip you should take a look round this website, where they have a very good list of brands such as Exus, Burton and Forum (snowboarding boots) and Atomic, Head and Nordica (skiing) with top line boards and skis to go with them. They also have some excellent discounts plus rental packages at good prices.

Prices:	Medium	Express Ship? (UK)	No
Delivers to:	Worldwide	Gift Wrap?	No
Based:	UK		

www.ellis-brigham.com

On its wonderful, clearly photographed website for mountaineers and skiers, Ellis Brigham offers brands such as The North Face, Patagonia, Ice Breaker and Lowe Alpine. Every possible type of equipment is very clearly shown and there are some good sporting gift ideas as well including items by Leatherman, Victorinox, Maglite and Toollogic.

Prices:	Luxury/Medium	Express Ship? (UK)	No
Delivers to:	Worldwide	Gift Wrap?	No
Based:	UK		

www.patagonia.com

As the sports that Patagonia specialises in are Alpine skiing, rock climbing, Nordic climbing and fly fishing you won't be surprised that this is a collection of really high-tech/high insulated products. They've also produced a really excellent range for infants and children, with jackets, vests, fleece, base layers, all-in-one's and gloves for ages from 3 months to 14.

Prices:	Luxury	Express Ship? (UK)	Yes
Delivers to:	Worldwide	Gift Wrap?	No
Based:	UK		

www.simplypiste.com

At Simply Piste there's a well laid out collection for men, women and children. Find ski suits, jackets, salopettes, ski pants, base layer and baby skiwear there plus lots of accessories such as gloves and goggles. This is a fun website from a group of sporting sites and where you can often find some very good discounts, particularly near the end of the season.

Prices:	Medium	Express Ship? (UK)	Yes
Delivers to:	Worldwide	Gift Wrap?	No
Based:	UK		

www.snowandrock.com

Snow and Rock is a well-known retailer for skiers, snowboarders and rock climbers, with a full range of equipment and clothing and accessories by brands such as Animal, Billabong, Ski Jacket, Helly Hanson, O'Neill, Quicksilver, Salomon and Oakley. There's also lots of advice on what to buy and on fit.

Prices:	Luxury/Medium/Very Good Value	Express Ship? (UK)	Yes
Delivers to:	Worldwide	Gift Wrap?	No
Based:	UK		

Watersports

www.andark.co.uk

Andark offers everything from skis to a full range of watersports clothing, power kites, inflatable dinghies, wetsuits and diving equipment, torches, knives and underwater camera accessories. So if you know someone who sails, water skis, wakeboards, dives and enjoys any other general messing about in or on the water, this is the place to come.

Prices:	Medium	Express Ship? (UK)	Yes
Delivers to:	UK	Gift Wrap?	No
Based:	UK		

www.henrilloydstore.co.uk

This is a beautifully designed website from a famous sailing brand now offering an increasing range including stylish sailing clothing for guys and girls, footwear, luggage and specific branded marinewear. Online you can't buy their technical sailing gear but the collection is chic and stylish and not overpriced.

Prices:	Luxury/Medium	Express Ship? (UK)	No
Delivers to:	UK	Gift Wrap?	No
Based:	UK		

www.purplemarine.com

Purple Marine is a seriously good marine store offering a full range of clothing for everyone and everything for the boat owner from bilge pumps and hatches to chart holders, boat covers and buoyancy aids. If you're a sailor yourself or you know someone who is you'll find an enormous choice here.

Prices:	Medium	Express Ship? (UK)	Yes
Delivers to:	Europe	Gift Wrap?	No
Based:	UK		

www.roho.co.uk

If you're into watersports or you know someone who is then this is the site for you, offering clothing and equipment for scuba, windsurfing, waterskiing, kayaking, surfing, sailing and jetskiing. It's an easy-to-navigate site with clear pictures of every item offered and it might even tempt you to take up a new sport.

Prices:	Medium	Express Ship? (UK)	Yes
Delivers to:	EU	Gift Wrap?	No
Based:	UK		

Fishing

www.fly-fishing-tackle.co.uk

From a full range of rods and reels by manufacturers such as Snowbee, Fulling Mill, Loop and Fladen to waders, hats, caps and gloves; everything for the keen fisherman is available here. If you're looking for a gift go past the fly tying kits unless you're sure they'll be welcome and concentrate more on fly boxes, tackle bags and rod carriers or fly tying tools, lamps and magnifiers.

Prices:	Luxury/Medium	Express Ship? (UK)	Yes
Delivers to:	Worldwide	Gift Wrap?	No
Based:	UK		

www.johnnorris.co.uk

John Norris of Penrith offers lots of choices for the fisherman including equipment and accessories by Snowbee, Orvis, Musto, Barbour and Le Chameau and lots more. They also offer a full range of shooting accessories from gun cases and shooting sticks to gun cleaning kits and they're happy to ship worldwide.

Prices:	Medium	Express Ship? (UK)	Yes, worldwide express is available
Delivers to:	Worldwide	Gift Wrap?	No
Based:	UK		

www.orvis.co.uk

Orvis has always been at the forefront of fly-fishing tackle and shooting accessories. You can buy all their equipment online plus their excellent luggage and travel gear, pet products and a wide range of clothing. Going back to fishing: from rods to reels, lines to waders there's an excellent choice and everything is really clearly photographed and described.

Prices:	Medium	Express Ship? (UK)	Yes
Delivers to:	EU this website	Gift Wrap?	No
Based:	UK		

www.tackleshop.co.uk

TackleShop was established in 1999 and has grown quickly to become one of the UK's busiest on-line fishing tackle stores. If you're interested in carp fishing, coarse fishing, game, match, pike, pole or sea fishing you must take a look round as the product range is extremely comprehensive.

Prices:	Medium	Express Ship? (UK)	No, but delivery is speedy
Delivers to:	Worldwide	Gift Wrap?	No
Based:	UK		

Golf

www.118golf.co.uk

With its excellent delivery service and its diverse range of products for the golfer this would be an excellent website to look for your next set of clubs or accessories. They offer the ranges of Callaway, Nike, Mizuno, RAM, Cobra and many more and frankly if you can't find it here, it's probably not worth looking for.

Prices:	Luxury/Medium	Express Ship? (UK)	Yes
Delivers to:	Worldwide	Gift Wrap?	No
Based:	UK		

www.clickgolf.co.uk

This is a very quick and easy site to use, although like most of the golfing websites it's very busy and offers a huge range of products which at first sight look almost too much. You can find top brand names and some very good special offers here as well, so check for discounted equipment first if it's a new set of clubs you're after.

Prices:	Luxury/Medium	Express Ship? (UK)	Yes
Delivers to:	EU	Gift Wrap?	No
Based:	UK		

www.county-golf.co.uk

County Golf is a golfer's paradise offering all the brands and some very good prices. They also have sections/departments for left-handed golfers, junior clubs and weather gear and you can order personalised golf balls and sweaters here as well.

Prices:	Luxury/Medium	Express Ship? (UK)	Yes
Delivers to:	EU	Gift Wrap?	No
Based:	UK		

www.onlinegolf.co.uk

Online Golf has everything for the golfer and delivers throughout Europe. It's a typical sports website with loads and loads of products and brand names from Nike, Wilson, Adidas and Pringle to name but a few.

Prices:	Medium	Express Ship? (UK)	Yes
Delivers to:	EU	Gift Wrap?	No
Based:	UK		

Horseriding

www.colemancroft.com

Coleman Croft are master saddlers established over 25 years ago and now offering on their website riding clothing, rugs, saddles, bridles and tack and safety equipment. They also sell Barbour jackets and Hunter wellington boots. They try to keep everything you see in stock so delivery is speedy and they're happy to ship worldwide.

Prices:	Medium	Express Ship? (UK)	No
Delivers to:	Worldwide	Gift Wrap?	No
Based:	UK		

www.dragonflysaddlery.co.uk

Here you can choose from army camouflage jods (!), Buddies jods and Saddlehuggers in loads of different colours from pink and blue to the more traditional neutrals. Then there are long and short jodhpur boots, body protectors, wellies, muck boots and rain proof jackets. There's a good choice though so it's worth a look.

Prices:	Medium	Express Ship? (UK)	No
Delivers to:	Worldwide	Gift Wrap?	No
Based:	UK		

www.theequestrianstore.com

This well-designed and easy-to-navigate website offers express worldwide delivery and sells just about everything for horse and rider. You'll find a comprehensive clothing section offering jodphurs and hard hats, jackets and boots and in the horse section all you need including saddles, bridles, horse rugs and accessories.

Prices:	Medium	Express Ship? (UK)	Yes
Delivers to:	Worldwide	Gift Wrap?	No
Based:	UK		

www.thesaddleryshop.co.uk

This is one of the best online saddlery stores, it's extremely well designed, easy to navigate and easy to find what you're looking for despite the huge amount of kit on offer for both horse and rider. I will say that once you zoom in on a product they're not all as clear as you would like them to be but this is made up for by the sheer amount of what's on offer.

Prices:	Medium	Express Ship? (UK)	No
Delivers to:	Worldwide	Gift Wrap?	No
Based:	UK		

BE ENTERTAINED

Tickets for Everything

Booking tickets online has never been easier, whatever you want to go to, to theatre, opera, musical or a concert at the O2. If at all possible book somewhere that shows the seating plan and exactly where you will be sitting – this is a facility that is being offered more and more widely.

Every opera house and auditorium has its own website and usually a booking facility so if you want tickets for Glyndebourne, the Royal Opera House or Barbican you can visit their dedicated sites too.

www.aloud.com

Aloud specialises in rock and pop concert tickets and the alphabetic index in the left hand column on the homepage on this website allows you to choose quickly from their Hot New Tickets or Best Seller collections. Ordering is clear and easy, although they only tell you the area your seats will be in rather than the row.

Prices:	Luxury/Medium/Very Good Value	Express Ship? (UK)	No
Delivers to:	UK	Gift Wrap?	No
Based:	UK		

www.seetickets.com

You can book just about everything music and stage-wise here, plus events such as the Good Food Show and Clothes Show Live, sporting events such as the Horse of the Year show and the Grand Prix, comedy shows and classical music performances. They also suggest places to stay.

Prices:	Luxury/Medium	Express Ship? (UK)	No
Delivers to:	UK	Gift Wrap?	No
Based:	UK		

www.ticketmaster.co.uk

Music, theatre and sport tickets are available on this – the original ticket website. If you want standing room tickets to see Robbie Williams, seats for England v Barbarians at Twickenham or firework and music tickets at Hampton Court or tickets for pretty well anything else then this is your site.

Prices:	Luxury/Medium	Express Ship? (UK)	No
Delivers to:	UK	Gift Wrap?	No
Based:	UK		

Also take a look at these individual sites:
www.barbican.org.uk
www.eno.org
www.glyndebourne.com
www.nt-online.org
www.royalopera.org
www.southbankcentre.co.uk
www.tate.org.uk

Books, Music, Movies and Games

There's pretty well nothing in this area that you can't buy online, but I expect that you've discovered that for yourselves by now. Always check and compare the prices before you buy, so many of these retailers are offering free delivery that it sometimes makes sense to buy from different places even when you're tempted to put everything into your shopping basket at once.

Specialist sites such as Abe Books are invaluable when you're looking for a signed or first edition and although, unless you've signed up for Amazon Prime (where you pay a fixed fee for a year's first class delivery no matter how many times you order) you may have to pay postage there, you may well find that their prices are the best of all anyway.

www.abebooks.co.uk
This is the worldwide marketplace for rare, secondhand and out-of-print books. You just need to know the title or the author and if it's available it'll be found immediately. You can then narrow your search to see only first editions, or signed copies among other options.

Prices:	Luxury/Medium	Express Ship? (UK)	No
Delivers to:	Worldwide	Gift Wrap?	No
Based:	UK		

www.amazon.co.uk
At Amazon you can buy not only books but so much more, including your new Kenwood food mixer or digital camera, baby products and tools for your garden, which can make life rather confusing. They have probably the most comprehensive range of books, music, movies and games available anywhere, frequently at the best price and their service is excellent.

Prices:	Medium/Very Good Value	Express Ship? (UK)	Yes
Delivers to:	Worldwide	Gift Wrap?	Yes
Based:	UK		

www.blackwells.co.uk
If you prefer a less busy book website then pay a visit to Blackwell's of Oxford, established in 1879 and an online store for over ten years. What you'll find here is a really excellent and more personal service with a clear path through to the various departments: Fiction, Leisure and Lifestyle, Science, Humanities, Arts, Medical, Business Finance and Law.

Prices:	Luxury/Medium	Express Ship? (UK)	Yes
Delivers to:	Worldwide	Gift Wrap?	No
Based:	UK		

www.bookdepository.co.uk

The Book Depository claims to be the fastest growing book distributor in Europe and there's certainly a huge selection available through their easy-to-navigate website. This is also one of the best places to search out books you've been unable to find elsewhere.

Prices:	Medium/Very Good Value	Express Ship? (UK)	No
Delivers to:	Worldwide	Gift Wrap?	No
Based:	UK		

www.borders.co.uk

This is a wonderful online bookstore where as well as finding your next great read you can sign up for Borders Email, which means that you'll be the first to find out about their promotions, take part in their competitions, find out about events in-store near you and join their new Book Group.

Prices:	Medium/Very Good Value	Express Ship? (UK)	Yes
Delivers to:	Worldwide, through amazon.co.uk	Gift Wrap?	Yes
Based:	UK		

www.foyles.co.uk

This is undoubtedly one of the world's most famous bookshops, where there's not only an extremely wide range of books but you'll also find sheet music and manuscript paper, tickets for in-store author signings and events and a selection of signed copies. As soon as you start to search for a book you can see exactly how many they have in stock at Charing Cross Road and you can select to buy online or to collect in store.

Prices:	Medium	Express Ship? (UK)	Yes
Delivers to:	Worldwide	Gift Wrap?	Yes
Based:	UK		

www.waterstones.co.uk

Waterstone's website is extremely clear and easy to use and one of the great things about buying here is that this company is just (for the moment) about books, and not every other product you can think of. Browse categories straight from the Home Page menu including Finance and Law, Computing, Education, Comics and Graphic Novels alongside the more usual Fiction, Children's Books, Food and Drink, and Sport.

Prices:	Medium	Express Ship? (UK)	Yes
Delivers to:	Worldwide	Gift Wrap?	Yes
Based:	UK		

www.whsmith.co.uk

On WHSmith's easy-on-the-eye website you can buy books, all the latest DVDs, music and computer games plus a selection from their stationery ranges. There are also lots of gift ideas including original historic newspapers and commemorative sporting books, you can subscribe at a discount to all your favourite magazines and order personalised school labels and wedding stationery.

Prices:	Medium	Express Ship? (UK)	No
Delivers to:	UK	Gift Wrap?	No
Based:	UK		

www.cdwow.com

You'll find some of the best prices around here and this site covers all mediums from CDs and DVDs to computer games. Because their prices are so good it would be worth purchasing gift vouchers here as you can be sure that the recipient will get a good deal, whatever they choose to spend them on. They offer free delivery worldwide for all items and regular special offers.

Prices:	Medium/Very Good Value	Express Ship? (UK)	No
Delivers to:	Free Worldwide	Gift Wrap?	No
Based:	UK		

www.game.co.uk

Whatever the latest gaming consoles are you'll find a huge range of games here for all of them plus the consoles themselves and accessories. They also offer a reward points system – a very good idea as loyalty to game sites is thin on the ground due to the amount of competition.

Prices:	Medium/Very Good Value	Express Ship? (UK)	Yes, for the UK
Delivers to:	Worldwide	Gift Wrap?	No
Based:	UK		

www.hmv.co.uk

The HMV shops on Oxford Street and within Selfridges are usually the first places that my kids want to hit on a trip to London and I quite understand why, because no matter if you're looking for chart CDs or DVDs or something a bit harder to find, they're bound to have it. The website is super easy to navigate and there's a superb choice.

Prices:	Medium/Very Good Value	Express Ship? (UK)	Yes, and Worldwide Express
Delivers to:	Worldwide	Gift Wrap?	No
Based:	UK		

www.play.com

Having ordered from this music, movies, books, games, gadget, electronics and now clothing website many times I can only repeat myself and say that they're really excellent, whatever you buy. They're based in Jersey so you can't have your order tomorrow but couple their very good service, range and discounts and you'll be happy to wait that extra day.

Prices:	Medium/Very Good Value	Express Ship? (UK)	No
Delivers to:	Free to most EU, Canada and USA	Gift Wrap?	No
Based:	Channel Islands		

www.sendit.com

At Sendit you'll find all the DVDs, games, CDs and small electronics (as well as iPod) you could possibly want plus when you buy you'll automatically be joining their loyalty scheme and collecting ipoints. You can also rent from their huge collection of DVDs with free returns and no late fees.

Prices:	Medium/Very Good Value	Express Ship? (UK)	Yes
Delivers to:	Worldwide	Gift Wrap?	Yes
Based:	Northern Ireland		

www.thehut.com

The Hut offers free delivery on everything and some extremely good prices on its attractive blue website. Named in *The Sunday Times* top 100 Tech Track sites and only launched a few years ago this is very much a site to buy from. You'll find DVDs, CDs, games, books and memory storage.

Prices:	Very Good Value	Express Ship? (UK)	No
Delivers to:	Worldwide	Gift Wrap?	No
Based:	UK		

www.zavvi.co.uk

On this easy-to-use Guernsey-based website your can order all the latest releases and pre-order the next 'must-have' CDs, DVDs and games, plus games consoles and accessories. This is a well laid-out and colourful website where it's extremely easy to find what you're looking for despite the amount of choice.

Prices:	Medium/Very Good Value	Express Ship? (UK)	No
Delivers to:	UK	Gift Wrap?	No
Based:	UK		

Subscribe Here

www.discountpublications.co.uk

If you'd like to give the gift of a magazine subscription then take a look at this website, which is not necessarily the most sophisticated but which offers some of the best prices of all. You'll find subscriptions for *Vogue*, *Vanity Fair*, *Tatler*, *Red*, *FHM* and *GQ*, *House and Garden*, *The World of Interiors* and most other glossy publications available at very good rates.

Prices:	Medium/Very Good Value	Express Ship? (UK)	No
Delivers to:	UK	Gift Wrap?	No
Based:	UK		

www.magazine-group.co.uk

With over 400 titles on offer and some very good discounts you could find something for just about everyone here, from the sportsman (*Rugby World, Dive, Inside Edge, The Angler*), food and drink lover (*Olive, Good Food, Decanter*) home interiors enthusiast (*Beautiful Homes, Elle Decoration*) and fashion addict (*Vogue, Harpers & Queen* and *In Style*).

Prices:	Medium	Express Ship? (UK)	No
Delivers to:	UK	Gift Wrap?	No
Based:	UK		

www.magazinesofamerica.com

Some of the magazine subscriptions here are extremely expensive, even when you take the fact that they include postage into account, however, if you can't live without your great American read, you'll be delighted to find the likes of *American Vogue, Glamour* and *House Beautiful* which complement their UK counterparts and which you can have sent to you each month.

Prices:	Luxury/Medium	Express Ship? (UK)	No
Delivers to:	Worldwide	Gift Wrap?	No
Based:	US		

Dine Here

www.toptable.co.uk

Whether you want to book at Asia de Cuba, New York, Maze, London or Chez les Anges, Paris, here you'll find the latest recommendations, hot places to eat at, as well as booking your table. They can organise parties or private dining too, and you'll find reviews on all new restaurant launches plus special offers.

GET EQUIPPED

The number of online retailers offering you TVs and hi-fis, cameras, kitchen and laundy appliances and in fact every type of equipment you can think of seems to be multiplying daily. Some are excellent and others fall by the wayside in terms of design and making it easy for you to buy from them (which I find astounding bearing in mind the sheer number of excellent examples they have to follow).

I have listed some of the good ones here but like everything else in this line you should compare prices before you buy at which point you'll be offered loads more places to buy even if you end up choosing to spend a bit more and buy from a retailer you know. You may not be able to save on this season's Jimmy Choos but you'll certainly save enough on your next fridge, washing machine or flat screen TV to pay for them. Take it from me.

Camera Store

There are an enormous number of online shops where you can buy digital cameras, and it very much boils down to identifying the one you want and then finding the best place, which may not necessarily be a photographic store.

Use the websites below, offline stores and photographic magazines to make your choice and then find the best deal and if you're not sure how, take a look at Where to Compare, on page 232. You'll find some stupendously different prices.

For more specialised kit by manufacturers such as Leica and Zeiss you need different stores with staff who really know their stuff. Try online shops such as The Classic Camera to get away from the everyday selections.

You may say that there are some high street chains not represented here and you'd be right, but the reason they're not here is because their prices are simply not competitive. Once they wake up to the fact that we don't want, nor do we need to pay their overinflated prices, I'll be delighted to include them.

www.cameraking.co.uk

There are, of course, lots of places you can buy a camera online but you might like to take a look here as this is a great place for real enthusiasts. They not only offer a huge range of cameras and show you straight away what's in stock, but the menu is very clear and there are some excellent accessories including camera bags and cases and tripods of all shapes and sizes. Don't come here if you're looking for the latest pink pocket sized marvel, but for real equipment this is a great place.

Prices:	Luxury/Medium	Express Ship? (UK)	Yes
Delivers to:	UK	Gift Wrap?	No
Based:	UK		

www.cameras2u.com

This is an excellent website to find your next camera, where you'll find all the new models at very good prices. Compare their prices on a comparison website such as kelkoo.co.uk and you'll find they're nearly always the lowest. There's a lot of advice on digital photography in general such as linking up with your PC and printer plus photo-taking tips.

Prices:	Luxury/Medium/Very Good Value	Express Ship? (UK)	Yes
Delivers to:	UK	Gift Wrap?	No
Based:	UK		

www.campkinsonline.com

There's an excellent range here including digital SLRs and camcorders, and compact digital cameras – some of which can be ordered in colours such as fuchsia pink, orange, wasabi green and bright red which would make great gifts for girls. They also offer the digital frames you need to show off your pics, memory cards and Sandisk MP3 players.

Prices:	Luxury/Medium/Very Good Value	Express Ship? (UK)	Yes
Delivers to:	UK	Gift Wrap?	No
Based:	UK		

www.fotosense.co.uk

Fotosense offers an excellent range of the latest cameras plus everything you need for digital video, MP3 players, binoculars, printers and studio lighting from a list of over 50 manufacturers as well as one of the largest photographic accessory lists available in the UK. Having bought from them several times I can tell you the service is very good.

Prices:	Luxury/Medium/Very Good Value	Express Ship? (UK)	Yes
Delivers to:	Worldwide	Gift Wrap?	No
Based:	UK		

www.pixmania.co.uk

Pixmania has a wonderfully slick, colourful and user friendly website and tells you straight away about their best-sellers and the newly released models. You can become a VIPix and receive a discount and free delivery for a year, plus 20% off extended warranties or give one of their gift certificates.

Prices:	Medium/Very Good Value	Express Ship? (UK)	Yes
Delivers to:	Worldwide	Gift Wrap?	No
Based:	France		

www.theclassiccamera.com

This is the place to come to for your Leica cameras and lenses and they also offer Zeiss and Voigtlander lenses, Metz flashguns and Gitzo tripods. This shop is very much for professionals and specialists and if you're not absolutely sure about what you're considering buying call them for advice. There's a small range of digital SLR cameras here as well.

Prices:	Luxury/Medium	Express Ship? (UK)	Yes
Delivers to:	Worldwide	Gift Wrap?	No
Based:	UK		

Large Electrical – TVs and More

Whether you're looking for computers, DVD players, washing machines or fridges the rules are the same for all of this type of 'equipment' shopping online. First decide which product you're interested in and then compare prices. You can visit a major department store or other offline shop to do your research, read reviews in *Which?* online (www.which.co.uk) or get all your information online.

Once you've found the best deal and checked out the merchant (make sure they operate a secure site, what is their delivery and returns policy and if you're shelling out quite a bit make sure that you talk to a real person) then you can decide if you want to order online or not. You'll almost always get a better price on the net, particularly for electrical goods.

Here are some electrical suppliers with very good websites – there are far too many good ones to list here so please don't forget to compare – and again if you're not sure how to do this, read the 'Where to Compare' section on page 232.

www.bennettsonline.co.uk

There's a wide range of clearly displayed electrical appliances here from computers and widescreen TVs to washing machines, dryers and vacuum cleaners. They aim for delivery between 3–7 working days and there's a small charge for delivery up to £300, after which it's free.

Prices:	Medium	Express Ship? (UK)	No
Delivers to:	UK	Gift Wrap?	No
Based:	UK		

www.dabs.com

Dabs offer an enormous choice of products for computing, home entertainment, in car products, photo and video. When you're comparing prices Dabs will almost always come up with a very good one, if not the cheapest. They're extremely reliable and their delivery is far cheaper than on most sites.

Prices:	Medium	Express Ship? (UK)	No
Delivers to:	UK	Gift Wrap?	No
Based:	UK		

www.laskys.co.uk

Laskys supplies premium brand vision and computing products at very competitive prices. They're part of one of Europe's largest electrical retail groups and one of the best things here is the amount of advice on offer. Call them if you need more help than is supplied by their comprehensive buying guides. Delivery is included in the prices online within the UK.

Prices:	Luxury/Medium	Express Ship? (UK)	Yes
Delivers to:	UK	Gift Wrap?	No
Based:	UK		

www.martindawes.net

TVs and DVD, complete home theatre systems and digital radios are just some of the products you can find here from brands such as Sony, Panasonic and Bose. There's a smaller selection here than you can see at some of the mainstream electrical retailers but it's a clear, well-designed website and less confusing than some.

Prices:	Luxury/Medium	Express Ship? (UK)	No
Delivers to:	UK	Gift Wrap?	No
Based:	UK		

www.shop.bt.com

BT has entered the home entertainment market with a comprehensive choice and some extremely good prices. Whenever you're comparing prices BT is sure to show up towards the lower end so they're well worth considering. Check their prices before you order from anywhere else.

Prices:	Medium	Express Ship? (UK)	No
Delivers to:	UK	Gift Wrap?	No
Based:	UK		

Where to Compare

Using price comparison websites is simple and once you've tried it (if you're not comparing already) you'll be amazed at the difference between retailers. Firstly do your research and narrow down to the exact product you're looking for, then use one of the comparison websites listed below.

Be aware of the hidden extras whatever you're comparing prices on. Do they stock the items on offer? How long will delivery take? How secure is the website with the best price? Can you speak to a real person when you call and do you get a quick response to an enquiry email? Will someone carry your new flat screen TV up to your fifth floor apartment and will they take away the packaging or leave you with the mess? Do you have to pay for delivery or is it included in the price?

Be firm about the services you want and if you're going to buy from a company you haven't used before make sure that everything is confirmed in writing/email before you place your order. Print out a copy of all your orders and keep them somewhere safe until you're entirely happy with your transaction. Alternatively you can establish an email folder just for outstanding orders and drag all the correspondence there.

For general products visit:

www.kelkoo.co.uk
www.uk.shopping.com
www.pricerunner.co.uk

For music, movies, books and games visit:

www.best-cd-price.co.uk
www.dvdpricecheck.co.uk
www.uk.gamestracker.com
www.bookbutler.co.uk
www.bookbrain.co.uk

For wines and champagnes visit:

www.wine-searcher.com

Section 10
Weddings

When I think about weddings, and my own, even though it was a while ago (putting it mildly), I think about my dress, the flowers, the cake, the bridesmaids and my mother's daft hat.

My instinct, when I started writing this, was to say that, as in every other area of shopping today, you can do it all online. Well, maybe. If you really want to yes you can. You can order your dress, the ring, the flowers and no, I won't go on, I'm sure you already have the list.

There are some major items you may well not want to buy online and for these I would suggest you have a browse here because there's plenty to see and lots of ideas to find. Forgetting the daft hat it's very much the list in my first few lines. You'll find in these sections that there will probably be a few places you can buy, more to have a walk through, and also suggestions of other places within this guide where you'll find a bridal range. Take Gina shoes, for example – they don't have two entries in the book but the mention in the wedding shoe section will direct you to where their main entry is so you can see the collection there.

I've looked far and wide for really good online wedding stores and they're few and far between in the UK at the moment. Unless I love them they don't appear here, however what I have discovered are the numerous, lovely wedding collections within mainstream online boutiques, a few beautiful, quirky stores you may like to have a look at and one or two superb online wedding shops based in the US but who will ship to you wherever you are in the world, at speed.

Where invitations, favours, gifts, wedding registries, jewellery, shoes, lingerie and groom's accessories are concerned you don't need to move an inch, so order online and then use all the extra time you've freed up to spend the hours you need to make sure your perfect dress is just that … perfect. Enjoy.

All about the Dress

I always think that deciding on a wedding dress is an almost impossible thing to do. You have that single choice and you'll probably be offered a collection of the most beautiful dresses you've ever seen, whichever wedding specialist you choose to go to. Fifteen shades from antique ivory through to white, beads, lace and embroidery, flouncing, ruching, boned bodices, trains and bows. How on earth can you know which to pick?

This is where these glorious websites can help. In the main you can't order directly through them and you may well not want to. However, they're wonderful places to get an idea firstly of different styles, such as column or full skirted, empire line, strapless or long sleeved and secondly to get an idea of shades and trims.

These are fabulous, glamorous and beautifully finished gowns and you may fall in love with one, in which case you can find out from the website where your nearest stockist is. Hopefully you already know which is the best shape for you so that when you do go offline you'll know what to look for and what not to gaze lovingly at.

All these wedding dress designers have beautifully designed websites and most do not retail online, therefore I haven't given any awards here.

www.alanhannah.co.uk

Marguerite Hannah has been designing wedding dresses for the past 14 years and in that time has won many awards including the Retail Bridal Association's Best Designer award in 2001, 2002, 2004 and 2005. The collection is often really beautiful and embellished with modern handcrafted jewellery and hand painting as well as delicate beadwork.

Prices:	Luxury/Medium	Buy Online:	No
Delivers to:	Worldwide		
Based:	UK		

www.amandawyatt.com

Here's a gorgeous range of mid to upper priced wedding dresses shown in really clear and pretty detail. Click through to the other collection here; Charlotte Balbier, which is younger and at a slightly higher price level. You'll also find her wedding accessories. Visit the stockists' listings and you'll be able to see if there's a special event happening near you, such as a designer evening or special showing.

Prices:	Luxury/Medium	Buy Online:	No
Delivers to:	UK		
Based:	UK		

www.benjaminroberts.co.uk

Award-winning Benjamin Roberts brings you gowns that are designed by young, European-trained designers who are encouraged to try new fabrics, silhouettes, colours and texture. The workmanship is exquisite and most dresses here are reasonably priced. Once you've selected the style of wedding gown you like his comprehensive stockist's directory will tell you exactly where you can find your dress.

Prices:	Luxury/Medium	Buy Online:	No
Delivers to:	UK		
Based:	UK		

www.jasperconran.com

The bridalwear collection by Jasper Conran continues the signature elegant style of a designer famous for creating costumes for ballet, opera and theatre. Having said that most of his designs are beautifully understated; think strapless corded lace bodices with silk tulle skirts, or a simple silk column dress worn with a pleated wrap to have some idea of what you'll find here. There is lovely jewellery here as well plus the bridegrooms' collection.

Prices:	Luxury/Medium	Buy Online:	No
Delivers to:	Worldwide		
Based:	UK		

www.jennypackham.com

Jenny Packham designs beautiful contemporary bridal and eveningwear, often bead and jewel encrusted and perfect for summer and on the beach weddings. The collection is extensive and exquisite and although it takes a while for each dress to download to its full size, once it has you can see it in all its gorgeous detail, so persevere.

Prices:	Luxury/Medium	Buy Online:	No
Delivers to:	Worldwide		
Based:	UK		

www.justinalexanderbridal.com

This is a collection of glamorous, extravagantly gorgeous wedding gowns which you can find at stockists throughout the world. The gowns incorporate high levels of craftsmanship and are made of the finest fabrics: pure silk, rich satins, soft laces and handcrafted beading as well as glittering Swarovski crystals. The corsetry is based on original Victorian patterns and techniques.

Prices:	Luxury/Medium	Buy Online:	No
Delivers to:	Worldwide		
Based:	UK		

www.phillipalepley.com

Phillipa Lepley has been creating beautiful wedding dresses for over twenty years, combining femininity and simplicity with enormous attention to fine detail such as embroidery, colour and flowers. When you look through the gallery of pictures on her website you'll immediately see that here are some of the most unique wedding dresses available.

Prices:	Luxury/Medium	Buy Online:	No
Delivers to:	UK		
Based:	UK		

www.pronovias.com

Pronovias is a Spanish bridal wear company specialising in top-of-the-range and couture wedding dresses by designers such as Elis Saab, Emanuel Ungaro, Badgley Mischka and Hannibal Laguna. On their stylish website you can look at their elegantly photographed online catalogues plus their cocktailwear and find out where your nearest stockist is wherever you are in the world.

Prices:	Luxury/Medium	Buy Online:	No
Delivers to:	Worldwide		
Based:	Spain		

www.stewartparvin.com

Stewart Parvin trained at the Edinburgh College of Art and went on to work with other designers before establishing his own studio. From day and eveningwear he launched his wedding collection which now includes couture and diffusion ranges and is available worldwide. He works with a small team and uses only the most luxurious fabrics and creative embroiderers and seamstresses to create unique, elegant designs.

Prices:	Luxury/Medium	Buy Online:	No
Delivers to:	Worldwide		
Based:	UK		

www.suzanneneville.com

Having studied at the London College of Fashion Suzanne Neville went on to win in the British Bridal Awards in her first year of working under her own name. Her client list now includes celebrities and brides in media, film and television. Her dresses are handcrafted using contemporary couture techniques and on her website you'll find her Classic, Deco and Renaissance ranges with stylish photography and close-up detail.

Prices:	Luxury/Medium	Buy Online:	No
Delivers to:	From Stockists		
Based:	UK		

Also buy ready-to-wear wedding gowns from:

www.monsoon.co.uk

The Monsoon bridal collection comprises a small but stylish and well-priced collection of bridal gowns, perfect for weddings on the beach. They also have an enchanting range of little flowergirl dresses here so that even if you want to have your dress made for you elsewhere you could easily have a bevy of really happy bridesmaids for far less than you would usually need to spend. There are pageboy outfits here as well.

Prices:	Medium/Very Good Value	Buy Online:	Yes
Delivers to:	UK		
Based:	UK		

www.debenhams.com

If you don't want to spend a fortune but you like the idea of a designer gown – and who wouldn't – then take a look at the Designers from Debenhams range of wedding dresses by J by Jasper Conran, Pierce II Fionda, Star by Julian MacDonald and BDL by Ben de Lisi. Prices start at around £250 and sizing is from 8–18. There are some beautiful dresses here so it's well worth considering, particularly if you don't have a lot of time.

Prices:	Medium	Buy Online:	Yes
Delivers to:	UK		
Based:	UK		

www.emptybox.co.uk

Established in 1988, The Empty Box Company first began reviving the old fashioned Edwardian Hat Box and then began to produce beautiful, handmade and pH neutral boxes after research into storage of fabrics and discussions with textile experts at The V&A. Their boxes are made specially for you with your choice of design and ribbon and you can also have your Wedding Dress Box personalised with your name and wedding date.

Prices:	Medium	Buy Online:	Yes
Delivers to:	Worldwide		
Based:	UK		

Also look at the following websites already in the guide above for wedding collections:

www.amandawakeley.com
www.brownsfashion.com

ACCESSORY HEAVEN

This is where the fun really starts. So you've chosen your dress, and if you went to buy it from a large bridal boutique you may well have bought everything else to go with it, from a hat, feathered comb or tiara to gloves, a faux fur stole, your shoes and special jewellery. Alternatively you may have decided to wait until your dress is ready before you choose everything else, so you can see how it looks all together with your dress fitting perfectly.

Either way there are lots of other accessories you're going to need and not just for your wedding but for your rehearsal dinner (if you're having one) your going away outfit and for your honeymoon.

On the websites below you can find a selection of tiaras and jewellery, sumptuous shawls in the softest faux fur, silk organza and velvet lined with satin, beaded satin slippers and beautiful lacy lingerie and many of the stores here will deliver to you anywhere in the world.

Jewels and Tiaras

www.andrewprince.co.uk

Andrew Prince has designed jewellery for celebrities and was also commissioned in 2002 by the Victoria and Albert museum to design a unique collection of costume jewellery to accompany their 'Tiaras Past and Present Exhibition.' He uses only the finest Swarovski crystal and Signity zirconia in the beautiful collection you'll find here, of tiaras and chokers, necklaces, earrings and brooches.

Prices:	Luxury/Medium	Buy Online:	No, call or email to order
Delivers to:	Worldwide		
Based:	UK		

www.bijoux-heart.com

Each piece here is handmade in Yorkshire to the standards of vintage couture jewellery. Having won six Condé Nast awards for Design and Manufacture, Bijoux Heart has worked over the years with Vivienne Westwood, Catherine Walker and Lulu Guinness. You'll find exquisite tiaras detailed with seed pearls, Swarovski crystals and Venetian glass and if you want something bespoke you should contact Tracy Graham for images and bead samples.

Prices:	Luxury/Medium	Buy Online:	Yes
Delivers to:	UK		
Based:	UK		

www.chezbec.com

At Chez Bec you'll find an excellent collection of very reasonably priced wedding jewellery, with the majority of the pieces having been designed and made exclusively for them. They also offer a bespoke service for brides looking for something totally special and unique. The collection features jewellery with freshwater pearls and Swarovski crystals for necklaces, earrings and bracelets and would make lovely gifts also for bridesmaids and flowergirls.

Prices:	Very Good Value	Buy Online:	Yes
Delivers to:	Worldwide		
Based:	UK		

www.floandpercy.com

Florence and Percy (who gave this website its name) were married for 80 years and held the record for the longest marriage in the world. Here you can find beautiful one-off original vintage bridal jewellery plus a collection of ready-to-wear which includes exquisite headbands, tiaras and combs, created and inspired by vintage jewellery and components, with the message being that if you see something you fall in love with, buy it straight away.

Prices:	Luxury/Medium	Buy Online:	Call or email to order
Delivers to:	Worldwide		
Based:	UK		

www.jothorne.co.uk

Jo Thorne offers a small but beautiful collection of vibrant, modern hair jewellery, comprising tiaras, pins and combs – a range which you won't find anywhere else. Designed to be worn by the independent woman who loves contemporary fashion, they create a very different look and feel to the bridal jewellery you normally find. You can see each item by itself and also what it will look like being worn.

Prices:	Luxury/Medium	Buy Online:	Yes
Delivers to:	Worldwide		
Based:	UK		

www.kellyspence.co.uk

Art and design graduate Kelly Spence has been designing wedding jewellery since 1999. Each piece is made by hand and combines Swarovski crystals, faux/freshwater pearls and semi-precious stones and you'll be encouraged to be part of the designing process by contributing ideas for customisation if you choose to buy from her. Tiaras, delicate crowns and coronets, unusual hair pins and feathered combs are just some of the items you'll find here.

Prices:	Luxury/Medium	Buy Online:	No, call to order
Delivers to:	Worldwide		
Based:	UK		

www.kirstengoss.com

After studying jewellery design in South Africa, Kirsten Goss moved to London and launched her own company where she currently creates exclusive, modern collections of bridal and everyday jewellery using semi-precious stones and sterling silver. Having been featured by *Harpers*, *Elle*, *Glamour* and *In Style* and described as 'the next big thing' by *The Sunday Times* magazine, this is a one to watch.

Prices:	Luxury/Medium	Buy Online:	No, call or email to order
Delivers to:	Worldwide		
Based:	UK		

www.miamasrijewellery.co.uk

This is a stunning collection of handmade tiaras and jewellery – a wonderful place for brides looking for something totally unique and special but also a treasure trove of jewellery for all occasions. You can create your own tiara online with their easy-to-use 'Design-a-Tiara' feature whereby you can almost magically transform their designs by changing the base metal and colour and size of the stones to match your dress and accessories.

Prices:	Luxury/Medium	Buy Online	Yes
Delivers to:	Worldwide		
Based:	UK		

www.yarwood-white.com

Award-winning bridal jewellery designer Claire Yarwood-White specialises in beautiful hand-made headbands and tiaras that are unique and reasonably priced. On her website you can order from her full range of jewellery which includes necklaces, earrings and bracelets for both weddings and other occasions.

Prices:	Medium	Buy Online:	Yes
Delivers to:	Worldwide		
Based:	UK		

Also take a look at the following jewellery retailers from the Jewellery section above, which offer bridal jewellery:

www.butlerandwilson.co.uk
www.emmachapmanjewels.com
www.astleyclarke.com
www.swarovski.com
www.mikimoto-store.co.uk

Shoes, Wraps and Gloves

Wonderful, glamorous shoes: glitzy strappy beaded shoes with killer heels. Flat silk hand embroidered ballet pumps. Palest pink satin shoes with bows on the back or sexy diamanté embellished ivory satin sling-backs. The choice is yours and it's a really, really wide choice.

There are several ranges that you'll come across more than once and these are the most popular UK designers. Prices range from the hundreds to extremely good value so take your time to look through.

There are also a couple of websites here based in the US. Don't be scared of buying your shoes here as shoe sizes are pretty standard and provided you use their conversion chart (or if in doubt go to www.onlineconversion.com, clothing and shoes) you should be fine. Some of the US ranges are really lovely, particularly Stuart Weitzman and Vera Wang so it's well worth having a look.

A few of the websites here will dye your shoes to match your dress and incorporate specific beading and embroidery which is an excellent service to take advantage of.

www.bellissimabridalshoes.com/

This US-based website offers a wide choice of really lovely designer wedding shoes (and matching handbags) by names such as Stuart Weitzman, Vera Wang, Cynthia Rowley and Kenneth Cole. You will have to pay extra for shipping and duty so don't expect to make any great savings but this is an opportunity to choose special and different shoes for your wedding which you can't find anywhere else.

Prices:	Luxury/Medium	Express Ship? (UK)	No
Delivers to:	Worldwide	Gift Wrap?	No
Based:	US		

www.elegantsteps.co.uk

There's quite a range to click through here from the simplest satin sling-back to lovely beading and embroidery and from gorgeous classic styles to contemporary heels. The number of designers on offer covers a wide selection of prices, and includes Benjamin Adams, Filippa Scott and Johnathan Kayne. You can call them to discuss having shoes dyed to match your dress and also choose from handbags and other accessories

Prices:	Medium	Express Ship? (UK)	No
Delivers to:	Worldwide	Gift Wrap?	No
Based:	UK		

www.emmyshoes.co.uk

You can order totally bespoke shoes here or you can shop from their online boutique and choose one of their ready-to-wear styles. Don't expect to save money, but if you want something truly elegant (and shoes that hopefully you'll wear after your wedding as well), you should think of shopping here. Expect to find seriously beautiful shoes that you can't buy anywhere else.

Prices:	Luxury	Express Ship? (UK)	No, but call them if you need rush
Delivers to:	Worldwide		delivery
Based:	UK	Gift Wrap?	No

www.josephazagury.com

Shoe designer Joseph Azagury creates a superb collection of beautiful and wearable shoes each season for all occasions. He's especially well known for his bridal collection, where you'll discover stunning and elegant designs that don't try to outshine your dress and that you'll be able to wear all day. Expect to pay designer prices for a wonderful pair of shoes.

Prices:	Luxury	Express Ship? (UK)	Email to order and call for urgent
Delivers to:	Worldwide		deliveries
Based:	UK	Gift Wrap?	No

www.katepennington.co.uk

Kate Pennington Designs specialises in hand-decorating bridal and bridesmaid shoes. Using their extensive range of trimmings they'll decorate your shoes to complement the theme and design of your dress. You can see lots of the styles on her website and then you need to contact her about a month before your wedding to confirm the style and sizes you want to order.

Prices:	Medium	Express Ship? (UK)	No
Delivers to:	UK	Gift Wrap?	No
Based:	UK		

www.lucymarshall.com

Lucy Marshall is a mother-and-daughter partnership who have been inspired by the beauty and skill to be found in traditional hand embroidery and beading. This is a bespoke collection, with each item being made by hand and tailored to the bride and fabric, beads and threads being chosen to complement the bridal gown. Originally having started out designing bridal gloves the collection now includes exquisite headpieces and hair jewellery.

Prices:	Luxury	Buy Online:	No, call to order
Delivers to:	UK		
Based:	UK		

www.my-wedding-wishes.co.uk

Here you'll find a very good choice of wedding shoes from designers such as Diane Hassell, Gabriella & Lucido, Else and Paradox, some which are very well priced and some quite expensive, so it's well worth spending some time. They also offer wedding petticoats and a small collection of jewellery. If you send them a swatch of fabric they'll dye your shoes to match and they deliver only to the UK.

Prices:	Medium	Express Ship? (UK)	No
Delivers to:	UK	Gift Wrap?	No
Based:	UK		

www.theaccessoryboutique.com

This is a really stylishly designed website offering you, as they put it, 'everything bar the dress,' so you can choose from their excellent range of shoes by Paradox, Filippa Scott, G&L and Benjamin Adams, jewellery and hair clips by Emma Cassi and Stephanie Browne, silk and beaded handbags and essentials such as Hollywood Fashion Tape and comfort shoe pads.

Prices:	Medium	Express Ship? (UK)	Yes
Delivers to:	Worldwide	Gift Wrap?	Yes
Based:	UK		

www.wonderfulwraps.co.uk

Established for over ten years, Wonderful Wraps have offered their accessories through major UK retail outlets such as Harrods, Selfridges and Harvey Nichols in London and Saks Fifth Avenue and Neiman Marcus in the US. They offer a collection of sumptuous velvets, silk organzas, chiffons and tulles, satins, faux furs, marabous and other luxury wraps, stoles and capes. To place your order you need to call them.

Prices:	Medium	Buy Online:	No
Delivers to:	Worldwide		
Based:	UK		

Also take a look at the following for shoes, wraps and gloves. For shoes try:

www.gina.com
www.lkbennett.com
www.emmahope.com
www.faith.co.uk
www.jimmychoo.com
www.envycouture.com

For gloves visit:

www.corneliajames.com

Lingerie

Most of the online lingerie boutiques offer a selection of bridal lingerie, below are a few that are particularly good but you should also take a look at the collections in the Lingerie and Swimwear section above. I've listed those with specific bridal collections for you so that you'll know where to go.

Whatever you've looking for, be it lacy nothings or the complete 'hold-me-up-and-keep-me-there' business you'll find everything at these stores, with a very good range. As always Figleaves will have the largest selection of all (when don't they?) but it's well worth browsing the other websites to find something special and different and perfect for your wedding day.

www.lingerie-company.co.uk

Based in Hinckley, Leicestershire, this retailer offers lingerie by a multitude of designers including Aubade, Lejaby, Chantelle, Charnos, Fantasie, Passionata, Panache and Triumph. Also Swimwear by Aubade, Freya and Fantasie. Click through to the Occasion section to see a wide selection of bridal lingerie.

Prices:	Medium	Express Ship? (UK)	Yes
Delivers to:	Worldwide		
Based:	UK		

www.sophieandgrace.co.uk

Sophie and Grace offer top quality lingerie, nightwear and swimwear including the bridal ranges of Honeymoon Pearls and Verde Veronica where you'll find garters, bras and briefs, basques and nightgowns with touches such as embroidered lace and pearl straps. This is a very different and luxurious range of lingerie and you'll no doubt want some to take away on honeymoon as well.

Prices:	Luxury/Medium	Express Ship? (UK)	No
Delivers to:	Worldwide		
Based:	UK		

www.vollers-corsets.com

This is, quite simply, an amazing collection of corsets, both for underwear and outerwear. The sexy and feminine designs include ruched velvet, satin, lace, leather, beaded brocade, gold and silver fabric, moire and tartan and with flower, feather, lace and velvet trims. Sizes go from an 18 to 38 waist or you can have a corset specially made for you. There are corsets perfect for weddings and special occasions and most are available in a range of colours.

Prices:	Luxury/Medium	Express Ship? (UK)	Yes
Delivers to:	Worldwide		
Based:	UK		

Also take a look at the following which are included in the Lingerie and Swim sections above:

www.agentprovocateur.com
www.bravissimo.com
www.figleaves.com
www.glamorousamorous.com
www.janetreger-online.com
www.mytights.co.uk
www.rigbyandpeller.com

Bridesmaids and Flowergirls

As with wedding dresses, bridesmaids' dresses, particularly for older bridesmaids, are difficult to buy online. However, there are just a few places where you can find them and particularly if your bridesmaids are very short of time or live quite a distance from your wedding dress designer, some of the stores below may solve the problem as everyone can have a look at what you've chosen, wherever you are.

You'll find dresses for tinies at Little Bevan and Qurna Creations and for older bridesmaids at www.monsoon.co.uk. Also, for the older variety, take a good look at www.coast-stores.com where there are gorgeous cocktail and full length dresses at reasonable prices and a beautiful range of colours.

www.eveningdresses.co.uk

This is an unsophisticated website. However, the range of dresses online, which includes those by Dessy and Alfred Sung, is excellent. Take a look first at the evening dress section which includes the designer (evening and bridesmaid) lines, and then click through to their other site at www.perfectbridal.co.uk. Call if you need a dress in a hurry.

Prices:	Luxury/Medium	Buy Online:	Yes
Delivers to:	Worldwide		
Based:	UK		

www.jlmeurope.co.uk

There's a lot to see here, so be prepared to spend some time. There are three ranges here for bridesmaids of all ages, from enchanting little flowergirls' dresses in pretty soft colours to chic and sophisticated dresses for older bridesmaids that'll hopefully be worn more than once. You can view the whole range here plus colour swatches for each style online right down to ribbon swatches, order their brochure and find out where your nearest stockist is.

Prices:	Luxury/Medium	Buy Online:	No
Delivers to:	Worldwide		
Based:	UK		

www.littlebevan.co.uk

Little Bevan offers clothes for girls, boys and tinies as flowergirls, bridesmaids and pageboys. The prices differ according to the fabric you choose and how much detail there is involved in the design. There are also lots of accessory options here such as sashes, petticoats, wraps and shoes to match the dresses. For boys there are waistcoats (in silk, velvet or cord), trousers and breeches, shirts and jackets.

Prices:	Medium	Buy Online:	No
Delivers to:	UK		
Based:	UK		

www.nickimacfarlanebridesmaids.co.uk

Nicki Macfarlane offers bespoke and ready-to-wear dresses for bridesmaids and flower girls, as well as smart pageboy outfits for both pretty country and smart town occasions. What you can expect here is a totally personal service – all the dresses have the child's name embroidered inside and arrive with a pretty bag containing their accessories, and she also offers flower alice bands, capes and satin sashes.

Prices:	Luxury/Medium	Express Ship? (UK)	No
Delivers to:	Worldwide	Gift Wrap?	No
Based:	UK		

www.qurnacreations.co.uk

Here you'll find a pretty collection of flowergirl dresses which you can order online. First you choose the style that you prefer and then you customise the dress with a choice of colours, bodice and sleeve styles and type of sash, so at each stage you can see what your dress is going to look like. If you want to be sure of fabric colours then order one of their sample packs, the cost of which will be refunded when you place your order.

Prices:	Medium	Buy Online:	Yes
Delivers to:	UK		
Based:	UK		

Flowers and Confetti

There are a huge number of florists online, many of which offer to show you a collection of wedding flowers. Now you and I know that you're unlikely to go buying your wedding flowers online unless a disaster occurs with your existing florist or you simply can't spare the time to go and choose elsewhere. So, here are a few where you can see some lovely options and order through the web.

Even so in most cases you'll need to allow some time for your flowers to arrive. In an emergency I would suggest contacting JW Flowers or The Real Flower Company to ask for their help.

If you don't know a really good local florist you can go to www.confetti.co.uk and look a few up in their supplier directory. Many of them have pictures showing you their style and some have websites you can visit which will give you even more information.

Regarding confetti and the throwing thereof: wherever you're getting married you need to know if it's allowed as some churches and other venues simply don't permit confetti of any sort to be thrown and others allow certain types only. If it's not allowed or if there's a specific rule make sure that your guests are aware of it (maybe by a note or line included with the invitation). That way they won't splash out on something they can't use.

www.confettidirect.co.uk

Charles Hudson's Wyke Manor estate is the British centre for real flower confetti and every year he plants an original design in a 10-acre field. He is in *The Guinness Book of Records* and his 2004 Delphinium Union Jack was pictured from the air by the national press and TV. For his real petal collection flower heads, rose petals, sunflowers and lavender are included as are a variety of different packaging ideas.

Prices:	Medium	Express Ship? (UK)	No
Delivers to:	Worldwide		
Based:	UK		

www.foreverandeverpetals.com

Forever and ever specialises in supplying beautiful biodegradable, freeze dried, rose petals and rosebuds, with each rose being hand selected and carefully preserved to the highest quality to retain its shape and form. There's a really lovely selection here, all beautifully photographed and you can order online, making sure that you allow two to three months for delivery. They also offer favour boxes and organza, rose-trimmed bags and rose-petal potpourri.

Prices:	Medium	Express Ship? (UK)	No
Delivers to:	UK		
Based:	UK		

www.kennethturner.com

Kenneth Turner is famous for his exceptional floral designs throughout the world. If you'd like to have them design your wedding flowers you'll first need to call them to arrange a consultation before you can place your order. Needless to say if you order flowers here you'll be paying for 'designer-quality' bouquets and arrangements but you'll also be certain of having something really special on your wedding day.

Prices:	Luxury	Express Ship? (UK)	No
Delivers to:	Worldwide		
Based:	UK		

www.miraflores.org.uk

Miraflores deliver brides' wedding bouquets, bridesmaids' bouquets, button-holes and matching table arrangements throughout England and Wales. They have a small but beautiful collection, shown in white or pale pink, and if you want them to use another colour you need to contact them by phone or email. Place your order at least two weeks before your wedding and the flowers will be delivered the day before.

Prices:	Medium	Express Ship? (UK)	No
Delivers to:	UK		
Based:	UK		

www.realflowers.co.uk

The Real Flower Company will deliver beautiful wedding bouquets, church and reception flowers wherever you need them in the UK, so if you live somewhere that makes it difficult for you to order the flowers of your choice then call them on 0870 403 6548 and ask to speak to their wedding expert, Karen Watson. You need to do this once you have chosen your dress and know what colour scheme you are looking for. Allow ten days for delivery.

Prices:	Medium	Express Ship? (UK)	No
Delivers to:	UK		
Based:	UK		

www.trulymadlydeeply.biz

You'll find freeze dried rose petal confetti here in gorgeous colours plus peony, delphinium and hydrangea petals and aromatic lavender grains. Choose from tiny sequinned straw or organza petal bags, envelopes or cones, plus freeze-dried rose buds and silk orchid blossoms to scatter on the table along with rose scatter lights and pretty candle surrounds. You can even order a Swarovski crystal encrusted 'Just Married' t-shirt here in white, black or fuchsia.

Prices:	Medium	Express Ship? (UK)	No
Delivers to:	Worldwide		
Based:	UK		

Also pay a visit to the following flower companies which have full reviews in the Flower section of this book:

www.designerflowers.org.uk
www.jwflowers.com
www.lambertsflowercompany.co.uk

Wedding Registries

Every one of your guests will want to give you something special and that they hope they'll be remembered for and I'm speaking from experience here, both as a bride and a wedding gift giver.

This can make things really difficult if you're having a very big wedding as several hundred individual items, some of which you almost certainly won't like, will be really irritating. First you have to thank for them, then you have to work out what to do with them if they simply don't work for you. Hopefully you can exchange some of them for what you do want.

I've included here websites where you can set up your wedding list online to make your life really easy, with clear lists and very good photographs of each and every item. Many of them offer lovely and unusual ideas for presents (some of which hopefully you'll have chosen) so that those who want can leave the toaster or ironing board to someone else.

For lots more wonderful wedding gift ideas and places to shop (speaking to your guests, now) you need to refer to your copy of *The Gift Book*, which you'll find at www.amazon.co.uk, which offers everything from antique silver and glass to contemporary tableware, luxurious bed linens and unique home accessories.

www.heals.co.uk

Heals is famous for its Tottenham Court Road store in London and the modern/retro styling for all the products you'll find there. Just register with them and you can set up your gift list online or if you want, in store with the help of one of their personal shopping consultants. Before you register take a look around the store website to make sure their style is for you. Once you've set up your list you can publish it yourself online or ask them to do it for you.

Prices:	Medium	Express Ship? (UK)	No
Delivers to:	UK	Gift Wrap?	No
Based:	UK		

www.johnlewisgiftlist.com

I'm sure that you won't be surprised to learn that John Lewis has one of the most popular wedding list services in the country. With its huge range of products at different price levels and the excellent service it offers this would be a very good place to set up your list (or part of your list, obviously you don't have to have it all in one place). You can register either online or at your local store but you need to actually select the items for your list in store, after which it can all be handled online.

Prices:	Medium	Express Ship? (UK)	No
Delivers to:	UK	Gift Wrap?	No
Based:	UK		

www.laywheeler.com/home/services/wedding.aspx

Lay and Wheeler offer a traditional and personal wedding list service whether you'd prefer to be given wine to drink immediately or looking to start a cellar plan. Their wines can be viewed either online and once you've made your selection, the list can be set up and despatched either by post or via e-mail. Use their sales team before you set up your list for advice on all aspects of selecting wines and contact them by email at weddings@laywheeler.com, or by calling 01473 313260.

Prices:	Luxury/Medium	Express Ship? (UK)	Yes
Delivers to:	UK		
Based:	UK		

www.mulberryhall.co.uk/GiftList.aspx

Mulberry Hall offers a wonderful range of tableware, home accessories and unique items from designers such as Vera Wang, Herend, Spoke, Christofle and Baccarat. There's an international bridal order service and the wedding list can be accessed and purchases made online. If there's a design you like that they don't stock they'll do their best to find it for you and they offer free delivery within the UK.

Prices:	Luxury/Medium	Express Ship? (UK)	No
Delivers to:	Worldwide	Gift Wrap?	Yes
Based:	UK		

www.onslowandridley.co.uk

To start with Onslow and Ridley will send you a copy of their 'memory jogger', a list of everything you may want to consider putting in your wedding list. They'll then give you as much or as little help as you want in compiling your wedding list. They're based in Scotland, which may or may not be perfect for you to visit, but if not you can call and ask them to send you their brochures so you can see whether you'd like to keep your list with them.

Prices:	Luxury/Medium	Express Ship? (UK)	No
Delivers to:	UK		
Based:	UK		

www.smallislandtrader.com/weddings/index.htm

Small Island Trader offers not only china, glass and silver from a wide range of designers and manufacturers including Waterford, Villeroy and Boch and Spode but also kitchen equipment from juicers and steamers to copper and Le Creuset pots and pans, Sabatier knives, baking trays, and unusual kitchen products and homewares. They have an excellent wedding list service which you set up online.

Prices:	Luxury/Medium	Express Ship? (UK)	No
Delivers to:	Worldwide	Gift Wrap?	No
Based:	UK		

www.weddingpresentsdirect.co.uk

Wedding Presents Direct offer a very personal wedding list service. To start with you need to visit one of their showrooms, either in Battersea, London, or West Harling, Norfolk (by appointment). Once you've selected your list, with as much help and advice as you want, they endeavour to provide you with a copy of it within just a couple of days. Your guests can then purchase from it online or by phone or email.

Prices:	Medium	Express Ship? (UK)	No
Delivers to:	Worldwide	Gift Wrap?	No
Based:	UK		

www.weddingshop.com

The Wedding Shop have selected over 250 suppliers from which you can compile your Wedding List, including Rosenthal, Villeroy and Boch, Arthur Price, Gaggia, Dualit, Mulberry Home, Bodum, Sabatier, Baccarat and Edinburgh Crystal. You need to make an appointment with them at one of their London showrooms and then after that everything can be handled online.

Prices:	Luxury/Medium	Express Ship? (UK)	No
Delivers to:	UK	Gift Wrap?	No
Based:	UK		

Invitations and Stationery

This is an area you really can save time and cover online as the choice is enormous and you're unlikely to find such a range anywhere else without spending a great deal of time and trouble.

Whatever your style you'll almost certainly find something you like, whether you're looking for modern invitations and orders of service, the highest quality card with traditional script or hand tied scrolls in high-quality boxes. You need to spend a bit of time visiting the different websites and checking out the designs and prices until you bring it down to the two or three which match your budget and style, and all the printers and designers need a specific amount of time, particularly if you're going for something like a handmade scroll.

The other huge advantage of choosing your invitations online is of course that if you're extremely busy you're not limited to the working hours of stores, printers and designers. This is one of the things you can do as a couple, in the evening or at a weekend with a glass of wine in your hand and no interference or unwanted suggestions from anyone else. Marvellous.

www.borrowedbluepress.com

This is a really attractive stationery designer to visit and totally different to any other. Their aim is to help you create the most beautiful bespoke range for your wedding, including everything from 'save the date' advices to invitations and envelopes and thank-you notes. Use their consultation service to help you with colour coordination, advice on wording and wedding etiquette.

Prices:	Luxury/Medium	Express Ship? (UK)	No
Delivers to:	UK		
Based:	UK		

www.brideandgroomdirect.co.uk

Here you can choose from a wide range of gift ideas, guest books, bookmarks, cake boxes, envelope seals, favours, keepsake books and photo albums. You can also use their invitation service where you select the style and quantity you need, then just follow the on-screen instructions for your personal details, wording styles, typeface and ink colours. There are some really pretty designs here from beautifully ribbon tied invites to simple and elegant.

Prices:	Medium	Express Ship? (UK)	No
Delivers to:	Worldwide delivery on request		
Based:	UK		

www.katkin-rose.co.uk

At Katkin Rose you can order unique wedding stationery where you choose from their very attractive ranges and then select the individual matching elements you want to include. You can buy straight from their off-the-peg collection or you can visit the Boutique section where you order pretty sets which include invitations and reply cards. There's a totally bespoke service as well.

Prices:	Luxury/Medium	Express Ship? (UK)	No
Delivers to:	Worldwide		
Based:	UK		

www.letterpress.co.uk/

The Letter Press specialises in traditional high-quality wedding stationery, offering a full service, covering engagement announcements, wedding and evening invitations, reply cards, orders of service, menus, place cards and thank you cards. Their designs are based on simple classical styles, which the customer can either adopt as they are or use as a starting point for their own designs.

Prices:	Luxury/Medium	Express Ship? (UK)	No
Delivers to:	UK		
Based:	UK		

www.twobytwoweddings.com

If you want to browse a collection of really special wedding stationery then pay a visit here. Expect to be seriously charmed by the different designs such as Lily; with watermarked flower images on a raised panel trimmed with satin ribbon and Hepburn, with photographs and entwined monograms. This is a very easy site to navigate and before you make your final decision anywhere you should take a look here too.

Prices:	Luxury/Medium	Express Ship? (UK)	No
Delivers to:	Most worldwide		
Based:	UK		

www.whole-caboodle.co.uk/

The Whole Caboodle Design Company offers you high-quality handmade stationery for invitations, reply cards, menus, place cards, favours and thank you cards, boxed handmade scrolls in exquisite designs and lovely contemporary designs. This is very much the top end of the range for invitations etc so expect to pay more here, but if you want something absolutely unique and special you must take a look.

Prices:	Luxury/Medium	Express Ship? (UK)	No
Delivers to:	UK		
Based:	UK		

www.wrenpress.co.uk

The Wren Press is regarded as one of England's leading high-quality stationers. They offer a beautiful, timeless range of stationery including albums and personal stationery plus traditional, romantic and contemporary wedding invitations, orders of service, reply cards and tissue lined envelopes. Order their sample pack to get a clear idea of what they can do for your wedding, the cost of which is refundable when you order.

Prices:	Luxury/Medium	Express Ship? (UK)	No
Delivers to:	Worldwide		
Based:	UK		

And …

www.theweddingfile.com

The Wedding File is a beautifully designed, covetable yet practical loose-leaf A5 planner for anyone who is organising a wedding. It contains over 200 pages divided into seventeen clear sections that cover every conceivable detail including budgets, flowers, checklists and table plans to help you make sure the wedding day runs as smoothly as possible.

Prices:	Medium	Express Ship? (UK)	No
Delivers to:	Worldwide		
Based:	UK		

Also take a look at the following, mentioned above, for wedding stationery.

www.smythson.com

WEDDING CAKES AND FAVOURS

You can choose and order your wedding cake online if you want to and this will work very well if you want something really different from what you're offered locally (unless you live in London, of course, where the choice is incredible). However, and it's a big however, you will probably have to pay quite a lot for delivery if you're miles away from your cake designer.

So think about this, and if you find a cake from somewhere a bit further afield, try to arrange for one of your guests to collect it for you the day before and bring it that day if at all possible (you don't want to be worrying about your cake arriving or not on your wedding day). Also choose a cake that doesn't need to be assembled with tiers and stands but that can be collected as it will be served. In that way your choice will widen considerably.

There are also lots of ideas for favours here, or those little gifts you can give to your guests that make the table look very pretty and again you can spend any amount you want.

In any case it's all here for you to browse through and choose from and the idea of having it all online is to make the whole process more fun and easier to manage than it would be if you had to choose everything in the shops when you're short of time.

Allow as much time as possible for your perfect cake to be created, cake makers get extremely booked up and the longer you can give them the better. Most will try and help you if you're in a hurry but they will say no if they don't think they can produce what you want in time.

Wedding Cakes

You're unlikely to want to order your wedding cake online, but before you turn the page swiftly I would say to you firstly that if you need to you can, and also that it's well worth having a look through the wonderful confections here to get some ideas. Then you can order from here or elsewhere. The galleries of photographs here will show you more wedding cakes than you could possibly find anywhere else, and who knows, you may just fall in love all over again.

www.lindacalvert.co.uk

Linda Calvert creates the most exquisite wedding cakes, decorated to the theme, style and colours of your choice. On her website you can see a selection of her designs and either choose from those or call her to discuss your ideas and request a brochure. She will deliver to anywhere in the UK but London and the Home Counties will have the lowest delivery charges.

Prices:	Luxury/Medium
Delivers to:	UK
Based:	UK

www.littlevenicecakecompany.co.uk

If you want to order a really, really special cake for your wedding (and you're not too far from London) you should visit the Little Venice Cake Company's website and have a look at the amazing creations on show. These are wedding cake designers to the stars, and you should expect the prices to be high accordingly, however it is a quite exceptional collection and merits its wonderful reputation, press coverage and star studded clientele.

Prices:	Luxury/Medium
Delivers to:	UK
Based:	UK

www.maisiefantaisie.co.uk

There's a really pretty range of wedding cakes here and they're all beautifully photographed so you can get some really good ideas. Designs range from the contemporary to the traditional, using a variety of flavours. They prefer you to have a personal consultation as each cake is totally made for you and they'll send your cake to you anywhere in Europe.

Prices:	Luxury/Medium
Delivers to:	Europe
Based:	UK

www.rainbowsugarcraft.co.uk

Don't be put off by the fact that this cake maker states that they only deliver to the North of England. If you ask them they'll actually deliver to you anywhere in the UK. This is not the most sophisticated of websites but they have a wonderful range of top quality cakes, whether you want floral embellishment, a novelty design, chocolate cake or traditional tiers.

Prices:	Medium
Delivers to:	UK
Based:	UK

www.savoirdesign.com

Celebrity pastry chef, Eric Lanard offers a service from the most spectacular chocolate creation or a 5ft croquembouche, to a glamorous fifties-style iced tiered cake. You need to visit him in his production kitchen in south west London for an initial consultation and then he'll deliver to you as far north as Cambridge and down to the south coast.

Prices:	Luxury
Delivers to:	UK
Based:	UK

www.toogoodtoeat.co.uk

With over 20 years' experience, Too Good To Eat specialises in creating unique wedding cakes specially for you. You can choose your cake by visiting their showroom or selecting from their picture gallery and calling them for specific requirements. They will ship anywhere in the world although delivery costs will inevitably be greater the further away you are from them.

Prices:	Luxury/Medium
Delivers to:	Worldwide
Based:	UK

Wedding Favours

A long time ago, French and Italian aristocrats would send their guests home with a small gift, which was then called a bonbonniere. This was a box made of porcelain, crystal or metal and in most cases would contain five almonds or pieces of candy, which represented fertility, health, wealth, happiness and longevity. The idea was that the bride and groom felt they were giving their good luck to their guests with such a gift and it is from this custom that we have today's wedding favours.

Nowadays there's a wealth of choice as to what you give as a favour and how they're presented and these are some of the best of the online retailers where you'll find a good selection.

www.diyfavourboxes.co.uk

This is just exactly as it sounds. Choose your boxes, bags or pretty nets, ribbons in a multitude of colours and everything can be personalised for you as well. Traditional wedding favours contain five sugared almonds, signifying health, wealth, happiness, fertility and long life. You can buy those here as well, alongside chocolate buttons and dragees in case you want to include something different.

Prices:	Medium	Express Ship? (UK)	No
Delivers to:	UK, EU and US		
Based:	UK		

www.talkingtables.co.uk

Talking Tables is not just a wedding favour store, but offers fun ideas for lots of other occasions as well. Click through to the Catalogue to find party sparklers, cake candles and confetti, Perfect Poppers, Blissful Bubbles, place cards and much more. There's an amazing amoung of choice here and you could find yourself spending a great deal more than you intended in an instant.

Prices:	Medium	Express Ship? (UK)	No
Delivers to:	Most worldwide		
Based:	UK		

www.thebridalgiftbox.co.uk

This is a very attractive website offering (you guessed it) lots of ideas for weddings including jewellery and tiaras for the brides, a wide selection of favours, gifts for pages and bridesmaids and well-priced and attractive wedding gift suggestions. Everything is beautifully photographed and you can use their Wish Mail service to send yourself a reminder if you've seen something you really like.

Prices:	Medium	Express Ship? (UK)	Yes
Delivers to:	UK	Gift Wrap?	No
Based:	UK		

www.treasuredfavours.co.uk

Wedding industry award-winning finalist Treasured Favours offers a really good choice, a helpful and efficient service and takes you straight to what you're looking for the minute you arrive at the site. Choose your colour and style from Romantic to chic black and white to tropical (and more) and then exactly how you want your choice to look and what you would like to put inside.

Prices:	Medium	Express Ship? (UK)	On request
Delivers to:	UK		
Based:	UK		

Also take a look at the following for wedding favours:

www.brideandgroomdirect.co.uk

Section 11
Click to Travel

Travel is one of the fastest growing areas on the web. The days when you had to wonder what a hotel lobby or bedroom would look like, phone to ask for the facilities or hope that your destination would be as lovely as the guide books said it would are over. Now you can see just about everything online and make your booking at high speed.

But stop a moment. Isn't it all becoming a bit too easy? How do you know you can trust the photographs that hotels and resorts place online? After all, they're selling themselves, aren't they? There are incredibly clever ways of making a swimming pool or room look a great deal larger than it actually is, taking pictures on the best days so that you're seduced by the sunshine and digitally creating a sandy beach where there actually isn't much of one.

So take care before you leap. With famous five star luxury you're usually safe although you should still read the travellers reviews. For anything else you should visit www.tripadvisor.co.uk and take an overview of the reports and pictures you'll find there. It is in my top ten of absolutely essential travel websites (along with www.kayak.co.uk). Learn how to use it and then never book without taking a look there first.

If you're in any doubt, or the information isn't online, ask for the measurements of the room you're thinking of booking, swimming pool (if it's as important to you as it is to me) and other facilities such as laundries, child care and wi-fi. The last thing you want is to be disappointed when you arrive, when it's probably too late to change. Create your own list of the things that really matter to you and then get the information before booking. Every time.

One final word: online tour operators wouldn't get your business unless they had really lovely websites, and it would be impossible for me to pick from these for a special award, so I've concentrated here on giving awards to those sites that are best for general information, the ones you're going to be using over and over again no matter where you're going or who you're travelling with.

On the whole here the photography is gorgeous, the layouts excellent and if you're anything like me they'll all make you want to leave tomorrow, well that's the general idea, anyway. The only question is, what are you in the mood for? Zebra watching? Sipping margueritas by the pool? Skiing in Vail? The choice is just too, too difficult.

Fly, Drive or Relax on the Train

Whatever way you choose to travel there are literally hundreds of tour operators wanting your business, some of whom will offer you a really good deal and others who won't offer quite such a good service. So how do you find your way through the choice you get offered if you click through to one of the major search engines – it isn't easy, I promise you.

Here you'll find, quite simply, the companies who will help you get to your specific destination when you don't want to book through one of the 'book it all here' operators. Even if you do, you should check the prices at the individual carriers. Sometimes Expedia or Lastminute. com will offer you the best deal, and sometimes because an airline or ferry company has made a last-minute adjustment to their prices, they won't. Booking any travel arrangements online is now so fast that it's worth spending just those extra few minutes making sure.

Bear in mind when you're ready to book that the time of year you travel, the day of the week and the time of day will all affect the prices you're offered. The best way to get the cheapest price is to book early enough and have a bit of flexibility. Don't just check one day or one time to travel, check several.

Passenger and Car Ferries

www.brittanyferries.co.uk

If you want to take your car to Caen, St Malo, Roscoff or Santander then this is the site to use to book your journey. Book early to ensure you get the cabin of your choice and really early if you're planning to go in the holiday season. You'll find clear route guides and timetables here and you can combine your crossing with one of their holiday offers for self-catering and hotel accommodation throughout France and Spain.

www.eurodrive.co.uk

Eurodrive is a comprehensive ferry and channel tunnel booking comparison website, so you just input your route and the time you'd like to travel and then view the available options. Be aware that prices will differ quite substantially depending on the time you choose so try a few different times to get the real picture.

www.eurotunnel.com

If you haven't already tried it this is a great way to cross the Channel. Eurotunnel will take you and your car from Folkestone to Calais (as well as other European destinations) and make the crossing in just 35 minutes. If you're slightly late for your train you can usually get onto the next one (except in peak times) as they leave every 20 minutes.

www.condorferries.com

Condor Ferries' giant, high-speed sea-cat sails from Poole and Weymouth to St Malo via Jersey or Guernsey. The company also runs a conventional five hour ferry crossing service for those who want to take a large vehicle or motor-home across. This is much the fastest way to get to St Malo but only runs during spring and summer months as the sea-cat does not suit rough seas.

www.poferries.com

P&O Ferries offers ferry crossings to and from the South to Calais, Le Havre, Cherbourg and Bilbao plus Zebrugge and Rotterdam from Hull and across the Irish Sea. Register your car details to make the site even quicker to use. You can book online and if you're thinking of using another website to make your booking with P & O check the price here before you do so as you'll often find excellent special offers at certain times of the year.

www.superfast.com

Superfast Ferries offer you a high-quality service whether you're travelling between Italy and Greece, Finland and Germany, or Scotland and Holland. You can download their Booking Request Form and fax it back to them, book online, or alternatively you can contact one of the many agents on the clear worldwide listings they supply on the site.

www.irishferries.com

Taking you from Holyhead and Pembroke across to Dublin and Rosslare and then on down to Cherbourg and Roscoff, Irish Ferries offer you an extremely modern fleet including Ulysses, the world's largest car ferry. There's lots of information on this website about timetables and fares, on board shopping and upgrades to their Club class and (yes you guessed it) offers for holidays in Ireland.

www.norfolkline-ferries.co.uk

Norfolkline is a new ferry company operating brand new cross channel ferries from Dover to Dunkerque which is more convenient than Calais for many destinations in France and is also better situated for Belgium and Holland as well as providing shorter drive times to Germany and Switzerland. They also offer Irish ferry routes from Liverpool to both Belfast and Dublin.

Car Hire Here and Abroad

There are an enormous number of car rental companies. You want the best price wherever you're travelling to, speedy pickup and no nasty surprises when you arrive after a long trip. These are probably the best-known companies and they all offer you the same thing:

- the ability to select your type of car
- a check on what you're going to have to pay
- special offers at certain times

www.avis.co.uk
www.hertz.co.uk
www.alamo.com
www.europcar.co.uk
www.nationalcar.co.uk
www.budget.com

If you have a favourite or you're on a loyalty scheme, you'll probably want to go straight to them. Alternatively use www.kayak.co.uk to run a check with just about all of the rental companies and find out what's on offer.

Travel by Train

www.amtrak.com

Thinking of crossing the US by train? Click onto Amtrak's website, use their station list to input starting points and destinations then book your Superliner Roomette (or normal seat) for the journey. There's lots of help on the site on how to book and what type of seat or accommodation to reserve plus anything else you might need to know before making your booking.

www.eurostar.com

Eurostar will take you to Paris or Lille at high speed and will also connect you to over 100 destinations across Europe. Always check the Eurostar site prices before booking it through anyone else, however there are very often good rates for upgrades to first class on websites such as www.driveline.co.uk and www.leisuredirection.co.uk.

www.nationalrail.co.uk

There's a great deal going on on this website, from train and coach ticket information for anywhere in the UK, times, fare types, luggage allowances and online booking to ferry crossings and the seemingly inevitable plane tickets, hotels and theatres. The train and coach service in particular is really excellent and easy to use.

www.orient-express.com

This is one you will have heard of, with the famous Venice Simplon-Orient-Express offering to transport you in the style of a bygone era to exciting cities such as Venice, Paris, London, Budapest, Prague, Istanbul, Vienna and Rome. Now through Orient Express you can also book The Royal Scotsman, The Eastern and Oriental Express in South East Asia, and PeruRail – one of the highest rail routes in the world.

www.raileurope.co.uk

Rail Europe specialises in selling tickets and passes for travel throughout Europe by train. Available to buy online or via their call centre, you can find some excellent deals on Eurostar, TGV and the French internal SNCF trains, overnight services to cities including Barcelona, Rome and Florence, French Motorail, InterRail passes and the snow trains which deliver you right into the heart of the French Alps.

Fly Away

Nowadays booking flights online is a breeze, and if you haven't started doing so yet you really should. The days of calling up your travel agent or going out to book your flights are well and truly over. Obviously you have the option of going to your favourite airline straight off to see what's on offer, such as:

www.britishairways.com
www.flybmi.co.uk
www.virginatlantic.com
www.easyjet.com
www.ryanair.com

In fact I never make my final booking until I have checked out my destination on the actual airline's site, just in case there's a time or a day that has a better deal.

Otherwise for booking flights you should go straight to www.kayak.co.uk who will show you where everyone is flying to and at what price. If that sounds complicated it's not – just input your preference and you'll be given all the choices. You can then narrow it down by airline, number of stops and even nearest take-off or landing time.

If you want to include the budget airlines remember to tick the 'show nearby airports' box on the home entry page so that for London, for example, Luton and Stansted will also be included.

Get used to using this website, as it brings together and compares all the other 'comparers,' such as Expedia, Travelocity, Cheap Tickets and E-Bookers.

Information

www.baa.com

The British Airports Authority website provides real time arrival and departure information for all UK airports together with excellent car parking information, travel insurance and a foreign currency ordering service. You can book Executive Lounge passes here whatever cabin you're flying in and check out the shop and restaurant listings for your airport and terminal. This is a great site to use before you fly and if you're meeting someone.

Budget Flights – a Word

Where flights only are concerned all the airlines are competing heavily with the cut price carriers such as **www.easyjet.com** and **www.ryanair.com**.

You can find some amazing prices here but please be aware of the following:

- There will be significant luggage restrictions and excess bags can cost you a small fortune.
- You may well have to queue both to check in and to board and end up feeling like one of a herd of cattle (I've done this several times so I can say this with truth). Be prepared for this, have your bottle of water and book to hand and try to stay relaxed.
- You always need to check exactly where you're flying to. Do not assume that you will be arriving at your destination's main airport, even if that's what they are calling it. You may have to bus, train or taxi for many miles at some considerable expense to get where you thought you were going in the first place.

Perfect Villas

If you're travelling with a group of friends or with lots of children a villa is often a very good option, you can have your privacy, your own private pool and as much luxury and service as you choose, from totally self catering 'clean and tidy yourself' villas to full-on chefs, chauffers, maids and the rest.

Here it's essential to book early, as the best villas will be booked year after year by the same families who often 'option' for the following year before they leave. Start thinking well in advance of the right number of rooms and facilities that you require and then make several choices that suit your party, possibly from several of the tour operators listed below.

Again it's really important to get measurements of rooms and pools and a list of the facilities confirmed before you book, particularly if you're travelling with tinies.

www.cvtravel.co.uk

CV started as 'Corfu Villas' in the 70s and has now grown up with a portfolio of some of the most sought-after villas throughout Europe, all with pools or right on the water's edge plus a boutique collection of hotels and ski chalets. The website is beautifully clear with lots of pictures of each destination. You'll find options in France, Italy, Greece, Morocco, Portugal, Spain, South Africa and the Caribbean.

www.individualtravellers.com

Use the easy interactive search facility at Individual Travellers to select your next perfect family villa. You tell them exactly what you're looking for in terms of distance from cities, number of rooms and facilities and they (hopefully) will come up with the answer from their portfolio of over 2000 villas in France, Italy, Spain, Portugal, Dubai and Croatia. The pictures are excellent and there are several for each property to help you make your choice.

www.meonvillas.co.uk

Spend too long on the home page of this villa travel company and you'll be getting out your passport before you know it; the pictures are so wonderful. Family travel company Meon offers family villas with special facilities such as gated pools for tinies and annexes with snooker tables, playstations and gyms for teens as well as a selection of luxury villas in the Algarve, Greek islands, Menorca, Majorca and Italy.

www.palmerparker.com

Palmer and Parker offer villas in destinations such as France, The Algarve, Jamaica and Spain. All their villas have pools and maid service and some have tennis courts as well. Once you click through to your chosen destination you can see exactly the facilities on offer, the size of the swimming pool and whether a snooker table and grand piano are part of the deal. This is one of the best villa sites for information on each property.

www.tapestryholidays.com

Tapestry specialises in luxury holidays to unspoilt resorts in Turkey, Crete and Kefalonia, as well as gulet cruises in the Med. They also have private villas with pools, boutique hotels and luxury apartments on their list and can arrange everything for you from travel insurance to car hire and nanny services. You'll find beautiful and sophisticated places to stay here.

www.thevillabook.com

The minute you arrive at this website you know you're going to enjoy having a browse, even if you don't end up booking anything. There's an extensive list of destinations including France, Cyprus, New Zealand and Italy. Turn the pages (for this is designed like a book) to find lots of information on each plus the choice of villas and then lots of pictures of each one.

www.wimco.com

If you fancy making your next villa holiday a trip to Mustique, St Barts or Anguilla, not to mention St John, Morocco or the Cayman Islands then take a look at Wimco (The West Indies Management Company) and be totally tempted by deep blue seas and luxury accommodation. They'll organise everything for you from babysitters to chefs and yes, you will pay a bit more, but you'll probably have the holiday of a lifetime.

Short of Time

Short breaks can do as much for you as long holidays and they're wonderful for de-stressing and taking your mind off everything else that's going on provided you're willing to switch off that mobile and leave your laptop behind.

Choose something that will be a total distraction, go skiing, visit a city you haven't been to before, attend a music or dance festival or just somewhere beautiful to chill out with a group of friends. Shopping of course is always an option so Paris, Milan and New York have to be on the list of possibilities. Anything that will take you away from the day-to-day for a short while can be bliss.

Many of the tour operators in this whole travel section (and particularly in Luxury Time) offer short breaks as well as the ones listed here so it's well worth a look right through.

www.coxandkings.co.uk

Cox and Kings organise high-quality group tours, private journeys and tailor-made itineraries to many of the most fascinating places in the world, ranging from the luxurious to the downright adventurous. There is a great deal to choose from here, with longer trips as well, but one area in which they excel is in their city breaks, which can take you to Venice, Florence, Helsinki or Istanbul and there's plenty of information to help you decide.

www.greatgetaways.co.uk

If you're keen to get away but you don't want to spend a fortune or go for very long, then take a look at this website, offering great value short breaks to cities such as Paris and New York. If you want to travel to Europe you can choose from Eurostar or flight options and hotels from two to five star. This is a very flexible company so if you want single supplements or flight or hotel only bookings you just need to give them a call.

www.inntravel.co.uk

On this easy-to-navigate website you can choose from several very different short break options, as well as the more usual city breaks to places like Bruges and Lille. You can, for example, go on a riding weekend in Spain, relax in a French county auberge, take a cycling trip through Spain or Italy or learn to cook traditional dishes such as Tarte Tatin in Normandy.

www.originaltravel.co.uk

Original Travel offers a collection of exclusive trips within easy reach of the UK, to Europe, Africa and the Middle East, with each destination specially chosen to minimise the amount of time you need and maximise your experience. You can select from 70 holidays set out under the sections for Adventures, Expeditions, Safaris, Escapes, Cities, Skiing and Classics and they propose itineraries for each.

www.short-breaks.com

This is a very clear and easy website to navigate, with the home page offering you all the options from luxury and cheap breaks to Disney, 'Shop till you Drop' and Kylie Live. For each event they offer you the tickets, travel and accommodation or just click on the country, city and hotel you want, input your dates and book your travel. There's a wide range of hotels and some very reasonable prices at all levels.

www.superbreak.co.uk

This fast, colourful and busy website offers all sorts of short breaks, including theatre breaks, golfing holidays to places like Goodwood Park and Edinburgh and spa breaks throughout the country at three and four star hotels and resorts. You can also book for events such as the Cheltenham Festival and Chelsea flower show and although there is a lot to choose from the website is very clear and easy to use so persevere.

And Teddy Came Too

Travelling with children, and in particular tinies, can be wonderful or dreadful and I know all about this having travelled both in Europe and the US with three extremely close in age (don't ask). The main thing is to be prepared. Know exactly what facilities will be on offer before you book and don't try to go somewhere stupendous and five star unless you're either taking your own childcare with you or you can arrange childcare before you leave.

The only good thing about travelling with real tinies is that you can choose where you go, rather than the slightly older variety who want to be involved in your decision making. After that, of course, they can wreak absolute havoc, so go somewhere where it doesn't matter too much so you can have a good time too.

www.adventurecompany.co.uk

The Adventure Company has searched the world to offer unique trips and experiences for all the family and for singles as well, with a balance of well-known highlights and places off the beaten track. They bring you the opportunity to go trekking, view wildlife, experience life in a tribal village, see the stars from a desert wilderness or try a new activity like rafting, dog-sledding or kayaking and have over 130 holidays to suggest worldwide.

www.babygoes2.com

If you're looking for a child-friendly escape, whether it's a luxury hotel or a budget holiday then you've just found your essential one-stop place to search. Created by parents looking for perfect 'breaks-with-baby' they've managed to put together an excellent guide for anyone travelling with children. They don't only tell you about the best places to stay and childcare options, but they offer tips, advice and checklists too.

www.clubmed.com

Club Med has one of the best travel sites on the web and an enormous offer of holidays throughout the world, whether you want to go sailing on its incredible five masted yacht, skiing, visiting one of the spas or taking a holiday at one of the family oriented resorts in Tunisia, Greece or France. They offer exceptional recreational facilities for everyone from babies upwards, including baby welcome packages and child supervision.

www.disneylandparis.com

You won't be at all surprised that this is a fun and colourful website where you can buy your tickets, arrange your hotel and find out how to get there. You can book all of this elsewhere too, but if that 'meet'n greet' by Donald Duck is important to you and yours then this is the place to start. For Disneyland California visit www.disneyland.com and for Florida go to www.disneyworld.com.

www.totstoo.com

Visit this beautifully designed website offering luxurious and child-friendly spa holidays. All the spas here offer babysitting services, cots, kids' clubs and five star luxury, so don't expect to save money but do expect to be able to both travel with your tiny and relax as well. Once you click through to the destination of your choice you can see immediately how much babysitting costs, what ages the crèche and kids' clubs cater for and if there's a separate children's pool. Bliss.

www.takethefamily.com

This is a bright, colourful and immediately child-friendly looking website with family breaks and holidays on offer throughout the world. For each destination there's information on why to go there, when's the best time to travel, how to get there, where to eat and what to do, plus essential reading. You can organise everything from sailing in Turkey and 'Infant Adventures in Egypt,' to a visit to the Ritz Carlton in Dubai, there's a wide range of prices to select from and there are lots of special offers as well.

Travelling Solo

This is an area where the web has made so much difference. No longer do you need to worry about single supplements or ending up in a group of couples – here you can pick the type of holiday you want to go on and know that you'll be with like-minded people, all of whom are travelling on their own.

Another very good place to look is in the Culture Class section, as if you like opera, art, architecture or cooking you'll find many of the websites there offer great ideas for solo travel as well.

www.coldfusionchalets.co.uk

The policy here is simple – no families and no children; they cater totally for individuals. Based in Chamonix, France, they have two quite large chalets and offer a full service from organising equipment hire, lift passes and lessons, providing daily shuttles to and from the slopes and setting up activities such as heli skiing and ten-pin bowling, so if you want to ski and you are on your own you can socialise (if you want to), ski and feel part of a friendly group.

www.justyou.co.uk

Just You offers escorted tours for single travellers including cruises, short breaks, safaris, skiing, wine tasting and whale watching with choices in Europe, the US, New Zealand and Australia, Central and South America, Africa, China and the Middle East. The website is extremely friendly and easy to navigate and with no single supplements and the opportunity to extend your holiday for extra days.

www.friendshiptravel.com

If you're travelling on your own, Friendship Travel will help you to arrange an un-structured holiday with like-minded people. They'll book you a cruise on the Royal Clipper – the world's largest fully-rigged five-masted sailing ship – or a skiing holiday in Courmeyeur and there's lots of choice in between. They also offer last-minute breaks and single-parent holidays with a 'vacation nanny'.

www.singulartravel.co.uk

This is a 'one-stop shop' for finding out about the best possibilities on offer for the single traveller. Use their search facility to enter your requirements, whether you're looking for kayaking, bridge, or sun and sand, and pick your ideal destination. Alternatively call them to chat through what you're looking for. This is a much calmer website than many and there's a lot on offer.

www.solitairhols.com

Solitair Holidays offer comfortable atmospheric resorts, a choice of good quality cuisine and plenty of things to do and experience with interesting company, all specifically designed for solo travellers. Every Solitair Holiday is organised so that you can be part of a group if you wish and not if you don't, so that you don't have to follow a set itinerary. There's a choice of places to visit including Florida, Mexico, Crete, Morocco and Italy.

www.solosholidays.co.uk

Solos Holidays is a long established expert in arranging holidays for those travelling alone. They offer a wide and varied range of holidays throughout the world including Chile, the

US, France and Switzerland and everything from skiing and golf trips to exotic breaks in Nepal. They specify that you must be single to join them so you can't just leave your other half behind.

Active Adventures

I have to say that I'm one of those people who can spend an entire holiday lounging on the beach or by the pool, and all I need is a good book, good company and somewhere great to eat in the evenings. Having two boys who are, at time of writing, 20 and 19 I know only too well that if I'm going to be able to have a good time they have to be fully occupied from when they wake up until they go to bed. My daughter, I'm happy to say, is still happy to lounge.

To me the best types of holiday are where 'active adventures' are accompanied by lovely places to stay and this is very much what you'll find here. Find somewhere beautiful, book white-water rafting, grizzly hunting or extreme skiing (just joking) for those who want and then everyone can have a good time.

www.activitiesabroad.com
If you fancy skydiving in Spain, an adventure weekend in France, a husky safari, a visit to the Ice Hotel in Lapland or kayaking in Costa Rica then this is the place to look, with many other family friendly and adult only trips to browse. To make the most of your free time you can also book adventure weekends here in France and Slovenia and you need to call them or email your requirements to book.

www.audleytravel.co.uk
Use Audley's specialist knowledge when you next decide to travel to Asia, Africa, India, New Zealand or Antarctica (and other destinations). You can either join one of their group tours, where you have a specific itinerary designed for that region and a guide, or let them help you create your own unique trip incorporating exactly what you want.

www.discover-the-world.co.uk
Discover the World offer specialist travel programmes to Iceland, Sweden, Lapland, New Zealand, Canada and Galapagos. Their itineraries include everything from superjeep weekends and skiing in Sweden to hiking in New Zealand and field study trips to the New York. You can ask for their brochures to be sent to you and there's a huge amount of information online as well.

www.explore.co.uk
Book your next adventure trip online here at Explore, and pay a visit to anywhere from Australia and the Antarctic to Greece, Turkey or Egypt. The amount of choice here is breathtaking and with everything from walks and treks, family trips, short breaks and wildlife tours on offer you're bound to find something. Then there are special interest options such as history tours, festivals and school adventures.

www.onthegotours.com

On the Go has been operating cultural and adventure tours since 1998, and specialises in holidays for people who want to combine culture with fun. They offer tours to a range of destinations including Egypt, India, Russia, Turkey, China, Jordan, Morocco, South America, Sri Lanka and Africa. Just click through to the country you're interested in to find what's on offer, such as Gateway to Tibet, Gorilla and Game Trek, Camels, Souks and Kasbahs or Vodka on Ice. Go explore.

www.viator.com

Viator is a US-based travel company (who will quote you in your own currency) offering lots of information and advice on where to go and what to do when you arrive just about anywhere in the world. There are literally thousands of activities available on this amazing website from helicopter tours in Las Vegas, hot-air balloon rides in Italy and swimming with sharks in Australia.

Safari Magic

Although many, if not most, of the tour operators in the luxury section offer safaris, here you'll find those who just specialise, rather than offering lots of other types of holiday as well. It's totally up to you which you choose and I would recommend taking a look at all of them. One thing you can be absolutely sure of, the people who run these travel companies are likely to be total safari enthusiasts, prepared to give you lots of time and advice. Try to find someone who has actually visited the country and camp you're interested in.

www.aardvarksafaris.com

Independent travel company Aardvark promises that they won't suggest a camp or lodge to you unless one of them has been there, and that they've walked with the guides, eaten the food and slept in the beds. They offer game drives, walking, riding and water safaris plus scuba diving, luxury train journeys and fishing in exotic locations. Read about where you can go and what you can do on this beautifully clear website with some amazing photos and then give them a call.

www.naturetrek.co.uk

Naturetrek is a specialist tour operator offering one of the largest selections of professionally-organised group wildlife tours and natural history holidays around the world. Here you can choose from travelling to see the Asiatic lions and tigers in India, orang-utans in Borneo and Polar Bears in Canada to whale-watching in Baja California. There's a huge amount to read about on this website with a marvellous choice of wildlife tours and safaris all over the world.

www.fmallen.com

If you're looking for a luxury safari stop right here – F M Allen are based in New York and offer personally recommended camps, lodges and hotels in destinations such as Mozambique, Botswana, Kenya, Namibia and Zanzibar. There are gorgeous pictures of all the places where you can stay and a great deal of information, so much so that I would recommend you send them an email outlining what you're looking for once you've had a browse.

www.realafrica.co.uk

Specialising in safaris and holidays in Africa, Real Africa can offer you everything from luxury lodges to remote mobile camps. On their website they showcase a wide selection of the most popular safaris and tours, giving details of the itineraries, prices and properties. They'll also tailor any itinerary to match your requirements for a special holiday or honeymoon.

www.scuba-safaris.com

This is a UK-based company specialising in luxury diving holidays around the world, from Micronesia to S E Asia to Central America. They pride themselves on the in-depth knowledge of each location offered and a very high standard of service. Whether it's a rainforest trek, white-water rafting, admiring ancient monuments or just relaxing on the beach you'll find everything here, plus the diving, of course.

www.tribes.co.uk

Tribes is an independent specialist travel company offering holidays in Botswana, Brazil, Ecuador, Galapagos Islands, India, Jordan, Kenya, Lesotho, Malawi, Morocco, Nepal, Peru, Rwanda, South Africa, Tanzania, Uganda and Zambia, and you're probably going to need some time, unless you've made your mind up beforehand, to decide exactly where you want to go. Click through to the Destination Guide to view the options in detail and then to their African Safari Guide to learn more.

SKIING, SAILING AND GOLF

If you like to take part in a specific sport there can frequently be nothing better than combining it with your next holiday – you get to do what you enjoy doing most, escape totally from the day to day and create your own perfect all round holiday – provided everyone else that you're travelling with likes to do the same thing, of course.

At most of these travel websites the tour operators themselves will be enthusiasts too at your favourite sport and will have a great deal of information to offer on your chosen destination. Still don't forget to visit www.tripadvisor.co.uk if you're going to be staying in a hotel to make sure you get absolutely unbiased reviews.

Skiing

www.mtmhols.co.uk

Made to Measure Holidays is owned and run by passionate skiers with a great deal of experience. They give you lots of information about places to take your next skiing holiday, whether you want to go to Courchevel, Beaver Creek or Klosters. With clear pictures of each place to stay and info about all the resorts this is a good place to have a browse and book your holiday.

www.skidream.com

Ski Dream offers luxury skiing holidays in the US, Canada, Japan and Chile plus France, Italy, Austria and Switzerland and operates from an exceedingly attractive and tempting website which is much less busy than most. Click on the destination that inspires you to find out all about it, from resort details and ski facts to hotel information and pictures that, if you're anything like me, will send you immediately rushing for your passport.

www.descent.co.uk

Descent International have been described as Britain's most upmarket operator by the *Financial Times* and their mission is to offer levels of comfort and service you'll be hard put to find elsewhere. Their luxury chalets are in resorts such as Meribel, Courchevel, Chamonix and Verbier. The prices are undoubtedly high but the gorgeous photographs may well have you making a booking before you know it.

www.powderbyrne.com

Powder Byrne specialises in personal service and luxury accommodation with world class facilities. Their expertise is in combining the highest quality hotels and resorts with a bespoke and flexible service that includes professional childcare for children of all ages. Ski destinations are across the Alps and Dolomites and they also arrange summer retreats across the Med, Indian Ocean and Caribbean.

www.igluski.com

Widely becoming known as one of the best online ski holiday companies, you'll find a very well laid out website offering a wide range of skiing holidays in different countries and resorts and at a range of prices. They offer good information about each resort and have an excellent, fast search engine which tells you exactly what's available at any specific time.

www.scottdunn.com

Very much at the luxury end of the holiday market, Scott Dunn specialise in tailor-made holidays to their 31 ski chalets in the alps where there are wonderful facilities, chefs and nannies, so if you fancy a luxury chalet with its own swimming pool, sauna and steam room, this is the place to come. They also offer holidays in Africa, Asia Pacific, Latin America and other destinations worldwide.

www.skiclub.co.uk

If you go skiing regularly it's a good idea to join the Ski Club of Great Britain, not only do you get lots of information but on those days when you don't want to pay for lessons but you'd like a guide to show you around you can join the Ski Club guide who'll give you the tour for free. This is for intermediate/advanced skiers only and who you get is very much the luck of the draw.

www.skifamille.co.uk

Skiing is one of those types of holidays that usually you can manage to continue as a family (usually because you're paying) far longer than most others. Clever Ski Famille specialise in holidays with childcare included in the price in Les Gets in France. They'll take your little ones to and fro from ski-school and offer qualified carers and experienced playroom helpers, all of whom are first-aid trained.

www.skiweekend.com

For the past 15 years, Ski Weekend have been running tailor-made, high-quality 2–4-day weekends in a selection of resorts in the Alps. They offer scheduled flights, luxury express transfers, well located accommodation and arrange and advise on equipment hire and instruction so that everything is ready from the moment you arrive.

www.snow-forecast.com

Inevitably once you've booked your skiing holiday you're going to be checking the snow reports for a few weeks beforehand, which can, of course, be wonderful and uplifting or totally depressing, depending on where you're going and how much snow they've had. Check up on all the resorts here and read up all about them as well.

Sailing and Watersports

Sail Yourself

www.sailingholidays.com

Sailing Holidays are an independent flotilla and sailing holiday specialist offering holidays round some of the most beautiful islands in Greece and Croatia, both of which have the advantage of being only a 2–3 hour flight away from the UK. You can sail your own boat or if you're not quite confident enough you can share a flotilla holiday with people more experienced. The choice is yours and on this website they make it easy for you to decide.

www.sunsail.com

This is one of the world's largest and most successful sailing and watersports holidays company, offering a great choice of water-based holidays throughout the world. They cater for beginners on the water through to seasoned sailors, with 6 Watersports Beach Clubs in the Mediterranean and an award-winning Club in the Caribbean, as well as sailing bases in 23 countries worldwide.

www.top-yacht.com

Family-owned company Top Yachts specialises in high-quality boats and good service, offering a range of options including bareboat charters, skippered charters, crewed charters and Turkish motor sailers or gulets. You can find out about sailing holidays in Turkey, Greece, Croatia, Italy, Spain, the Caribbean, Whitsundays, Seychelles and Polynesia. Just click on their Boat Search button to find yachts in all their destinations.

Cruise and Relax

www.discovercruises.co.uk

Discover Cruises has been created by the Passenger Shipping Association, and through it you have access to over 40 different cruise lines and hundreds of accredited cruise agents. You can check out all the destinations and itineraries and whether you want to circumnavigate the globe or take a short break in the Med you'll find everything you could possibly need right here.

www.pocruises.com

With P & O you can cruise just about anywhere in the world on their luxury liners and choose from total relaxation to something much more energetic. There are clear descriptions of everywhere they go to, and full details of the ships and activities on their extremely well laid out website, plus an easy-to-use online booking facility.

www.onlinecruiseagency.com

Cruise to Hawaii, Alaska, Mexico, the Carribean or the Bahamas on the cruise line of your choice and the amount of choice is enormous. This US-based site makes it easy to choose by breaking cruises down into destination, date, length of time and price so if you're thinking of cruising take a good look here. There's a very good question and answer section too.

Golf

www.chakatravel.com

This is quite a lot more sophisticated than many of the golf holiday websites, and so it should be, as it specialises in golf tours at luxury resorts and exotic destinations such as Mauritius, Dubai, Cyprus and Sri Lanka, so if you're celebrating something special and you want a golf trip totally out of the ordinary, you've come to the right place. Chaka will not only tell you the best places to stay and play, but also organise golf tournaments themselves.

www.exclusivegolf.co.uk

The list of golfing destintions at ExclusiveGolf is extensive, and includes China, Indonesia, Egypt, Mexico, Portugal and Spain. Click through to the country of your choice and then the area to find the list of hotels and courses available, with star ratings and all the information you could possibly need. With famous courses such as Quinta do Lago, St Andrews and La Manga to choose from you're really spoilt for choice here.

www.golfbreaks.com

Golfbreaks.com is one of Europe's largest golf travel companies with an aim to save golfers time and money by providing a one-stop service at great value prices. Their experienced staff are happy to recommend a number of appropriate golfing venues to fit your specific budget; check availability; book accommodation; reserve the tee-times and get the best rate for you possible.

www.longshotgolf.co.uk

Whether you want a full time golfing holiday or just to have golf as a part of your relaxing break you'll find a great choice here. You can visit, amongst others, Portugal, Spain, Barbados, Cyprus and South Africa. Check on their calendar of tournaments to find out what's happening where or book your next golfing trip to Sun City, South Africa, Lisbon or Myrtle Beach, USA.

www.sogogolfing.com

If you can cope with the busy home page here you may well find an excellent deal, with most of the offers being displayed immediately you arrive at the site. Once you've picked your destination you can choose to join one of their organised groups, book one of their luxury hotels with their own courses, select a short break, arrange tuition and check out all the individual places to stay from apartments to hotels, for which there are excellent details and lots of photographs.

Culture Class

As short breaks become more and more popular there are a number of travel tour operators emerging offering you the opportunity of doing everything from wine tasting and cookery to visiting famous opera houses. Then you could join up with a group keen on anything from archaeology and art to photography and sculpture. This is a particularly good area to browse if you want to go off on your own to follow your particular hobby as you can join groups of like-minded people who enjoy the same things you do (and totally escape from those who don't).

www.andalucian-adventures.co.uk

This innovative holiday company offers specialist art, photography and walking holidays in Europe with the aim of bringing like-minded people together in active or cultural breaks. You don't just 'turn up' here, once you've decided on the holiday you want to go on you'll be contacted by the relevant activity director to discover exactly what you're hoping to achieve so that they can help you to do just that.

www.inscapetours.co.uk

Inscape is dedicated to teaching adults art history actually in front of works of art, whether paintings, sculpture, architecture or decorative art, and their expert tutors take small groups on journeys of artistic discovery all over the world. With them you can visit the treasures of Minoan Crete, St Paul de Vence on the Cote d'Azure, the Picasso museum in Spain and many other famous galleries, buildings and museums. Alternatively you can join one of their study days or tours in Britain.

www.martinrandall.com

Art, architecture, gastronomy, music, archeology and history tours are on offer here, so if you're culturally minded you're going to be really spoilt for choice. Choose by category, country or date and you can immediately see what's on offer, from journeys by rail from

LA to San Francisco and visits to the Napa Valley or the Danube Music Festival. There's an enormous range so have a look round.

www.jmb-travel.co.uk

For opera lovers this is the perfect website to browse through and you'll almost certainly be tempted as there's such a wide choice of towns and opera houses to visit, from Warsaw to the Met in New York. You select your destination first, input the dates you're interested in and they'll tell you which operas are on offer. Make your choice, then decide which hotel and flight you want and you'll be off to see *Cavalleria Rusticana* in Verona in no time at all.

www.travelforthearts.co.uk

Long-established tour operator Travel for the Arts offers opera and dance trips catering for all musical tastes and with destinations including the Opera de Paris, La Scala Milan, and the New York Met. Dance schedules include the Bolshoi and Mariinsky (Kirov) companies and they'll also take you to a wide selection of the world's great music festivals including Verona, the Schubertiade and the Havana ballet festival.

Food and Wine

www.activegourmetholidays.com

Specialising in food and wine holidays as well as art and painting, Active Gourmet will take you cooking in Southern Tuscany, Lousada, Italy, Arles or in Provence. You can also choose joint cooking and biking holidays (so that if your travelling companion doesn't want to cook, they can pursue other activities at the same time). Prices are in euros on this site and they offer a currency converter.

www.cellartours.com

Cellar Tours offers luxury food and wine vacations throughout Spain, Portugal and Italy, so you can choose from Florence, Portofino and Ferrara, Barcelona, Madrid and Seville or Lisbon or Oporto (and that's just a taste of what's on offer). Their tours focus on wine tastings, traditional and creative cuisine, history, art, and architecture.

www.gourmetontour.com

Whether you want half a day or a two-week break, Gourmet on Tour provide over 80 culinary and wine appreciation adventures and holidays in countries such as: Italy, France, UK, Ireland, Spain, Morocco, USA, Australia, Indonesia, Singapore and Thailand with a diverse selection of venues deep in the countryside or in the thick of the city and with accommodation in cosy farm houses or urban designer hotels.

www.tastingplaces.com

Voted by Condé Nast Traveller as one of the best ten cookery holidays in the world, Tasting Places offer you holidays in Italy, Greece, France, Spain or Thailand where you can improve your cookery skills and relax at the same time. They also offer masterclasses in a top London restaurant such as The Ivy or Nahm or the Manoir aux Quatres Saisons.

www.flavoursholidays.co.uk

Here you'll find Italian cooking holidays and cookery courses and you can choose from luxury weeks of food indulgence in places such as Rome, Puglia, Ravenna and Sicily or short-break cooking holidays in Tuscany. They show you exactly where you'll be staying and give the individual itineraries for all the courses on offer. Most of the holidays on offer have no single supplement if you're travelling on your own.

www.grapeescapes.net

For those who enjoy wine and travel this website is a must, as it gives you the opportunity to visit vineyards and wine makers both small and large, most often selected smaller growers who are passionate about their wines. Accomodation runs from 2* family run hotels to secluded 4* chateax with impeccable service and accommodation and there are self catering options too.

www.winetours.co.uk

Arblaster and Clarke offer more tours and destinations each year and include Opera and Wine tours (and opera holidays), Vineyard Walks, an annual Wine Cruise and visits to explore the vineyards of South Africa, Languedoc Roussillon, Veneto and Cognac amongst others. The website is beautifully clear and the combination of wine and opera totally irresistible, although obviously wine is the main theme here so ignore the opera if it's not for you.

Pamper me Please

Many of the tour operators will offer you spa breaks but here you can explore for yourself the different options from spa hotels to available therapies and treatments. Offering everything from girly short breaks to luxurious holidays these are all perfect places to find the ultimate stress relieving holiday. At most of the best hotels with spas there are lots of other activities available as well, so everyone can have a wonderful time and you can totally relax – particularly while the rest of the party if off golfing, sailing, skiing or sightseeing.

www.thermalia.co.uk

Thermalia specialise in spa holidays all over the world, and whether you want to travel to Jordan, or Sri Lanka, Italy, or Greece they have a choice of beautiful and luxurious places to stay and be pampered. Just click on the destination of your choice to find out what's on offer in terms of accommodation, facilities, therapies and treatments.

www.kuoni.co.uk/spa

Luxury operator Kuoni can offer you gorgeous spa breaks in the USA, the Far East and the Indian Ocean where you can wash away the stresses of life back home, with massages, mud baths, facials and saunas. With such a well-known luxury tour operator handling all your arrangements you know that you'll be getting the best.

www.lajoiedevivre.co.uk

Here you can arrange tailor-made spa holidays in Europe, the Indian Ocean, Far East and the Caribbean of whatever duration you choose and including short breaks, two centre breaks and long-haul holidays. They offer a concierge service to pre-book any spa treatments you may wish for, make restaurant reservations, book golf tee times and arrange concert and opera tickets.

www.lhwspas.com

All you need to know here is when you want to go, roughly where you want to go, i.e. which country, and you're away. Use their excellent search facility to find the most luxurious spas throughout the world, where you can choose from spas with hydrotherapy, Ayurvedic spas, spas with yoga, Pilates and t'ai chi or somewhere gorgeous to just relax and be pampered.

www.spabreak.co.uk

Dedicated to UK spas only, Spa Break offers excellent and comprehensive information on luxury spas all over the country. There's plenty of advice and pictures to help you make up your mind where you want to go, and once you've decided you can purchase a gift voucher for a specific monetary value or type of break, which will be sent to you or whoever you want together with the relevant colour brochure.

www.spafinder.co.uk

Here you can easily discover spas anywhere in the world offering the specific services you require and contact them directly through the website's links. You can see so many wonderful pictures of each spa that, if you're anything like me, you'll want to book something immediately. You can order the Worldwide Spa Directory here or the Luxury Spa Finder Magazine, check out day spa deals and group specials and buy vouchers to spas throughout Europe.

Luxury Time

Who doesn't love luxury? I certainly do and I would love to travel with any of the tour operators listed below, offering the most fabulous, individually tailored holidays. They're all delighted to be at your service and we're talking about real service here, from chefs, chauffeurs and maids to private pools and the ultimate in accommodation. Take a look here when you're thinking of booking a honeymoon or just that trip of a lifetime and start saving now.

You'll notice that there are quite a lot more travel companies here than in most of the other sections. Is that because I'm such a luxury lover? Yes definitely, but it's also because there are frequently such a diverse range of holidays on offer here, from skiing to safaris and short breaks to long-haul trips as long as you want them to be that they all deserve a serious mention.

www.abercrombiekent.co.uk

Abercrombie and Kent are one of the most famous luxury travel operators, and one of the major differences here is that they aim to offer you experiences you're unlikely to find anywhere else. These might include gaining access to the Medici's private art collection in Florence, exploring Udaipur in one of the Maharana's own classic cars or discovering local culture hidden down a small tributary of the Yangzi River.

www.westernoriental.com

Here you'll find tailor-made holidays to some of the world's greatest resorts and destinations, and insider's expertise that allows you to really experience a country, rather than just visit it. Luxury beach resorts, chic hideaway hotels, hillside retreats and prestigious city addresses are just some of the options to choose from, with holidays from pre-Christmas shopping breaks to Hong Kong to family holidays in the Caribbean.

www.destinology.co.uk

Search the database of flights, hotels and holidays here for a wide range of luxury holidays and hotels, including last-minute deals. Most of the trips offered are long haul from city breaks to beach holidays, and destinations include Dubai, Mauritius, the Maldives and Thailand. You can book all-inclusive and family holidays or choose from their 'top ten' breaks. One of the best things at Destinology is that you can, sometimes, really find luxury for less.

www.elegantresorts.co.uk

'Effortlessly Stylish Holidays' is the mission statement at Elegant Resorts, where they offer to help you find your idea of paradise, wherever in the world you want to visit and whatever type of holiday you're looking for. Choose from skiing, city living, beach holidays, African tours, visits to India or spa retreats and for each they're just waiting to take care of every single detail for you.

www.itcclassics.co.uk

Experienced bespoke travel operator ITC Classics will arrange your holiday in destinations such as Mauritius, Antigua, the Italian Lakes and South Africa. Through building personal relationships with each of the hotels and resorts on offer they're able to bring you special care and attention and create trips for you that are perfect in every detail. There are excellent flight offers here as well such as free upgrades and half price child flights.

www.kuoni.co.uk

Luxury holiday company Kuoni offers you a range of holidays throughout the world, including safaris, beach resorts, spa breaks, cruises, city breaks, golfing trips, diving holidays and so much more that there's simply no way I can tell you about them all. Visit their beautifully designed website, select the type of holiday you're looking for and go from there.

www.carrier.co.uk

The moment you arrive at this website you know that you're in for a treat as this is without a doubt one of the most carefully thought out and beautifully designed. Travel with privately owned Carrier to Africa, the Far East, India or the Caribbean (and more) and choose from Luxury Chic, Desert Adventures, Safaris and Island Escapes as examples of your holiday theme. Expect a superb, personal service.

www.cazenoveandloyd.com

Winner in the Favourite Specialist Tour Operator Category in Condé Nast Traveller's 2007 awards, Cazenove and Lloyd specialise in three destinations; Latin America, Africa and the Indian Ocean, and India and Beyond. This is a much smaller tour operator than many that are listed here and probably know these challenging areas of the world as well as, if not better than, anyone else you could travel with.

www.harlequinholidays.com

Harlequin specialises in luxury holidays and short breaks to Europe, the Carribean, North Africa, the Indian Ocean and Dubai. Click through to their site, choose your destination and then be totally tempted by the wonderful collection of hotels. There are lots of pictures and information on each from number of rooms, restaurant details, sports facilities and nightlife.

www.exsus.co.uk

Exsus offers luxury tailor-made holidays and short breaks in Europe, Africa and the Indian Ocean (but look at Europe and Dubai preferably for short breaks). They offer an extremely personal service and organise everything for you, from your flights and hotels, to restaurant bookings, private transfers and personal sightseeing tours.

www.mrandmrssmith.com

Rated in the Top 50 Travel Websites in the *Independent*, Mr and Mrs Smith offers a collection of wonderful and exclusive places to stay plus special added extras for members. Just click on 'Hotel Search,' and let them send you on your perfect trip, whether you're looking for a quirky city boutique hotel, stylish country guesthouse or luxury spa.

www.seasonsinstyle.co.uk

At Seasons in Style you'll be allocated your own personal travel consultant, who'll look after you throughout the booking of your trip and from one holiday to the next. Destinations include Bermuda, South Africa, Dubai and Europe and whichever you browse you can immediately see the hotels and resorts on offer and then be totally seduced by the outstanding photographs.

www.relaischateaux.com

For lovers of luxury everywhere Relais and Chateaux offers the essential guide on where to find the best hotels and restaurants around the world, from large resorts to hidden gems. On their beautifully designed website you can select your perfect destination or choose your holiday by themes such as culture, sports, family or oenology (wine tours to you and me). There are also special offers and a gift shop.

Luggage and Essentials

I remember a few years ago going into Selfridges, buying a large rolling holdall and then working my way home with it on the tube and train. Now of course you don't have to do that, with free delivery and speedy service all your new luggage can arrive at your door in an amazingly short amount of time.

Then there are the essential luggage straps, adaptors, chargers and all the other bits and pieces that go into your ready-to-travel list as well as laptop bags, baby bags, mini iPod speakers and mosquito nets. They're all here and you won't have to look very far, or wait very long until you're totally ready to leave.

Two brief words: we usually travel in a pack of five and use brightly coloured straps to ensure that we can recognise our bags when they come off the belt at the airport. It certainly beats trying to spot them amongst the sea of black. Secondly, if you're a female like me who likes to take everything around with her, even in town, such as sports gear and laptop plus (oh dear) hairdryer and more you should check out www.midwestbags.com for their totally different rolling totes that no one else will have in zebra or giraffe prints. Totally glam.

www.billamberg.com

Bill Amberg designs a seasonal collection for men and women in carefully selected fine leathers and suedes. Expect to find a very contemporary and beautiful quality collection of handbags and luggage, jewellery boxes, laptop bags and baby and home accessories, plus wallets, belts and gloves for men.

Prices:	Luxury	Express Ship? (UK)	No
Delivers to:	Worldwide	Gift Wrap?	No
Based:	UK		

www.bagsdirect.com

This is an excellent luggage and general bag website where you can shop from ranges such as Antler, Kipling, Eastpak, Timberland and more and you'll find everything from lightweight holdalls to luxury computer cases and large hard-sided suitcases. They offer free UK delivery on orders over £35 and very good discounts as well.

Prices:	Luxury/Medium	Express Ship? (UK)	No
Delivers to:	UK	Gift Wrap?	No
Based:	UK		

www.ebags.co.uk

Ebags is almost certainly one of the largest travel bag stores online and there's a great deal to choose from, with everything from luggage, business and travel accessories to backpacks, sport bags and baby bags. There are some excellent brands here including Mandarina Duck, Samsonite, Kipling and Victorinox and mainland UK delivery is free.

Prices:	Luxury/Medium	Express Ship? (UK)	Yes
Delivers to:	UK	Gift Wrap?	No
Based:	UK		

www.itchyfeet.com

This is a great travel clothing and essentials store started by a couple of adventure travel addicts, and aimed at everyone from new travellers taking their first adventure holiday to old hands looking for the latest developments. They stock ranges by Patagonia, Berghaus, Mountain Hardwear and The North Face (plus more) and everything from base layer to down jackets and adaptors to mosquito nets. Use their packing list section as well.

Prices:	Medium	Express Ship? (UK)	Yes
Delivers to:	Worldwide	Gift Wrap?	No
Based:	UK		

www.goplanetgo.co.uk

Here's the perfect place for travel gadgets and essentials and for gifts for travellers as the range, of both products and prices, is enormous. There's everything from Mini Compact iPod speakers and DVD players, clever chargers and gadgets, essentials from leather organisers to stylish toiletry bags and their own well edited selection of gifts such as tiny camera tripods, aluminium travel games, TVR multi function tools and spirit level cufflinks.

Prices:	Medium/Very Good Value	Express Ship? (UK)	No
Delivers to:	Worldwide	Gift Wrap?	No
Based:	UK		

www.essentials4travel.co.uk

Essentials4Travel is one of the best travel products and luggage websites, offering everything from classic and well-priced luggage by brands such as Antler, Travelpro and Skyflite to business cases and laptop bags, travel wallets, backpacks and wheeled duffles. You can also order your Michelin Red Guides and road atlases here plus electric and PDA adaptors.

Prices:	Medium	Express Ship? (UK)	No
Delivers to:	Worldwide	Gift Wrap?	No
Based:	UK		

www.magellans.co.uk

This is the UK arm of one of the US's largest travel supply stores and the selection on offer is wonderful. Brands such as Eagle Creek and Case Logic (plus their own) offer luggage and totes that are otherwise hard to find here. As well as the bags there's everything you could possibly need for travel including clothing, toiletry kits, padlocks and tags. Everything is shipped from the US but all duties are included.

Prices:	Medium	Express Ship? (UK)	3–5 days
Delivers to:	UK this site, also www.magellans.com	Gift Wrap?	No
Based:	US		

www.nomadtravel.co.uk

If you know someone who's about to take off on safari or into the jungle you'll need to introduce them to this website, which offers a good, highly edited range of efficient and well-priced travel clothing including lightweight trousers, zip-offs and vented shirts, base layer fleece and thermals plus lots of advice on health abroad and on travelling with children.

Prices:	Medium	Express Ship? (UK)	Yes
Delivers to:	Worldwide	Gift Wrap?	No
Based:	UK		

www.rohan.co.uk

Rohan are specialists in easy care (easy wear, easy wash and dry) travel and casual clothing for men and women, which you can select depending on the type of activity, clothing or climate. There's a very good selection, lots of information and fast service. If you're planning a visit to the jungle this is an excellent website as you can buy not only your clothing but also clever washbags, microfibre towels, dry wash, travel bottles and lots of other accessories.

Prices:	Medium	Express Ship? (UK)	Yes
Delivers to:	Worldwide	Gift Wrap?	No
Based:	UK		

www.sandstormbags.com

If you're a luxury consumer on the lookout for products that not only work well, but have a high degree of authenticity, Sandstorm fits the bill. Sandstorm is the only range of authentic premium safari-style bags out of Africa. These beautiful bags are handcrafted in Kenya and are perfect for your next safari, walking in the Cotswolds or smart weekend breaks.

Prices:	Luxury/Medium	Express Ship? (UK)	Yes
Delivers to:	Worldwide	Gift Wrap?	No
Based:	UK		

www.travelsmith.com

This US-based website must be the ultimate online travel clothing store. They offer a really comprehensive and well-priced range of travel clothing and accessories for men and women, from outerwear including washable suede, tailoring and safari jackets to easy-care separates, hats, swimwear and luggage. You can't place your order directly online for international delivery but you can fax it to them at 001 415-884-1351 and they'll send it to you anywhere in the world.

Prices:	Medium	Express Ship? (UK)	No
Delivers to:	Worldwide	Gift Wrap?	No
Based:	US		

www.zpm.com

ZPM specialises in travel accessories that are always easy to spot, they're cleverly designed and all come in really pretty fabrics. There's everything here from small zip purses to hanging weekenders, classic washbags and vanity cases plus shower caps and beach bags as well. Nothing is over priced so when you're buying that Barbarella Mag Bag for a friend you can slip a Fashion Girls zip purse in for yourself too.

Prices:	Medium	Express Ship? (UK)	Yes
Delivers to:	Worldwide	Gift Wrap?	No
Based:	UK		

A Way through the Travel Maze

There are so many places to compare the prices of flights, hotels and more, and now websites were you can compare the comparers too, such as Tripadvisor and Kayak. These are tools you want to use to get really good deals. Take a quick look at them all and find the one which suits you the best. Kayak is the best at the moment for checking all the flight prices from everyone and includes the budget airlines in its search so it's well worth using every time you want to jet away. Whether you end up clicking through to book is totally up to you.

You'll also find that you can book absolutely everything else as well, from car hire to hotels, theatre tickets, rugby matches abroad and restaurants. If you need it they'll probably already have thought of it for you.

Always check flight prices with the individual airline of your choice as well – you may find a better deal (not always, but sometimes) and you may get offered flight times that suit you better, after all, the cheapest flights here will be out of peak times and the combinations are usually fixed.

Book Everything Here Together

www.expedia.co.uk

This is probably the largest of the multi travel booking websites and in my opinion the easiest to use. Just key in the destination you want, dates and number of people who are travelling and you can almost immediately see which flights are applicable and at what prices. Then you can go on and book hotels all over the world and car hire as well. Register so that your details are stored for your next trip.

www.lastminute.com

On this well-known and multi-tasking website you can compare flight prices, book hotels and car hire plus restaurants, theatres, sporting events and much more, including hotel, flight and fixture tickets for rugby in Sydney or dinner for two at The Ritz in London. Sometimes the amount of choice can seem a bit overwhelming but there are frequently very good deals.

www.travelocity.co.uk

Travelocity has a clear, easy and friendly website, where you can compare flight prices for anywhere in the world, with excellent short notice offers and almost always the same prices you will find on the individual airline sites. Register and they'll remember you when you return to make your next booking even easier. You can also find deals on hotels (mainly the large groups) and car hire.

www.ebookers.com

This is a very clear and easy-to-use website offering you everything to everywhere (don't they all?) they frequently have the best offers on flights and upgrades so you always need to check prices here. You can also use their Travellers Tools to book your airport parking, a car to pick you up from home and reserve your place in the airport lounge.
Compare prices for flights and car hire here:

www.kayak.co.uk

This is a quite amazing website, which will tell you who's operating on which routes for most places in the world, plus how much the fares are with each airline and where to click through to book to get the best deal. They claim to have the industry's most powerful flight search engine and collate real time prices and itineraries from more than 120 travel websites, including airlines and online agents such as Ebookers.

www.traveljungle.co.uk

'It's a jungle out there' is the motto here and where travel booking is concerned they're absolutely right – just who should you use to book? Travel Jungle will search all the last-minute offers and discounted holidays available through other websites for flights, hotels, car hire and insurance and when searching for flights it includes budget carriers as well as traditional airlines. It's well worth taking a look when you're in a hurry.
Find personal reviews here:

www.tripadvisor.co.uk

Filled with USG (User Generated Content) and links to where you can book, this is the place for totally unfiltered and personal views on hotels and places to visit with visitors' own photographs, so those hotels trying to hide behind professionally taken pics and their own reviews can no longer do so. It's important to look at all the reviews for a specific place and not just go by the one or two exceptionally bad or good ones, the average ratings will tell you more than anything else.

Driving Directions in Europe

www.viamichelin.com

Via Michelin will help you with all your European travel planning; whether you want to find a restaurant in Paris, a road map of Zurich or a hotel in Milan. This is the online version of the famous Red Guides but unlike the Red Guides here you just key in your starting point and your destination and it'll tell you exactly how to get there, no matter how many borders you're crossing. You can find hotels and restaurants on the way and even how much the tolls are going to be.

Online in the USA

www.frommers.com

If you're planning a trip to the USA you'll need this website (they also cover other areas but this is their main area of expertise). Frommers are the experts on trips across the pond, helping you with hotels, flights, cars and cruises. They offer you a wealth of information; once you've decided on a city or place to visit you can find out about nightlife, restaurants, shopping, walking tours, activities and everything else you can possibly think of.

Section 12

The One-stop Christmas Shop

To me the web has revolutionised Christmas. I don't have to trek out to the shops and carry large parcels home. I don't have to buy any of my food in the stores. I don't have to fight for a place to park nor spend hours trying to battle my way out of the carpark and through the traffic to get home. I never have to queue any more. I do have to think ahead just a bit and I do have the panic of hearing my kids, the day before Christmas Eve, say that they haven't done any of their Christmas shopping, let alone wrapping things up, and do I have spare cash/wrapping paper/ribbon/time to help them. Of course I do, I say through gritted teeth (ha!). All I said was that the web made Christmas so much easier, it'll never be a perfect world.

I've brought all my favourite retailers together here who either offer specific Christmas products, as in trees, crackers and decorations or those of the more general variety who are also elsewhere in this book. This is very much your one stop shop. Some of the sites may not be the most sophisticated but just the best range you'll find anywhere so have a good browse round.

Whatever you're ordering here do allow enough time. You can book your Christmas cake, pudding and turkey to be delivered on a specific date so place your orders right at the start of December. The best products will run out just before. The same goes for the supermarkets which are not listed here, but in most cases you can order several weeks in advance and you need to do this to be certain of your delivery date.

Below you'll find websites divided into the following categories:

- Christmas cakes and food (including the turkey)
- The Christmas Table – candles, crackers, linens and more
- Christmas trees, decorations and lighting.

For the following you need to go to other places in the Guide:

- Wines, champagne and spirits
- Extra Christmas food
- Tea and Coffee

Christmas Cakes

www.bettysbypost.com

At bettysbypost.com you can order hand decorated Christmas cakes in a variety of sizes, their family recipe Christmas pudding with fruit soaked in brandy and ale and seasonal favourites such as Christmas Tea Loaf, Pannetone and Stollen.

www.botham.co.uk

Here you'll find a simple collection of cakes for Christmas and other occasions which you can personalise with your own message or buy un-piped. All cakes are hand decorated and iced so they ask you to give them plenty of notice. You may well also be tempted by the plum bread, biscuits and preserves on this website and they're happy to ship to you anywhere in the world.

www.megrivers.com

The traditional fruit cakes and Christmas cakes here, including a chocolate Christmas cake, are lovely to look at and taste delicious (and I know, I've tried them). If you can't be bothered or don't have the time to bake yourself this Christmas then shop here. You won't be disappointed.

www.thechristmascake.com

Pandora, Portia and Scarlett Edmiston have created their own unique celebration fruit cake from a secret family recipe, perfected over three generations. Using personally selected fruits soaked in cognac the cakes are slowly and carefully baked and matured, ensuring a shelf life of at least a year.

Christmas Puddings

www.georgieporgiespuddings.co.uk

These traditional Christmas puddings are made with all the ingredients you'd expect from the home-made variety, including currants, sultanas, raisins and orange peel, brandy, rum and spices. They're available in a choice of sizes, from a tiny one person pudding to one large enough to feed 15.

www.thecarvedangel.com

At thecarvedangel.com you'll find their famous Christmas pud, which you can order in three sizes to feed up to a dozen people. All the puddings are traditionally presented in a re-usable earthenware bowl that is dishwasher and microwave safe and then hand tied with a muslin cloth and ribbon with cooking instructions attached.

Turkeys

www.kelly-turkeys.com

Recommended as the turkey du jour by celebrity chefs, you can order your traditionally farmed Kelly Bronze turkey directly from their website. Select your turkey by weight on their order form and it will be delivered to you, close to Christmas, in their insulated cool boxes.

Also from:

www.daylesfordorganic.com
www.eversfieldorganic.co.uk
www.healfarm.co.uk

Also take a look at the butchers listed in the Meat section as most will offer turkeys as Christmas approaches.

Online Delis and Specialities

www.canapeum.com

Canapeum create delicious canapés using ingredients such as lobster, foie gras, tapenade and pastrami. You just calculate how many canapés you need then choose which ones you want to order. Prices range from reasonable to quite expensive but when you think of all that fiddling in the kitchen you won't have to do at your next party you may well think them worth a go.

www.formanandfield.com

Forman & Field is a luxury delicatessen specialising in traditional British produce from small independent producers. You'll find a delicious selection of luxury cakes and puddings, smoked salmon, ham and cheeses all beautifully photographed and extremely hard to resist.

www.lakelandlimited.co.uk

A selection of chocolates, Bay Tree Turkish Delight, Apricots in Moscato, Candied Fruits, Marrons Glace, olive oils, jalapeno spiced nuts are just some of the goodies Lakeland offer at Christmas. Couple this with Lakeland's emphasis on quality and service and you certainly won't go wrong when you place an order here.

www.mrshuddleston.com

Christine Huddleston makes unique home-made preserves each season from high-quality fresh ingredients and is frequently adding new products to her excellent list. Here you'll find a wide range from Hot Chilli with Cider and Vodka Jelly, and Strawberry and Rose Petal Conserve to Pink Grapefruit Marmalade.

www.paxtonandwhitfield.co.uk

You can buy a mouthwatering selection of speciality British, French and Italian cheeses here and join the Cheese Society to receive their special selection each month. They also sell biscuits, chutneys and pickles, York ham and pates, beautifully boxed cheese knives and stores, fondue sets and raclette machines.

www.christmasdinnercompany.co.uk

If you really don't have the time to order all your Christmas ingredients online and prepare your feast yourself then let The Christmas Dinner Company do everything for you. They'll select the best ingredients and pack them off to you with ready peeled spuds, brandy butter and mince pies. Cooking guidelines, a suggested time plan and recipe leftover ideas are included too.

www.donaldrussell.com

You can buy just about every type of meat here, from free range goose and game (in season) to pork, beef and lamb plus natural fish and seafood. Most of the pictures show the products as you'd like them to arrive on your plate and you can either buy from their ready prepared dishes such as Salmon en Croute, Smoked Salmon Pate or Bolognese sauce or you can follow their excellent receipes.

www.dukeshillham.co.uk

Dukeshill was founded over 20 years ago with the aim of producing the very best hams, cured the 'old fashioned' way (where flavour and texture are more important than speed or yield). Today, alongside their hams, you can also buy bacon and other cured meats, fish terrines and smoked salmon, regional cheeses, condiments and preserves and mouthwatering looking cakes.

Candles

www.candlesontheweb.co.uk

This is an unsophisticated candle website but offering an amazing range of dinner candles and t-lights, church and pillar candles, hand dipped beeswax candles and a gold and silver range. They also have a very good choice of extra large candles which you can pay a fortune for elsewhere and a Christmas collection which includes gold and beaded candles and Christmas fragrances.

www.thecandlelightcompany.co.uk

Here's a very clear and easy-to-use candle website offering not only high-quality dinner and church candles but also an interesting selection of novelties, pretty candles in boxes, scented candles and gel fish bowl candles which would be very good children's gifts.

Garlands and Table Decorations

www.festive-dresser.co.uk

There are some really different and beautifully made decorations here including both circular and heart shaped wreaths incorporating beads, feathers, jewels and even marabou plus the more traditional autumn foliage and berries. You'll also find exquisite table decorations – beaded and feathered napkin rings, glass decorations and candle rings and garlands to decorate your home.

www.mithus.co.uk

This online home retailer offers mainly Scandinavian style home accessories including chic table linens, candleholders and vases, photo frames, cushions, and rugs plus an excellent range of dinner and pillar candles in an unusual selection of colours. For Christmas there are wreaths and garlands, enchanting lights and candles and traditional decorations.

www.pier.co.uk

For really gorgeous and unusual Christmas ribbon and wrap, decorations and candles, pretty tableware for Christmas day, beaded and sequinned cushions and throws you should really take a look round here, where you can not only decorate your tree, wrap your presents and create the perfect festive table for but do a lot of your Christmas shopping as well.

Table Linens

www.purpleandfinelinen.co.uk

As well as traditional white and ivory you can also choose from their range in deep chilli red and damson (purple), which would be lovely for Christmas. These are investment linens and very beautiful.

www.thewhitecompany.com

Every year The White Company's range increases and improves and there are far too many lovely and tempting things to buy. If you're buying for your Christmas table here you'll be investing in timeless table linen, crockery, glassware and candles that will not only be perfect for just about any Christmas table but also last you right through the future seasons.

www.volgalinen.co.uk

Update your table linen this Christmas with the exquisite collection of Russian table linen from the Volga Linen Company. The collection consists of richly coloured paisley, white and natural double damask and bordered linen table cloths, placements and napkins, with all tablecloths available in a selection of sizes.

Crackers

www.christmascrackershop.co.uk

However you want your table to look this Christmas you'll almost certainly find some crackers here to match your theme. You can select from jumbo and 'fill your own' crackers to their excellently priced choices in gold, red, green, glittered sprinkled silver and Santa embellished together with their range of sizes. They ship worldwide and aim to despatch everything within 48 hours.

www.gocrackers.co.uk

Don't wait until the last minute to order your crackers online from this excellent website. You'll find a wide selection here from the unusual (leopard print) crackers to much more traditional red and gold, burgundy and green script and holly design and there's also a wide range of high-quality Christmas paper napkins to choose from.

www.froufrouandthomas.co.uk

Here you'll find 'couture' crackers, totally handmade and utterly luxurious. You choose your cracker design from their selection and then whatever you want to go inside from Jasmine scented bath confetti to a mother-of-pearl caviar spoon. They also offer matching wrapping papers and ribbons and other Christmas treats.

www.simplycrackers.co.uk

On this innovative website you can choose from their standard ranges which go from luxury crackers at £36 for six to mini gold and silver after dinner crackers (and in some cases you can select different types of gifts) to their 'Create your own Cracker' range where you literally choose everything from the paper colour, wording (or photo) and decoration to what goes inside.

Christmas Trees, Decorations and Lighting

www.chatsworth-dec.co.uk

If you're fed up of spending a lot of money on Christmas decorations or having to go round the heaving stores to buy them then you should take a look at this website, mainly designed to supply the leisure industry but with no minimum order value; happy to sell to you too. You'll find lots of very inexpensive Christmas decorations, baubles, and tinsel as well as party hats, novelties and lights.

www.christmastreeland.co.uk

Christmas Tree Land have a very clear site offering trees from 3ft to 45 ft and delivery to anywhere in the UK. There's a wide range of trees from Noble Firs to Norwegian Spruce (plus artificial trees) and your tree will be delivered to you well in time for Christmas. They will take your order very close to Christmas but I would suggest you allow plenty of time.

www.peeks.co.uk

Peeks is a family company established in 1946. Originally retailers of cards and toys, they have now developed their products to include themed party items (for occasions such as Halloween) games and other gift ideas and just about everything for Christmas including tree decorations, tinsel and garlands, artificial trees, crackers and balloons.

www.xmastreesdirect.co.uk

There's a great deal to look at on this Christmas website; from high-quality real and artificial trees, tree stands, lights (including bulb testers, transformers, motors and sensors), to artificial wreaths and holly, tree baubles and a lovely selection of unusual ribbons and Christmas stockings.

Ribbons

www.carnmeal.com

This site is a must for anyone who has more than a few presents to wrap up. They specialise in a wide choice of beautiful ribbons and craft accessories for all occasions and rather than buying those small irritating balls of gold and silver ribbon, here you can choose from wired and unwired ribbons, organzas and tartans in lots of different widths and a wide selection of colours. The prices are reasonable, the service excellent and the selection enormous.

www.theribbonshop.co.uk

There are wonderful ribbons here for all occasions (including Christmas) and what's different about this online retailer is that they're all beautifully photographed and decoratively wrapped around parcels, hat boxes, candles and treats so you can really get an idea of what they are going to look like. Prices are reasonable and they'll deliver worldwide.

Prices:	Medium	Express Ship? (UK)	No
Delivers to:	Worldwide	Gift Wrap?	No
Based:	UK		

Section 13
Useful Information

Driving? Traffic, Directions and Road Tax

Royal Mail, BT, Directory Enquiries and yell.com

Citizens Advice Bureau

Conversion Tables and Currency Conversions

Online Dictionaries and
Encyclopaedias Plus
Language Translations

Passports, Visas and
Replacement Certificates

Weather Reports

International Dialling Codes and
World Time Zones

Worldwide Email Access

Worldwide Parcel Delivery

To Buy or Not to Buy?
All the Essential Information You Need
about Buying Online

UK, European and US Clothing Size Conversions

There's so much information on the web and probably several dozen sites that'll give you the answer to any question you may have: what would this measure in metric? How do I convert US shoe sizing to EU? Where can I replace my tax disc online? How do I find my way from Helston to Nairn? Let alone what's 200 Euros in Yen? Or how many hours difference is there between here and Hong Kong?

These are the websites that I use all the time for all of the above and more, taking you straight to the quickest answers on easy-to-use and well-designed sites. Bookmark them all, you're almost certainly going to need several of them soon.

Driving? Traffic, Directions and Road Tax

www.vehiclelicence.gov.uk

Here's another totally essential and often left-to-the-last-minute facility that's now online. Once you have the new form of MOT document (if you need it) plus your car insurance document you can use this website to apply for your new road tax disc, so no further need for that trek to the Post Office. If you haven't had the reminder letter you can just use the reference code and registration number from your car log book instead.

www.getamap.co.uk

This is a really speedy website containing all the Ordnance Survey maps. You just click on the area of the UK you want a map for then click again to get as close as you want. You can also search for maps anywhere in the UK simply by entering the place name, full postcode or National Grid reference – and print the maps or copy them for use on your personal or business web site. Buy maps online here too from detailed explorer maps to historical maps showing you how your town looked a hundred years ago.

www.maporama.co.uk

Here's a very easy way to find a route from one place to another with clear directions and zoom in features and this works for just about anywhere in the world. You can also see exactly where major airports are throughout the world with maps which you can zoom in on, send by email, export to your PDA or print out and use their quick links to maps of New York, Chicago, Los Angeles, London, San Francisco and Hong Kong.

www.multimap.co.uk

Multimap.com is one of Europe's most popular mapping websites, offering a range of free, useful services including street-level maps of the United Kingdom, Europe, and the US, road maps of the world, door-to-door travel directions, aerial photographs and lots of local information.

www.streetmap.co.uk

If you're looking for a particular road or street then this site will provide clear and detailed maps of exactly where you want to be. It's a simple website and although it seems to be also trying to offer you lots of other services what you really want to do here is type in the postcode, street name or even telephone dialing code and what you'll get is an excellent, clear street map without any of the frills.

www.cclondon.com

Use this site to register your car for the congestion charge and then don't, don't, don't forget to pay it when you drive into London. Although it's a complete nuisance this is by far the easiest way of paying and you can book days, weeks and months ahead. You can also get set up to use SMS text messaging so that you can pay from your mobile phone.

www.rac.co.uk

For traffic news go to the main RAC website and click on Traffic News in the left hand margin. Key in the area and road your interested in and you'll get comprehensive information about what's going on (some of which you probably won't want to hear). Roadworks, delays, accidents – it's all there, giving you a chance to change your route. You can also visit the RAC main website from here.

Royal Mail, BT, Directory Enquiries and yell.com

www.royalmail.com

Go to their 'Buy Online' section and order your books of stamps here (or your Special Editions, ready stamped envelopes or personalised stamps). You do have to order quite a lot of stamps but it's the easiest way if you're going to be posting lots of mail in the near future. You can also find the package and letter weights and costs table here for the UK and overseas and look up addresses and postcodes.

www.bt.com

Provided you have enough information this site will, through its directory enquiries link, provide you with telephone number, full addresses and postcodes for people and business anywhere in the UK. You can also get UK and international dialing codes and a great deal of other information including online billing, reporting and tracking faults and help with moving your phone number if you're changing address.

www.yell.com

Just in case you haven't already discovered it, and you may well have, Yellow Pages is now online and it's so much easier to use than the tiny printed thin paged directories. Just put in what you're looking for, where you want it to be and you'll be straight there.

Citizens Advice Bureau

www.adviceguide.org.uk

This is not the most exciting of websites, and one which maybe you'll never have cause to visit but if you want any information on benefits, housing and employment, plus civil and consumer issues you'll find it all here, right up to date. It also tells you who to contact if you need further help and how to make a small claim in the courts should you need to, plus there are loads of fact sheets you can print off.

Conversion Tables and Currency Conversions

www.onlineconversion.com

You know that moment when you want to change miles into kilometres, inches into metres, or ounces into grams, or when you're using that marvellous cookbook you picked up in Williams Sonoma in the US and don't have a clue about the difference between a US teaspoon and the UK version. Well on this useful website you can convert just about anything including temperature, speed, volume, weight and fuel consumption plus some more unusual options.

www.xe.com

Don't go anywhere without using this website to check on how much you should be getting for your pounds and pence. You can convert any kind of currency into another instantly and even if you're going to order your currency elsewhere online or go down to the bank you should check the rate you're getting here as well. Just go to the Home Page, scroll down to the XE Quick Currency Converter and you're away.

Online Dictionaries and Encyclopaedias Plus Language Translations

www.askoxford.com

You can search *The Compact Oxford Dictionary*, *The Concise Dictionary of First Names* and *The Little Oxford Dictionary of Quotations* here. Find out about and order all the books published by Oxford University Press or sign up for a free trial of the Oxford desktop One Click dictionary. It's quite a busy website to use but the search facility is excellent.

www.dictionary.com

The next time you're doing a crossword, playing Scrabble (I know, I know, you're not allowed dictionaries here, but every once in a while to check something up you'll need one) don't bother to go through the book version but go on to this fantastic website where you'll find every word and every spelling for every word plus alternatives for every word. American and UK spelling is given in each case.

www.britannica.com

It's no surprise that the *Encyclopedia Britannica* is now online and if you subscribe to the full service rather than order the volumes you'll save an enormous amount of shelf space. If you're not a member you can use their condensed service for free, however if you subscribe you can access the full encyclopedia online. You can also order the books, the world atlas and other reference products from their online shop.

www.wikipedia.org

Over the last few years Wikipedia has rapidly grown into the largest reference website on the Internet. The content is free to access, and is written collaboratively by people from all around the world. This website is a 'wiki,' which means that anyone with access to an internet-connected computer can edit, correct, or improve information throughout the encyclopedia. There are over 1.15 million articles in English alone so you'll be able to obtain lots of information and I suggest that you also use Britannica.com for the full picture on any subject you're researching.

www.wordreference.com

This is your online French, Italian and Spanish dictionary so the next time you're hunting for that elusive word click here and your problem will immediately be solved. It's quick, clear and easy to use and well worth remembering. For German/English translations go to www.quickdic.org, where you'll also find links to other online dictionaries so you can find whichever one you're looking for.

Passports, Visas and Replacement Certificates

www.passport.gov.uk

When you next need to replace your passport and provided you're not in too much of a hurry (as we were when my son left his passport in his to-be-washed sweatshirt pocket ten days before we were due to go skiing) then use this website to download the application form, fill it in and submit it to the Passport office. If you're in a hurry you need to call for an appointment for their fast track service, details of which again you'll find here.

www.ukdocuments.com

If you, like me, at some time have had a panicked moment realising that you can't find a copy of your (or one of your children's) birth certificates and you need it urgently then click to this website where you can use their two day priority service for replacement certificates. It's extremely easy to fill in their forms and your certificate will be sent by special delivery to the UK or Airsure worldwide.

www.visaworld.co.uk

Visa World are based in London and offer passport and visa services around the world. Although I'd always recommend that you allow as much time as possible for applications they also offer a speedy facility in case you've left things a bit late. Call them up and you'll be speaking to a real, helpful person in no time at all.

Weather Reports

www.weather.co.uk

Although you can never be sure of the weather forecast (putting it mildly) and you can never totally rely on what you read here (as the situation can change so easily) you can at least get some idea of what is expected for the next ten days, hour by hour if you want and for anywhere in the world.

International Dialling Codes and World Time Zones

www.countrycallingcodes.com

This website will give you the dialling codes for anywhere in the world plus major city extensions so wherever you are you can discover what you need to dial anywhere. There are also reverse codes, so that if you know the code but don't know the country you can find that out as well.

www.worldtimeserver.com

Travelling any distance can become really confusing when you take into account the time zones. Use this website to calculate the time at your destination and time difference depending on where you are. There are a lot of other facilities here, such as downloadable clocks, a meeting planner and weather reports for all major cities.

Worldwide Email Access

www.mail2web.com

You may well already have established this invaluable tool but if you haven't, and you want to stay in touch wherever you are, you can use it next time you go away. You need to know your main email address and password (and exactly how this appears) and then you can access your email from any internet linked computer.

Worldwide Parcel Delivery

www.parcel2go.co.uk

Hitwise award winner Parcel2go uses FedEx, DHL, City Link, UPS, Home Delivery Network and Royal Mail to provide a fast, efficient and well-priced collection and delivery service throughout the world. Having used them to deliver golf clubs to the US and large packages to both Edinburgh and Newcastle I can only say if you want to send anything anywhere, try them.

To Buy or Not to Buy? All the Essential Information You Need about Buying Online

Many of us have now become totally used to buying online, and several of us, myself included, find it all too easy to add items into that virtual shopping basket. So easy, in fact, that we often don't stop to think, having leapt from online review guide to comparison website to the cheapest deal at an online retailer we've never heard of, let alone used before.

So I suggest that just before you part with your credit card details and click on 'buy now' you stop and think for a couple of seconds, run a few very simple checks and make sure that you know as much about the retailer and the security of your shopping as you really should do.

1 Before You Buy

1 Make sure that when you go to put in your payment information the padlock appears at the foot of the screen and the top line changes from http:// to https://. This means that your information will be transferred in code. If this doesn't happen, don't buy.

2 You should always be able to access a retailer's full contact details, not just their email address (unless they're a household name). Ideally these details will be available from the 'Contact Us' button on the Home Page but sometimes it's hidden within 'Terms and Conditions.' Be wary of retailers who only give you a PO Box number as their address and who don't reply to calls or emails very fast.

3 If it's the first time you're buying from a retailer you should check their Privacy clause telling you what they'll be doing with your information; I suggest you never allow them to pass it on to anywhere/anyone else. It's not necessarily what *they* do with it that'll cause you a problem, but if they pass it on…

4 Returns Policy – what happens if you want to return something? Check the retailer's policy before you order so that you're completely informed about how long you have to return goods and what the procedure is. Some retailers want you to give them notice that you're going to be sending something back and others don't. Make sure you know.

5 Check your bank statements to make sure that all the transactions appear as you expect. Best of all keep a separate credit card just for online spending which will make it even easier to check.

6 Check out the delivery charges. Again, some retailers are excellent and offer free delivery within certain areas and others charge a fortune. Make sure you're completely aware of the total cost before you buy. If you're buying from the US you will have to pay extra shipping and duty, which you'll either have to fork out for on delivery, or on receipt of an invoice. My advice is to pay it immediately.

7 Take advantage of the new MasterCard SecureCode and Verified by Visa schemes when they're offered to you. Basically they offer you the extra facility of using a pin when you use your registered cards to buy online from signed up retailers.

8 Look for the ISIS logo and shop from signed-up retailers whenever you can. ISIS, or Internet Shopping is Safe, not only indicates that the retailer has gone through more

intensive security checks than some but also if you have a problem IMRG (Interactive Media in Retail Group), who manage the scheme, will act as a go-between.

9   Buy a shredder. Most online and offline card fraud is due to someone having got hold of your details offline. Don't let anyone walk off with your card where you can't see it and don't chuck out papers with your information on where they can be easily accessed by someone else. You have been warned.

10   For extra security pay online with a credit, rather than a debit or any other type of card as this gives you extra security from the credit card companies on goods over £100 in value.

11   Don't ever pay cash, don't pay by cheque (unless you've got the goods and you're happy with them), don't ever send your credit card details by email and don't give your pin number online to anyone EVER. I'm amazed at the stories I hear.

12   Make sure that your computer is protected by the latest anti virus software and an efficient firewall. Virus scan your system at least once a week so that you not only check for nasties but get rid of any spyware.

13   Be very careful using an auction website. Make sure that you know absolutely what you're doing and who you're buying from. This is not to say that everyone who sells on auction websites is waiting to get you but remember to stay secure and don't get carried away in the excitement of bidding.

14   Be wary of anyone selling you 'replica' products – don't go there. If you're tempted to buy from someone selling you something that looks too cheap to be true, it probably is. If you're buying expensive products, always check on the retailer's policy for warranties and guarantees.

15   Don't give any information that isn't necessary to the purchase. You're buying a book, for goodness sake. Why do they need to know your age and how many children you have?

16   Don't buy in a hurry. Take the time to check the above before you click on 'Confirm Order'. If in any doubt at all: don't buy.

2   Deliveries and Returns – What to Look for and How to Make Them Easier

Deliveries

Deliveries from online retailers are getting increasingly better and more efficient. In many cases you can have your order tomorrow. Find a retailer you like who's stating the old 'within 28 days' policy and call them to find out if they're really that daft (being polite here). With most companies offering express delivery who on earth is willing to wait for 28 days unless something is being specially made for them (in which case it may well take longer but at least you'll be aware before you order)?

Most companies offer some or all of the following:

- Standard Delivery
- 24 Hour delivery (for a small extra charge)
- Saturday delivery (very occasionally)
- EU delivery and sometimes EU Express
- Worldwide delivery and sometimes Worldwide Express.

The problem is that you very often don't find out about all these and the relevant charges until you've put something in your basket (note to online retailers: please make 'Delivery Information' a key button on your home page, it saves so much time). Yes I have researched this information for you but sometimes I had to practically place an order to discover a retailer's policies – ridiculous.

Returns

This is an area that often puts people off buying online (or from catalogues, for that matter). Well don't be put off.

You will, of course, have read up the company's Returns Policy before you bought so you know how much time you have but you might like to know the following:

- You are entitled to a 'cooling off' period (usually seven days), during which you can cancel your order without any reason and receive a full refund.
- You're also entitled to a full refund if the goods or services are not provided by the date you agreed. If you didn't agree a date, then you are entitled to a refund if the goods or services are not provided within 28 days.

Having said that and assuming that once you've started you're going to become a regular online shopper, these things will make your life easier.

Buy a black marker pen, roll of packing tape and some different-sized jiffy bags (I use D1, H5 and K7 which are good for most things) just in case you only want to return part of an order and the original packing is damaged or too big.

Keep these where the rest of the family can't get at them (and that tells you something about my family, doesn't it? Why doesn't anyone, ever put things back?).

Make sure that you keep the original packaging and any paperwork until you're sure that you're not sending stuff back and keep it somewhere easy to find.

If you want to be really clever go to www.vistaprint.co.uk and order some address labels. They're really cheap and incredibly useful for returns, Recorded and Special Delivery postings and lots of other things.

Don't be put off if a premium retailer wants you to call them if you're returning something valuable. It's essential that the item is insured in transit and this is something they usually arrange – for really expensive goods they may well use a courier service to collect from you.

Rejoice when returns are free. Standard postage and packing is more and more free of charge from large online retailers, we'll be ordering far more when returns are free as well.

If you have a large box to return consider using www.parcel2go.co.uk. Not only are they extremely reasonable, use recognised carriers such as City Link and DHL but they'll come and collect from you.

3   Comparison Websites and How to Use Them

You're most likely already using comparison websites as they're such an excellent way of getting the best online deal and you'll find them mentioned throughout this book.

Use them for electrical equipment, computers, cameras and everything photographic plus books, DVDs, CDs and games and make sure that you know the specification of the product you want to buy first.

These are the ones I always use and find the best so rather than giving you a huge choice I've just selected a small number to make things easy.

General comparison websites
www.uk.shopping.com
www.kelkoo.co.uk

Food and wine price check sites
www.tesco.com/pricecheck
www.wine-searcher.com

Books, games, CD and DVD price check
www.bookbrain.co.uk
www.best-book-price.co.uk
www.best-cd-price.co.uk
www.dvdpricecheck.co.uk
www.uk.gamestracker.com

Motor and Home Insurance
www.confused.com

Flights and Car Hire
www.kayak.co.uk

4   Once You've Bought

- Very quickly after you've made your purchase you should receive email confirmation about your buy including all necessary purchase details – order number, date, details of the goods you've ordered and purchase price plus in most cases a link back to the website you've ordered from.
- You are entitled to a 'cooling off' period (usually seven days), during which you can cancel your order without any reason and receive a full refund.
- You're also entitled to a full refund if the goods or services are not provided by the date you agreed. If you didn't agree a date, then you are entitled to a refund if the goods or services are not provided within 28 days.
- Keep an email and paper folder into which you can save all relevant information about your online purchases. Call it something like 'Web Orders Outstanding.' Whittle it down to just the confirmation email with the order number and purchase details once you've received you're order and you're happy. There's truly nothing more infuriating that not having the right information if something goes wrong later.
- Note that the above entitlements do not apply to financial services such as insurance or banking, online auctions, or purchases involving the sale of land.

5   Help If Something Goes Wrong

If something goes wrong, and you've paid by credit card, you may have a claim not only against the supplier of the goods, but also the credit card issuer.

This applies to goods or services (and deposits) costing more than £100 but less than £30,000 and does not apply to debit, charge cards or Amex.

Contact the retailer with the problem initially by email and making sure you quote the order number and any other necessary details.

If you don't immediately get assistance ask to speak to a manager. Note: push hard. Contact the company's owner if you can or press office if need be and tell them what's going on. Do not allow yourself to be fobbed off by a customer service person no matter how helpful they're trying to be.

If after all of this you do not get a satisfactory result to your complaint you can contact www.consumerdirect.gov.uk (for the UK) or call them on 08454 040506 for what to do next. If your problem is with a retailer based in Australia, Canada, Denmark, Finland, Hungary, Mexico, New Zealand, Norway, South Korea, Sweden, Switzerland or the USA you can click through to www.consumer.gov/econsumer, a joint project of consumer protection agencies from 20 nations for help.

If (horrors) you find that someone has used your credit card information without your authorisation, contact your card issuer immediately. You can cancel the payment and your card company should arrange for your account to be re-credited in full.

UK, European and US Clothing Size Conversions

Here's a general guide to the clothing size conversions between the US, Europe and the UK. If you need size conversions for other specific countries, or other types of conversions, go to www.onlineconversion.com/clothing.htm where you'll find them all.

To be as sure as possible that you're ordering the right size, check the actual retailer's size chart against your own measurements and note that a UK 12 is sometimes a US 8 and sometimes a 10, so it really pays to make sure.

Women's clothing size conversions

US	UK	France	Germany	Italy
6	8	36	34	40
8	10	38	36	42
10	12	40	38	44
12	14	42	40	46
14	16	44	42	48
16	18	46	44	50
18	20	50	46	52

Men's clothing size conversions

US	UK	EU
32	32	42
34	34	44
36	36	46
38	38	48
40	40	50
42	42	52
44	44	54
46	46	56
48	48	58

Women's shoe size conversions

UK	3.5	4	4.5	5	5.5	6	6.5	7	7.5	8	8.5
EU	36.5	37	37.5	38	38.5	39	40	41	42	43	43.5
US	6	6.5	7	7.5	8	8.5	9	9.5	10	10.5	11

Men's shoe size conversions

UK	7	7.5	8	8.5	9	9.5	10	10.5	11	11.5	12
EU	40.5	41	42	42.5	43	44	44.5	45	46	46.5	47
US	7.5	8	8.5	9	9.5	10	10.5	11	11.5	12	12.5

Website Index

belindarobertson.com 31
belladinotte.com 36
bellissimabridalshoes.com/ 242
benefitcosmetics.co.uk 87
benjaminroberts.co.uk 235
bennettsonline.co.uk 231
berkcashmere.co.uk 31
besselink.com 172
bettysbypost.com 187, 291
beverlyhillsbakery.com 187
bexley.com 118
bibendum-wine.co.uk 209
bijoux-heart.com 239
biju.co.uk 155
billamberg.com 282
biotherm.co.uk 77
birstall.co.uk 176
biscuiteers.com 188
black.co.uk 69
blackface.co.uk 190
blackorchidinteriors.co.uk 170
blacks.co.uk 217
blackstonelewis.co.uk 107
blackwells.co.uk 224
blaguette.com 63
blisslondon.co.uk 82
bloom.uk.com 181
bloomingmarvellous.co.uk 137
blossommotherandchild.com 137
bobbibrown.co.uk 77
boden.co.uk 26
bodieandfou.com 160
bodyshop.co.uk 90
bombayduck.co.uk 161
bookdepository.co.uk 225
boots.com 87
borders.co.uk 225
borrowedbluepress.com 252
botham.co.uk 291
boucheron.com 62
branded.net 54
bravissimo.com 36
brideandgroomdirect.co.uk 252
brissi.co.uk 161
britannica.com 301
brittanyferries.co.uk 261
brittique.com 13
brooktaverner.co.uk 110
brora.co.uk 31
brownsfashion.com 9
bt.com 300
shop.bt.com 232
burberry.com 10
butlerandwilson.co.uk 67

byelise.com 63

cambridgewine.com 210
cameraking.co.uk 229
cameras2u.com 229
campkinsonline.com 229
canapeum.com 292
candlesontheweb.co.uk 293
caramel-shop.co.uk 133
carluccios.com 198
carnmeal.com 296
carrier.co.uk 280
carterandbond.com 120
casacopenhagen.com 161
cashmere.co.uk 32
caspiancaviar.co.uk 196
cathkidston.co.uk 155
caudalie.com 90
cazenoveandloyd.com 281
cclondon.com 299
cdwow.com 226
cellartours.com 277
celtic-sheepskin.co.uk 26
chakatravel.com 275
champneys.co.uk 98
chapmansjewellery.co.uk 64
chatsworth-dec.co.uk 295
cheapsmells.co.uk 103
cheesecake.co.uk 188
chezbec.com 239
childrenssalon.co.uk 133
chilternseeds.co.uk 178
chococo.co.uk 203
chocolatetradingco.com 203
christmascrackershop.co.uk 295
christmasdinnercompany.co.uk 293
christmastreeland.co.uk 295
christy-towels.com 155
ciel.co.uk 45
circaroma.com 94
clarins.co.uk 77
clickgolf.co.uk 221
clinique.co.uk 78
clubmed.com 268
coast-stores.com 14
cocobay.co.uk 39
coconuttrading.com 36
cocoribbon.com 20
coffeeandcream.co.uk 161
coffeebypost.co.uk 207
coggles.com 14
coldfusionchalets.co.uk 269
colemancroft.com 222

cologneandcotton.com 168
completeoutdoors.co.uk 217
comptoir-sud-pacifique.com 82
condorferries.com 261
confettidirect.co.uk 247
conran.com 165
cooksknives.co.uk 165
cookware.co.uk 165
cordings.co.uk 114
corneliajames.com 71
corneyandbarrow.com 210
cosyposy.co.uk 134
cotswoldoutdoor.com 217
countrycallingcodes.com 303
county-golf.co.uk 221
cowshedonline.com 83
coxandkings.co.uk 266
crabtree-evelyn.co.uk 83
cravematernity.co.uk 137
cremedelamer.co.uk 78
crewclothing.co.uk 41
crocandco.co.uk 14
crocus.co.uk 178
crombie.co.uk 110
cross.com 124
cruiseclothing.co.uk 14
crumpetengland.com 32
ctshirts.co.uk 107
cucinadirect.co.uk 165
cvtravel.co.uk 265

dabs.com 231
dalvey.com 122
dartington.co.uk 158
davidaustin.com 178
davidlinley.com 162
davidmellordesign.com 158
daylesfordorganic.com 201
deadfreshfish.co.uk 193
debenhams.co.uk 3
debenhams.com 238
decorativecountryliving.com 162
delinostrum.com 198
descent.co.uk 273
designerflowers.org.uk 181
designersguild.com 156
deskstore.com 125
destinology.co.uk 280
dibor.co.uk 153
dictionary.com 301
diesel.com 29
diningstore.co.uk 166
dinnyhall.com 64
dior.com 49